My Escape

My Escape

AN AUTOBIOGRAPHY

Benoîte Groult

TRANSLATED BY NICHOLE GLEISNER

OTHER PRESS
NEW YORK

Production Editor: Yvonne E. Cárdenas
Text Designer: Jennifer Daddio/Bookmark Design & Media, Inc.
This book was set in 12 pt Filosofia by
Alpha Design & Composition of Pittsfield, NH.

10 9 8 7 6 5 4 3 2 1

Library of Congress Cataloging-in-Publication Data

Groult, Benoîte.
[Mon évasion. English]
My escape : an autobiography / by Benoîte Groult ; translated by Nichole Gleisner.
p. cm.
ISBN 978-1-59051-543-3 (trade pbk.)—ISBN 978-1-59051-544-0 (ebook)
1. Groult, Benoît.   2. Authors, French—20th century—Biography.
3. Feminists—France—Biography.   I. Gleisner, Nichole.   II. Title.
PQ2667.R6Z4613 2012
848'.91203—dc23
[B]   2012018409

To my lovely, utterly feminine, line of descendants

BLANDINE, LISON, AND CONSTANCE

my daughters

VIOLETTE, CLÉMENTINE, AND PAULINE

my granddaughters

AND ZÉLIE

my great-granddaughter

Prologue

Young people today can't truly imagine the extraordinary course of history that belonged to women of the twentieth century.

As someone born in 1920, who grew up well behaved in a Catholic institution and who reached adulthood without possessing the legal means of expressing an opinion about my country's direction (I didn't have the right to vote until 1945, when I was twenty-five years old!), and who realized, around the age of forty, that I had lived a good part of my life without contraceptives or legal abortion (which is not to say, unfortunately, without abortions),[1] without being able to attend the schools of my choice, or attain political power or the higher offices of government, and as someone who did not even possess parental authority over my own children, I know the feeling of being condemned to a never-ending series of obstacles.

At an age when it's high time to write one's autobiography, I see my past life as a long march toward an autonomy that always seemed out of reach, and toward an independence that could no longer be limited by others but conquered, step by step, by going in the direction of my choosing.

With *Story of an Escape* in 1997, I had wanted to take stock of the feminist revolution that sought to transform the lives of women. I also wanted to shake up human relations, and to impact, little by little, men the world over, whether they liked it or not. Rather than my life story, this book was a self-examination, never completely finished since prison bars and fences have a maddening tendency to crop back up again, like bamboo.

I retold the stages of my second birth, which go back to "Year Zero of Feminism," as the press called it at the time, to the day when the nascent MLF[2] protested under the Arc de Triomphe in front of the Tomb of the Unknown Soldier, in homage to someone even more unknown than the soldier himself: his wife! That was August 28, 1970. I was already fifty years old and I still felt as if I were fresh off the boat, as if my position had been gained from on high in a world that, for all eternity, had belonged to men. I couldn't imagine that it would be so hard to break free from the straitjacket of tradition, from all these ties that ensnarl so tightly that you can't even make them out from your own flesh.

I discovered that freedom isn't just picked up naturally. It's something you have to learn, day after day, and very often painfully.

For this apprenticeship, I didn't need philosophy, or science, certainly not religious faith. I didn't need men either. They might bring me marvelous things but not the things I needed at this stage of my life. For these times, I needed other women, those models who had been carefully hidden from me during the course of my education. I finally discovered their existence and I realized that these women had all toiled for me, each in her way, according to her era—Christine de Pizan, Olympe de Gouges, George Sand, Flora Tristan, Pauline Roland, Jeanne Deroin, Hubertine Auclert, Marguerite Durand, Séverine, and so many others—so that we could finally shake up the traditional division into first and second sex[3] in order to become one class of human beings, plain and simple. I needed their journeys, their difficulties, the heroic choices that some had to make.[4] Acting alone, against their loved ones and against society, these women made their choices in spite of the need for love and recognition that they carried in their hearts like anyone else, perhaps more than anyone else.

Is feminism anything but this "transfusion of souls," moving from those who dared to act to those who accepted the rules of the game?

Today it's fashionable to proclaim that misogyny doesn't exist anymore.

But where did patriarchy go?

In the words of Marie-Victoire Louis, the founder of the AVFT,[5] it's staring you in the face. It's invincible.

We could say the same exact thing about misogyny. I belong to a pivotal generation in which practically no woman dares to call herself a feminist, as if it were a shameful disease. To pride oneself on being antifeminist, however, remains an excellent calling card in most social circles and in this way our success is more easily tolerated. Even men appreciate our antifeminism; it lets them off the hook so they don't have to be macho because we give ourselves this dirty job.

Every time I see a capable or powerful woman appear on television, I know that she will soon announce that, naturally, she isn't a feminist. If we forget—for just one moment even—that her presence on television is the result of so many past battles for women and that her presence is by no means a spontaneous gesture from one of her masculine partners, we continue to discredit a cause that we should all be proud of.

In the same way, a self-proclaimed feminist book will never be considered a *normal* book, one which could possibly interest readers of both sexes. Instead the book is seen as some sort of missal reserved for a few old-fashioned devotees, basically a work of patronage. Some women flip through its pages, others will read the entire thing. But 90 percent of men, according to my personal experience, won't even crack it open. It doesn't cross their minds that a feminist book could, like any other book, be good or bad, well or poorly written, brilliant or horribly boring. It's, quite frankly, really galling: the word itself reflects their base thinking. At least husbands no longer discourage their wives from reading such a book, as if to protect them from a virus (which quietly runs its course, in spite of them).

From what I can tell, all of our battles have been too recent (some so late that I could not take advantage of them in my lifetime) and this allows me to forget that our war for independence is still not yet won. In fact this war is just beginning for hundreds of millions of my fellow creatures across the world's continents. This is why I take measure of what each right, what each new step forward, means in all its precious, essential, fragile, and precarious ways.

Nevertheless I have benefited from a great stroke of fortune—namely that women are the ones who buy books and essays today. Without them, I would be left for nothing within the ranks of literature. Smoking kills, but so can feminism![6]

After seven or eight novels where I mixed the real and the fictional (as so many novelists do), I wanted to tell the true story of my life. Novels are convenient, especially when dealing with loved ones, since reality can often be harsh or hurtful. But the time has come now, sadly, when those once close to me have become scarce, especially my contemporaries. One day you suddenly find yourself in open country, in a desertlike state of semiliberty. On the other hand, one of the rare advantages of age is that you're no longer afraid of anything and you know that it is too late to change course now. The picture is more or less definitive. In sum, it's the moment of truth.

Is it the whole truth? In any case, it's nothing else but the truth. But can you ever claim to know the entire truth about yourself? Doesn't the way you go about telling the story of your life reveal just as much as your life itself? Writing is as much about the joy of writing as it is about giving birth to those characters who you didn't know how to become, or didn't dare to be. It is, in fact, a form of revenge against everything that you might have missed in life. And it's the opportunity to begin your own story just like a fairy tale: "Once upon a time a little girl was born in Paris on the thirty-first of January, 1920, and she was called Rosie."

My Escape

CHAPTER 1

Rosie Groult

In the rare moments when I think back on my child-hood self, I'm disappointed. From the start I didn't go by my real name. My parents, no doubt hoping for a Benoît, christened me Benoîte on all the official documents, but this name soon became unsuitable for such a fat, placid baby, so my parents turned to my middle name, Rosie. Neither one of them ever called me Benoîte. I was a conventional child: a shy, obedient, and good student, much closer in spirit to Camille and Madeleine de Fleurville, two exemplary and boring young daughters from Countess de Ségur's 1858 novel, than to the insolent Sophie of her second work, *The Misadventures of Sophie*. My parents, in their role as father and mother, were much more interesting than I in my role as child. They were excellent parents whose only flaw was to remain themselves, and they never sacrificed their strong personalities under the pretext of becoming better role models for my sister and me. Quite simply they led their lives, and then we were there, and they loved us. At the time, there weren't any therapists to pore over delayed bed-wetting or to defend dyslexia, which we dared to call a lack of effort. No one to stop us from chalking up mediocre classwork simply to laziness, and we didn't worry about scarring the guilty party. There weren't any theoreticians of least resistance, no camouflaging school subjects under fraudulent and ridiculous names (social studies?), leading students to believe that they could learn without studying. There weren't any early-learning "stimulation activities," which only imply that the other activities must be boring. No school psychologists to forbid all forms of punishment or traumatizing low grades, or to explain, and therefore even justify, insulting the teacher. These behaviors, which once represented what we believed to be arrogance and the refusal of discipline, have become today, maybe rightly so (I would add), a sign of anguish among young people, a cry for help that should be heeded, not punished, that ultimately challenges teachers, the educational system and all of society. Those of us of the prewar generation were children, *infans* (etymologically those who do not speak) who didn't express their opinions. And our parents were The Parents, a breed that wasn't judged or questioned.

The majority of writers today, both men and women, return incessantly to their childhood, like Ali Baba to his cave, where they might unearth, depending on the situation, plenty of treasures or horrors, moments of tenderness or inexpiable grievances. Whatever the case, they claim to find the reasons for their success and especially for their failures by interminably analyzing the words of Mom or Dad, unceasingly trying their case against their progenitors, for their laxness or their authoritarianism—even interrogating the way they made love the day they conceived their child. They denounce with equal bitterness the parental disinterest that their parents showed them in spite of the exciting promise they possessed, or the intolerable parental demand for better results.

Personally, unless the writer has an exceptional way with words, childhoods bore me and the trend of accusing one's parents, whether they happen to be biological or adopted, present or absent, loving or indifferent, is beginning to nauseate me. I realized that classical writers, as well as writers from the Renaissance and Romanticism, are so pleasant because they have left their childhoods behind. Was the playwright Pierre Corneille hit as a child? Did Plato masturbate when he was ten years old? Did the poet Alfred de Musset cry himself to sleep in his bed because his mother didn't come kiss him goodnight every evening?

It's certainly interesting to know these things and it's indispensable for psychoanalysts who must confront patients suffering from their childhoods, as from wounds that just won't heal. However, in the past, everyone moved quite simply out of childhood and it didn't occupy such a primordial place in our existence.

My childhood doesn't occupy a primordial place in this book either since I don't have any case to try, any grudge to reconcile, nor any reason that I could possibly invoke to explain why I wasn't brilliantly talented or one of those magnificent curmudgeonly types that so many writers claim to have been. The education that I was given, on the other hand, and the people who meted it out to me, shed an indispensable light on how I became such a timorous teenager, utterly unable to make use of my talents, despite the guardian angels that had watched over my cradle.

I was a nice little girl with very big, glassy blue eyes. I had mousy brown bangs which hung straight down my forehead and a mouth too ample for the times. I often let this mouth hang open, a faintly imbecilic habit that irritated my mother. Since she wasn't a woman prone to lamentation but rather to action, she reminded me constantly to mime the heart-shaped pout that was so popular for women in the 1930s. She would even whisper to me in public, in a murmur which I found booming, the words *Attention! Pomme, prune, pouce, Rosie!*

And yet I never retorted, "Hush Mother!" I must have well been a bit of an idiot at one point . . . Docile, I brought together my two lips so that they would resemble my sister's, which were perfect (like the rest of her being, in my mother's eyes). "Aha," the shrink thinks to himself, "she exposes her jealous side!"

But no, not really. I didn't even suffer from that. I loved my little sister, four years my junior. I certainly never hated her. Sure, I tortured her with innocent pranks. After all, I never claimed to adore my mother like she did, so it's normal that Mother preferred Flora's beauty as well as the passionate devotion that Flora always lavished upon her throughout her life.

Even today, twenty years after my mother's death, Flora says to me sometimes, "I saw Mother last night in a dream. She looked well." I hardly dream of her, probably because I look so much like her.

Yet, thanks to *Pomme-prune-pouce*, my mouth doesn't sag today. In spite of my age and my profession, my back isn't hunched, thanks to the torturous chair that my mother custom ordered for me from a store that specialized in accessories for the handicapped. It was a massive wooden chair, as straight and heavy as Justice. In the center of the seat, there was one long plank the length of my back and it forced me to sit very straight, almost at the edge. The chair had straps I slipped my arms through, giving me the posture of silent film star Erich von Stroheim. My elbows were thrust so far back that I was barely able to bring my fork to my mouth.[7]

"Chew, Rosie, chew! Look, André, she's pretending to swallow but she's hoarding it all in her cheeks like a hamster!" Rosie never thought to spit out her food . . . she must have surely been an idiot at one point.

Because I picked at my food (fortunately, these puerile displays weren't yet labeled anorexia), to compensate I was given Bemax cracked wheat, Gaduase brand cod liver oil that was supposedly odor-free (but the cod fish frolicking on the label was enough to make one gag), Phytine Ciba for my bones, and Russet apple syrup for my lungs.

I really had a marvelous mother.

Yet when it was my turn, I didn't know how to be such a marvelous mother. Or perhaps the mold for perfect little girls had been broken because I was never able to command the same meek submission from my own three daughters, a submission that didn't nurture any revolt until a much later age.

Unperturbed, my mother toiled for our well-being. And how can you deny that? She must have been right. She was beautiful, with the same large, glassy blue eyes that I had. "The Poirets have cows' eyes," my father, whose own eyes were like boot buttons, liked to say. My mother was impeccably, if not a little overly, made-up, as "pretty women" of that era so often were, especially the ones who worked in fashion. She was never sick and she left the house each morning to conquer the world, with her red nails and large gemstones studding her fingers. She wore her hair short and crimped, a hairdo that she perfected each morning with a curling iron that I heard clink in the bathroom when she took it up off the holder, where underneath a Meta alcohol tablet burned.

She only liked the city (specifically big cities). She hated Brittany, country houses, and sneakers. She didn't swim and didn't know how to drive. She was only happy when she was drawing sketches for her fashion line, or surrounded by artists and writers who would come to the house to partake in Nicole's cheekiness and André's leg of lamb *en croûte*. I often caught her at night writing to any one of her many lovers, with her pretty, curlicue handwriting, which had a force and uniformity that was striking. Having learned to write from nuns, her script slanted toward the contorted capital letters in the same style that was forced upon all young girls of that period. Born Marie Poiret in 1887, she decided to become Nicole Groult when she married in 1907. Since she was changing her civil status, she also wanted to shake up, in one swift motion, the whole picture: her handwriting, her style, and her aspirations.

I didn't yet know that I was going to do the same thing when I was twenty years old—except for the handwriting (mine has always been the same as my mother's), and the aspirations: hers crowded my own horizon. Left with only the first name, I decided to return to Benoîte. That was a start. Meanwhile I was supposed to follow in her footsteps. Since I was incapable of this, I decided to make my own way.

So who else could I possibly emulate? In my mother's circles, I came across the wives of artists and writers. But they intimidated me, each a sorceress, like the dancer Elise Jouhandeau. They all dressed in vibrantly colored, flowing robes, their short hair styled in a bob. They spoke with purpose; they didn't cling to the sides of their important husbands. And there was Marie Laurencin, noted avant-garde painter and my godmother, who looked me over each time, her myopic eyes behind her lorgnette, as if she had never seen me before, and had just discovered a vaguely repugnant, unknown insect.

And then, in the outside world, there were normal women, my classmates' mothers. They wore their hair in buns, clad their feet in low, stacked-heel shoes and knit socks for their many offspring. They came to pick up their daughters after school dressed in dark suits or, in winter, Astrakhan coats. Mother hated Astrakhan. To my horror, she wore for the longest time an absurd coat made from a monkey, with its long black hair stiff from battle. Knowing that she could show up at the door of Sainte-Clotilde's, on rue de Villersexel in the chic 7th arrondissement of Paris, with her high-heeled pumps ringing out indecently on the sidewalk and her regal allure, dripping with affectations and "yours trulys," was enough to induce a nightmare.

Fortunately she never came willingly to school and so it remained for me a place of refuge, shielded from her eccentricities. It became a place where I could cultivate a true taste for learning, a love fostered by my dogged and sheepish demeanor. Later, at the Sorbonne, I racked up degrees in Greek, philology, practical English usage, and biology. All of these degrees allowed me to remain a student for as long as possible and to delay the grand entrance into the arena where one should "hold out for as long as possible" (another one of my mother's expressions), when it came to boys, who were in my eyes a fearsome tribe with mysterious customs and thoroughly hostile to girls. I needed to "land" a husband (once again note the performative nature of the vocabulary), a feat that seemed completely out of reach to me, given the state of my arsenal. Always out of touch, my father often quoted the writer and politician Maurice Barrès: "I like young people who enter into life with an insult on their lips," to me, a girl who didn't even know how to say "darn!"

With all of my complexes, I was surely better suited to keep harmony among God's little flock of lambs. Wouldn't it have been simpler for me to enter a convent where a divine spouse waited? I would be done with the obligation to be pretty, to finish the battle in order to succeed. Done with high heels and Guitare rouge. Done with the botched perms for my hair, the horrible hot rollers. No matter how you looked at it, I was at a disadvantage from the word go; gentlemen preferred vapid blondes and superficial coquettes. For almost a year I nurtured this plan for religious life without any true sincerity, no doubt motivated more out of desire to scare my parents.

Several of my acquaintances (at the time, girls didn't use the word "copine"; only boys had "copains"[8]) prepared to take their vows. From the time they were little, they belonged to the Children of Mary, a group whose membership prematurely gave them that sad and dignified composure seen in women just after receiving communion. A few, those who had lost a loved one, were "dedicated to blue and white."[9] I would have been happy with this life. After all, I had also lost a little sister two years younger than I was. But my mother loved bright colors too much, and the Virgin Mary not enough, to accept this sartorial constraint. She loved life too much, and *my* life, to agree to my renunciation. Even the very word horrified her.

I was so afraid to leave the free and indeterminate realm of childhood that I clung to that awkward, in-between age, a syndrome that no longer exists today. To me, adolescence seemed to be a novitiate that led ineluctably to marriage, in other words, to the feminine condition. Just thinking about it made me break out with pimples. Since I didn't see any way out, in spite of all the ozone and scarification treatments and the special sulfur lotions, I hung onto my acne for two years, and it flourished in tandem with the cold sores that flowered on my lips each time I was invited to a dance or party.

One day, however, in spite of all my delay tactics, I had to resign myself to my lot in life as a female, and I was forced to submit to the conditions of the marketplace.

The first condition was to have a "pretty little face." That's what boys appreciate, everyone said. I preferred to sulk, a strike against me.

Next everyone said that a girl shouldn't advance too far in her studies. It makes her ugly (a consequence reserved uniquely for girls) and she is treated like a bluestocking.

Lastly a girl shouldn't harbor any shocking ideas, or really, any ideas at all, especially none of a political nature. Men dump stuck-ups and you could quickly become an old maid, that poor creature who merits only pity or sarcasm. There wasn't any alternative. I could stir things up in my little fishbowl, but it was the guys, and only the guys, who held the keys to my future. Every boy began to appear to me like a destiny.

It wasn't that I considered myself worthless; I even had some self-esteem. I just didn't see how I was going to convince a man of my worth. If they didn't know how to spot me, to distinguish me in the crowd of young women to marry, it was because they were idiots. My father, who had a Latin saying for every occasion, shared my opinion. "*Margaritas ante porcos* [pearls before swine]," he offered me as consolation. I was well ahead of the game!

My mediocrity was sealed the day when Marc Allégret, a well-known director and screenwriter who had come out to the country and was staying with some mutual friends, picked me out. (When out in the country or at the seaside, I came across as less obstinate.) He was looking for some young ladies to appear in a film he was making and he asked my mother if he could take some test shots of me. She was enthusiastic. I turned to jelly.

The night before the appointment at the studio, I told him that I was incapable of facing the camera. "I'd rather be cleaning house," I told him somberly. And so, once more, I was considered completely incompetent. My education had been, most decidedly, a failure.

Thirty years later, after my mother died, I leafed through her thick journal, bound in red Moroccan leather, where she wrote down her thoughts and poems, and where she recopied her most beautiful letters, those to Marie Laurencin, Jean Cocteau, Pierre Benoit, her brother Paul Poiret, and so many others. Stopping at one page, I found ten lines that revealed her disappointment in her oldest daughter, who was then only sixteen years old: "Rosie's more engaging than creative. I know now that she doesn't have any major gifts. She doubts herself and believes too much in books. She thinks she's lively, but she's really just stubborn and I'm beginning to lose hope for her future." My poor mother—I was going to disappoint you even more and it took years for me to come out of my lethargy.

It was only much later that I understood what paralyzed me: the impossibility of being like my mother and the absence of any other role model. Nicole Groult was one of the only women I knew who had succeeded in her career without the help of a man. She earned a good living for herself, for us all. She was loved her entire life by her husband, though various admirers and lovers weren't lacking either. Until her later years, she knew how to keep herself thin and seductive. She had lost a daughter at eighteen months, her second child, but instead of sinking into despondency, she brought another child into the world twelve months later. In those days, just like today, it's rare that a woman should succeed on all fronts. In our bourgeois milieu, she wasn't forgiven for this either. They would have preferred that she was somehow punished. "She's an eccentric!" my aunts would say, their faces puckered into a disapproving frown. "Try not to be the wrong kind of girl," Grandmother periodically advised my sister and me, herself weighing over 200 pounds and dressed in all-black mourning attire ever since the death of her oldest son at the Battle of Verdun in 1917.

I didn't have the courage to be an eccentric, nor the capabilities.

And I didn't know anyone who could rescue me, especially not my books. The more I read, the more the evidence indicated that an independent future for girls did not exist. I didn't have the slightest inkling that someone like Virginia Woolf could have existed. *A Room of One's Own*, written in 1929, would not be translated into French until 1951.[10] I was completely unaware of women like the iconic Marie Wollstonecraft, or Olympe de Gouges, Flora Tristan, or Louise Weiss. Simone de Beauvoir wouldn't write *The Second Sex* until five or six years later, and I didn't utter the word "feminism" until I was twenty-five or thirty years old. And without a word to give it a name, how can one conceive of the thing itself? My mother scoffed at the right to vote and at politics in general. And so I did the same.

I lived in a sort of innocence, like the village idiot. Almost all of us of the prewar generation, who were eighteen in 1939, were the idiots of a planetary village. And it was worse elsewhere. When it came down to it, wasn't I one of those pierced African tribeswomen, like the Mursi women that I saw displayed like female monkeys on a platform at the Colonial Fair in Paris in 1936. I was sixteen, but the idea that these women were also subjected to demeaning conditions barely crossed my mind. Like us, these women were forced to submit to the dictate of pleasing men, those who set the standards according to their whims, even the cruelest ones, and marriage was only achieved in the event of compliance.

In this fashion, twenty years went by before I noticed anything abnormal in how society works. I had a degree in literature in my pocket; I privately taught Latin and English. Why couldn't I vote as the taxi drivers and street sweepers could? Why couldn't I open a bank account without marital authorization or have an abortion without risking legal charges, being condemned by society, or even perhaps to death?

The question just wasn't asked.

And during the Occupation, why did only men have the right to tobacco rations, while women were treated once more like minors?

The question just wasn't asked.

(Yet, on a minor level, an answer was found! None of us smoked during the Occupation and we sent my father's tobacco ration to some farmers in Morbihan,[11] who sent us in exchange butter and some rabbits.)

Why, finally, did I stop at my bachelor's degree and not try for the *agrégation*[12] or the École normale[13] like the other young people around me? I watched them take off while I stayed on the ground. Where did this defeatism come from? It made me give up even though I had the time, means, health, and the love of learning necessary for the task.

Once again the question just wasn't asked. Renunciation often passes for a virtue in girls, even the renunciation of happiness.

I found the answer when I discovered, years later, a passage in *The Second Sex* that seemed as if it had been written for me: "The woman first finds herself in a state of inferiority during her period of apprenticeship . . . What is extremely demoralizing for the woman trying to be self-sufficient is the existence of other women of her class, having from the start the same situation and chances, and who live as parasites. . . . It seems to her that the further she advances, the more she renounces her other chances; in becoming a bluestocking, a cerebral woman, she will either displease men in general or humiliate her husband or lover by being too dazzling a success. . . . The girl is convinced that she has limited capacities. . . . Resigning herself to this inequality, she exacerbates it; she persuades herself that her chances of success are related to her patience and assiduity. . . . This is a bad calculation. . . . Crushed by respect for those in authority and the weight of erudition, her vision blocked by blinkers, the overly conscientious female student kills her critical sense and even her intelligence."[14]

This terrible analysis echoed my mother's own assessment. At last, I could explain the deep sleep of my intelligence. Simone de Beauvoir traced my likeness so exactly that I wanted to slap the poor young girl that I had been, and then embrace her with tears in my eyes.

How did the other women do it, those rare few who, in the twentieth century, forged their own way and succeeded in making a name for themselves? I admired them with amazement: Conchita Cintron, the first *torera* in 1937; Marie Bashkirtseff, who my father admired, who died of tuberculosis in 1884 at the age of twenty-four, already famous for her *Diary* and her paintings; my godmother Marie Laurencin; Colette, queen of scandal; and Elsa Triolet, who received the Prix Goncourt in 1945, the first given to a woman in forty years. Let us not forget others like Maryse Bastié and Hélène Boucher, wonders of French aviation, who were never hired to fly regular routes in spite of their international record-breaking and their heroism. Admittedly some women succeeded in cracking the wall of prejudice and breaking the taboo of silence, but society rushed to denigrate them or erase them from our memories. These women didn't truly gain entrance into the world of men, and they didn't reach any positions of power. Perhaps only artists and actresses were able to do so; but their status was precarious, at the mercy of a trend, their age, and public favor. It was really a man's world that they inhabited. Besides to succeed in that realm meant possessing a talent that I didn't have.

It's worth mentioning that I had spent most of my life up to this point in Catholic schools where we were carefully monitored so as not to grow any wings. The very structure of our religion should have sufficed to convince us of our insignificance. There weren't any fertility goddesses or queens of the harvest, like Demeter, that my beloved Greeks, with their multiple gods, possessed. There wasn't any trace of a goddess-mother like the Egyptians had, nor the Hindu Kali, an incarnation of life and death. Our own gods were nothing but bearded men.

At the foot of our masculine trinity, you could make out a prostrate form, the Virgin Mary. But, because of her immaculate conception and her virginity, she consti- tuted a two-fold challenge to nature—a fairly impractical model for women. The sad fate of this Mater Dolorosa, overcome with humility in front of God and His Divine Son, was hardly meant to encourage us along the road to emancipation.

We did have several saints and martyrs, who were mainly celebrated for having lost their breasts or their head, but these women hadn't written any Gospels or Epistles. There weren't even any prophetesses like the Delphic Oracle, not one feminine author of any founda- tional text. The rare texts that had been written by women were kept secret.

I believe that I lost my faith when I was twenty years old because of this glaring absence of women in the Church. It spans from the evangelical message, to the hierarchy, and to the liturgy. The ritual formula offered at the beginning of the homily each Sunday, "My dear brothers," excluded me from the conversation from the very beginning. Not knowing how to analyze this in feminist terms, I felt disgraced by the exclusion. At Sainte-Clotilde's, a priest came each morning to say mass but he was always accompanied by two choir boys, as if, from among the hundreds of little girls kneeling before him, none were considered worthy enough to serve at his side. The presence of these rascals, clad in red and called to tasks that appeared exalted to us (and they in turn surveying the bleating flock of what they saw as "ninnies"), perhaps most assuredly led me to feminism more than any discourse.

So much for my Catholic background.

On the Greek side, in spite of the joyous confusion of Mount Olympus, there wasn't anything better for my ego. Aristotle and Plato warned me two thousand years earlier that I was nothing but "a man manqué, a failed man, an error of Nature." In response to other similarly irrefutable authorities, the only thing left for these "failures" of humanity to do was to bow down to the successful specimens: men! Here, there was no shortage of heroes, and we admired them hopelessly. Clever Ulysses, Achilles with his swift feet, handsome Hector—they aroused our imaginations but only in the way that a marathoner fascinates a legless amputee confined to his little seat on wheels.

Our heroines seemed resigned to tragic destinies, their lives cut short by God, their father, or an oracle. Each of us could have dreamed of emulating Antigone, who inspired so many authors, but for only one brief moment, before the laws of the city condemned her for disobedience, sentencing her to be buried alive when she was twenty!

We had Helen, whose beauty caused the Trojan War, where the most worthy Greek sons died; Jocasta, who unknowingly married her son Oedipus; and Iphigenia, who was sacrificed at sixteen thanks to trivial meteorological patterns. There was Ariadne, seduced and abandoned on a desert island by Theseus; Medea, perpetrator of infanticide and a sorceress like her sister Circe (even magical powers did not prevent them both from being abandoned); and brave Andromache—all emblematic figures of vanquished destinies, and victims of fate. Furthermore Aeschylus, Sophocles, Euripides, and the others illustrated their lives in such terrible and magnificent tragedies that their very beauty formed one more argument against women.

So much for my Greek background.

In the end, whether pagan or Christian, women remained the wretched halves of the Earth, and the Church Fathers, with less skill but more fanaticism than the philosophers of antiquity, confirmed the same sad truth:

Plato, Aristotle, Saint Paul, Tertullus, Benedict XVI—two thousand years of the same battle!

All that was left to me was the Golden Age of French culture.

But here once more, from its very beginning, the history of France insisted on our exclusion. Not least through Salic law,[15] a unique French specialty, that deprived us of great queens like Elizabeth in England and Catherine in Russia. Marie de Médicis in the seventeenth century was our last crowned queen. Catherine de Médicis and the others were nothing but regents or repudiated spouses.

For us girls, who were just as eager to dream as our brothers, there were no archetypal heroines like those heroes from whom plenty of boys drew their inspiration, their vocation, or simply their self-assurance. They had the fortune of belonging to the gender that provided many glorious examples, so they harbored the feeling that a bit of this prestige lived on in each of them. Where were our own legends, when compared to Little Drummer Boy Bara of the French Revolution; to the Hundred Years' War hero Grand Ferré; to "the fearless and irreproachable" Knight of Bayard; to the Three Musketeers; to noble Gavroche from *Les Misérables*, the wonderful hooligan? Where was our own General Dumouriez, who saved the people and the Revolution at Valmy; or Louis-Lazare Hoche, the handsome twenty-year-old general; or the "Father of Victory," Prime Minister Georges Clemenceau, whom my father venerated? And I can't forget Napoleon, whom you can't resist when you're twelve years old. The line "Waterloo, sad plain"[16] brought tears to my eyes every time. Even defeated and exiled, he still loomed large. I collected busts of his head in plaster, in bronze, in ceramic—even in the form of a candle, with the wick planted in the middle of his two-horned hat. He held court for a long time on my nightstand, my dear Napoleon! But what example could he have given to Rosie? I had to break up with my great man, and with grandeur at the same time.

For us girls, there also weren't any "great authors" of our gender. At no stage of my studies, not even during my bachelor's degree in literature, was one of our sacred "great authors" a woman!

Erica Jong says that at Barnard, a college founded by American feminists and dedicated to educating young women, female authors, novelists, and poets weren't even studied. At the library, you couldn't find the novels of Colette (they were supposedly out of print) or Simone de Beauvoir or Emily Dickinson. In 1960! In the land of feminism! Imagine, then, the desert that was the Sorbonne in 1941. In fact, our pantheon was empty with the exception of one exalted heroine: Joan of Arc. Yet she was also incidentally a virgin, the sole descendant of the mythic Amazons, and the only one who had the audacity to break the chains of her feminine condition and traditions. As everyone knows, she was punished for it and, just like Antigone, Iphigenia, and Jocasta, doomed to a precocious and tragic end.

We can all agree—a rather dissuasive model.

In the twentieth century, in order to void the suffragists' claims, the French press quickly nicknamed them the Suffragettes, a name that made them go down in posterity like some sort of gleeful majorettes for the right to vote. In England, meanwhile, women fought heroically by chaining themselves to the gates of Westminster, throwing themselves under the horses' hooves during the Epsom Derby in front of a dumbfounded crowd, and taking up hunger strikes to win the right to vote twenty years before French women.

It was the same strategy with literature. By treating women like *précieuses ridicules*[17] or as *femmes savantes*,[18] the titles of two of Molière's comedies, women were made fun of for harboring the inclination to do something that appeared most noble for a man: the desire to educate themselves and to speak well. These shocking stock phrases, launched by Molière in 1659 and 1672, became the embossing tools needed to discredit women's creative ambition for a long time.

It's hard to imagine the impact of such stock phrases when they come historically at the right moment. From that moment on, the connection between *learned* and *ridiculous* has been suggested and the tone for talking about it has also been determined: it will be with derision.

Molière's Bêlise, flanked by her sister-in-law Philaminte and her niece Armande, will serve to disqualify both those devoted women, who turn toward hysteria when their man goes missing, and the snooty dames who pride themselves on their writing instead of ironing their doublets.

The patriarchal seventeenth century put order back into families. Despite the bright spot offered by the Lumières in the eighteenth century, despite chin-wagging from the architects of the Revolution, who, though intoxicated by the articulation of so-called universal principles, decided not to apply these principles to women, one can hardly find a female intellectual who is not marginalized and deprived of the chance to impact the ideas of her time.

Laws were needed to bring girls and wives back to their sacred duties. Rightly judging that education was the first step toward emancipation, the Jacobin Sylvain Maréchal proposed in 1801 his famous law to forbid teaching women to read. Napoleon's civil code went even further, establishing "the perpetual and obligatory resignation of women" by barring them from becoming civilians and forcing them to remain minors for their entire lives.

The term *femme savante*, having done its time, ceded to a new expression: "bluestocking," which came to France from England in the nineteenth century. The dictionary informs us that a bluestocking designates "a woman with literary pretentions." For, as we're meant to understand, when a woman writes, the result is always pretention, never literature.

"I don't want any bluestockings in our house," Madame Dudevant told her daughter-in-law Aurore Dupin, the future George Sand.

"I will not accept the fact that my daughter should become a bluestocking," declares the mother of one of the Ladies in Green Hats.[19]

"No petticoats here!" the Goncourts proclaimed, refusing to award *Marie-Claire*, Marguerite Audoux's beautiful novel, the prestigious prize in 1906, because of . . . a petticoat!

Just like *femme savante*, the term "bluestocking" caused an uproar, undermining the reputation of those "deserters" who abandoned their homes in order to have a career. A few words can occasionally kill and cause greater harm than a long diatribe. Barbey d'Aurevilly, an author that my father praised to the heavens, along with J. K. Huysmans, another notorious antifeminist, titled one of his most venomous novels *Les Bas-bleus* (The bluestockings). Albert Cim did the same ten years later. Curiously, this expression never applies to men, however pompous they may be.

Philosophers, scientists, poets, and men in politics[20] are never asked to affirm the equal dignity of both sexes. The ones who do remain isolated examples (Condorcet was practically the only defender of women during the Revolution), and they are labeled gentle oddballs or dangerous utopists (amiable Fourier spent his whole life in destitution). They were never praised in our schoolbooks for their defense of women's rights. Feminism was a whim, an unimportant detail, a nonthought.

Like all of my peers, I remained deprived of any point of reference, of any analysis of my situation, thus without any sort of exit door from the patriarchy.

"If I had to break with tradition, I would have needed heroic courage and I am not a hero," Virginia Woolf wrote.

I wasn't one either and I continued to revel in books that only destroyed me. Without television, it was truly literature, both past and present, that provided young people with the images, models, and fantasies that took shape in society. Gide and Montherlant, along with Malraux and Martin du Gard, were my gurus during the war.

The young people that I met quoted Montherlant at will and guys thought they could share in his grandeur by adopting his obsession with virility. The majority of them were practitioners of that particularly French "parlor room misogyny," and this allowed them to find themselves witty whenever they rattled off the most clichéd remarks about bimbos. To not laugh with them was considered a lack of humor . . . an especially feminine one. So I laughed along with the others . . . you aren't a silly twit for nothing. It took me a while to understand that through acceptance, you participate in misogyny.

My family home, where matriarchy happily ruled, along with my father's perfect consideration afforded to his wife, his daughters, and womankind in general, sorely prepared me for the undisturbed expanse of misogyny that I found in the outside world. More than merely just a belief, it was a way of being, a sort of worldly obligation, a national pastime. A young man had to be either truly intelligent, vaguely daft, or an oddball in order to speak normally about women. And to women.

I was even less hardened since at the Lycée Victor-Duruy, even in my philosophy classes, I was never in a mixed-gender class, and I never had to confront the in-stinctive cruelty or brutality of boys. I arrived completely fresh, without any weapons or armor, at an age when wounds can do harm. Fortunately I scarred well and formed solid calluses where I habitually met with friction.

All the while I waited in order to gain enough audacity to hurt others in my turn.

Dreaming isn't forbidden: the nascent field of psychoanalysis could have based itself on new criteria and saved us from this resignation to our subaltern destiny. But it only mired us further. Freud and his disciples finished locking down our destiny by giving woman a definition that bolstered dramatically those already furnished by Plato, Aristotle, and Tertullus—the ones that had begun to fade. Cloaked in modern dress and wrapped in an impressive theory overall, the same malediction struck us. We became once more "males manqués, castrated men, beings deficient in body and soul." The ideal human model remained the masculine one, so this idea was set in motion again for another century.

Freud was the father of psychoanalysis but we don't acknowledge often enough that there was no mother. Just like Christianity with its long line of popes, this new science was defined by a long line of lay pontiffs. Among this group, a few women filled the role of respectful daughter (so as not to call them submissive): Anna Freud, who became her father's Antigone; Hélène Deutsch; and Marie Bonaparte, who had her clitoris operated on in order to reach orgasm according to Freud's dictate.

It's difficult to go without founding mothers, especially when you are buckling under the weight of the founding fathers,[21] beginning with our eternal Father; the Roman paterfamilias; our Holy Father the Pope, in line with the Church Fathers; without forgetting the folkloric figure Black Peter, a small-scale despot; Father Christmas; the good dons of our colleges; and our father confessor to whom we revealed the depths of our childlike souls before prostrating ourselves before God the Father and consuming God the Son in the form of the Holy Eucharist that only the male abbot, the male chaplain of our school, could bring to our lips. Even in police stations, the women's holding cell is regulated by female personnel. Yet the Church has not followed this policy: no nun, even an abbess, is authorized to hear a woman's or young girl's confession, nor can they give them their last rites.

Thus, the right men come along at the providential moment to legitimate masculine domination. In the nineteenth century, less than in our evolved societies, a few women began rightly to reflect, and to emancipate themselves. Freud did his utmost to bring them back to the fold. Each attempt to escape from the traditional roles was condemned outright: "A woman's desire to succeed is a neurosis, the result of the castration complex which she can only heal through total acceptance of her passive destiny." The "perpetual resignation" inscribed in the laws by Napoleon found its intermediary with Freud in social and psychological life.

Fortunately, I had never read Freud. Otherwise I would have taken feminism for a neurosis or I would have become a neurotic myself.

Even though I wasn't a neurotic (it wasn't my nature), I was still contaminated by this education because inequality is learned from childhood on. For twenty years I had swallowed it up in daily doses without grimacing and I was completely assimilated. I never spoke of the "problem without a name" that Betty Friedan described later.[22] I accepted the rules of the game and I even turned out to be a good loser. I just had the taste of humiliation in my mouth without knowing why.

It took me another twenty years and three marriages to realize that I was playing with loaded dice while men entered into life with the best cards dealt to them, even before they began playing. I was trapped, bound up in an unforgiving network of laws, interdictions, religious traditions, and moral injunctions from which it would prove difficult, painful, and even dangerous to extricate myself.

And you've got to begin again a hundred times over. Each woman must bring herself into the world, without listening to soothing speeches that sap the drive for change. She can't listen to men's stonewalling (and the women who act as their backup) who announce after every stumble and hop that feminism no longer has any reason to exist because equality has finally been achieved.

The only advantage of ignorance and docility is that they allow you to live through anything without too much injury. I was able to survive certain moments as a young woman (which appear to me retrospectively as odious or intolerable) with chagrin but without major drama, revolt, or true suffering.

However strange that might seem in this apparently modern environment, I remained, like so many others, a young woman of the nineteenth century. In many ways, the twentieth century did not truly begin until after the Second World War.

Little by little, blow after blow, through mistakes happily accepted and sacrifices that I tolerated less well, I finally emerged from the gangue of conventions in order to become someone whom I had never imagined, but who would also never abandon me.

CHAPTER 2

Simple Pleasures

November 16, 1939

André Groult
Interior decorator

25, faubourg Saint-Honoré
Paris 8th
Tel. Anjou 26-28

Dear Rosie,
I don't think that you need to focus all of your efforts on
translating Greek and Latin. However brilliant you may
be at these languages, you could get it wrong. Tell me if
you can find a knowledgeable tutor who can teach you
how to write an essay in Greek or Latin. If not, I will try
to find you a fellow of this sort in Paris.

I feel that you should work on it every day. Don't be
satisfied just by reading the great authors of the cur-
riculum, but try working on enlarging the circle. You're

*preparing for your college degree as if it were high
school! Now you must know inside and out the history
of Greece and Rome, and their literature. Don't study to
pass your qualifying exam, but study in order to become
a Hellenist or a Latinist and, you'll see, you will pass
with flying colors.*

*If you translate the two passages included, I will
correct them,* doctus cum libro. *The Seneca is easy,
but there are some delicate nuances. To be honest,
translation is never easy.*

*Yesterday we went to the movies at Saint-Lazare
with the Galanis. Around ten o'clock, dinner at home:
French onion soup, scrambled eggs, asparagus tips,*
choucroute garnie, *and several desserts. But this
morning, vegetable broth!*

I love you, my little dove. Work hard. Kiss Flo for me.
Vale et me ama.

Pater

There, you have all of my father: our quirky relationship,
out of touch with the times and the mundane, confined to
the speculative and a few other limited subjects, but marked
by an infinite richness: antiquity, sports, botany, the sea.
Basically any arena where my mother never set foot.

Flora was extremely maternally dependant. She also would never learn how to drive a car, read a map, distinguish a *Pteris aquiline* (eagle fern) from a *Scolopendrium officinale*. But she skillfully maneuvered among boys, sketched with an airy grace, trembled at the slightest breeze like one of Giraudoux's young girls,[23] and happily put runs into the silk stockings that I had bought with money earned from my first tutoring sessions!

I didn't realize it at the time, but it was with my father that I learned to love, and to practice all of the activities that brought me happiness for the rest of my life.

Like I did, he respected a good effort, whether physical or intellectual. My mistake was that I favored effort over success. "Overcome with respect for authorities and the weight of erudition," Beauvoir wrote, "the female student is too conscientious." My father diagnosed the same sickness in me.

"Reading outside your curriculum, taking a walk, those rich moments when studying and fun come together, these can be more useful, even for the translation of a Greek text, than the dreary memorization of dense syntax."

It sometimes seemed that Pater had read Beauvoir! But I only knew how to "memorize dense syntax" and so I failed my Greek exam twice and didn't receive the highest honors in Latin or philology. The only exams I passed at the top of my class were in literature and English. Falling behind in school was perhaps the equivalent of those cold sores that guaranteed my romantic failures, which in turn allowed me to prolong my beloved studies.

I was able to forget my regimented future during lovely diversions like the long hikes on cross-country skis with my father, with sealskins strapped under the enormous, prewar Scandinavian skis with turned-up points, which were outfitted with straps as coarse as those on a work horse's harness.

Beginning with Father's penchant for telemark skiing, followed by the unwieldy snow plow move, and encompassing the Christiana turn as well as the wedeln, my career as a skier had to accommodate a number of changes to both the material and style, each one turning out to be more and more painful, especially for my feet.

Yes, I certainly miss those horribly ugly Norwegian ski pants to which the snow clung, and the leggings wrapped tightly around the upper half of my boots to keep them watertight.

Yes, I miss those long glacial climbs in the shady trails that led to the lake at Tignes and to the town that has been swallowed up today. With Pater in front of me, brandishing his balaclava like a polar explorer, I followed behind in his footsteps, fortified with ginger ale so that I could keep his pace.

Yes, I miss my ash skies that were so very heavy. Father's were made of hickory. One day I'd get a pair like that, when I passed my baccalaureate exam!

And how I miss those moments once we finally reached the summit: our jackets hung up on our crossed skis, the sealskins stuffed in our backpacks to use as seats upon the snow. We were alone, in all that whiteness, without signposted trails, without preformed jumps or the crowded bars where busloads of shouting, athletic tourist types congregated. We snacked on Meunier chocolates, which have never tasted the same since. We ate a banana. We drank a little orange juice from a metallic-tasting flask. We filled ourselves with this cocoonlike silence while our muscles throbbed with fatigue.

Flora claims today that day lifts and cable cars were already in existence on Mount Geneva and elsewhere in 1936, but our father made us hike up on the sealskin skis so that we "earned" the descent. For so long, I have found effort to be a virtue in itself that I don't even remember if I had been deprived of the relief of the ski lift.

Thinking back on the same hikes, Flora undoubtedly would describe the tortuous early-morning ascents, the snot frozen to the tips of our noses, the angry blister that flared with each step in our cold-stiffened leather clodhoppers, the way the sealskin stubbornly tried to separate from the skis, and the anguish of losing a mitten in the deep while you were trying to retie the straps with numb fingers. She would recall that ultimate moment, when you think you've reached rock bottom: the ski separates and escapes all by itself down the descent, almost mockingly, condemning its owner to give up the other one in order to act out a Station of the Cross in the fresh snow, the sole surviving ski slung over the shoulder like the crucifix itself. Unless, if Pater still happened to be nearby, and then he would take the remaining ski himself, but that wouldn't stop him from descending majestically downhill, despite the crushing stare from the aggrieved party who suddenly weighed two hundred pounds!

All of that is certainly true. It all must have happened to me as well. But memory is selective and my story is my truth only.

And I saw myself triumphantly, shaking the snow out of my boots, which were what they were, and readjusting the straps for the descent (that's when you're most likely to lose a ski), trying to spot the uneven places that were the most likely to cause a fall, trembling with excitement to soon blaze a trail through this virgin surface with the zigzag of my skis.

Even in this moment of happiness, as with all of life's pleasures, a pang of melancholy will strike. The tide will recede once more, curtailing the fishing . . . the party will end and everyone will make their way into the night . . . the last morsel of caviar will be eaten . . . the lover will take the last Métro home . . . The crest you ride after such a laborious ascent will fizzle after the all-too-brief exultation of the descent, just as, face-to-face with the first half of your life, you may hesitate for a moment while the other side is revealed, and then you realize that you will no longer be the master of your own speed, or of your own destiny.

When the skier comes back to the valley, when the fisherman returns to land, these moments share that feeling of superiority to the *vulgum pecus*.[24] The reflection of solitude, the beauty of the unknown shines in your eyes. Your muscles had obeyed, your technique hadn't failed you, your body rose to the occasion. The hunger and thirst that you feel are all the better.

At the opposite end of that exhilaration lay the many humble pleasures of your backyard.

We never had one ourselves. Mother feared having to prepare picnics, dreaded having to dust off and close up a country house. She was afraid of mice and spiders, of mold growing on the walls, and of drafty windows. She preferred visiting other people's houses or staying at home in her large bed, with the half-moon headboard upholstered in shagreen, where she would sketch dresses or paint her nails while singing little ditties from the penny operas that gave me chills.

When she was eighteen years old, she had dreamed of becoming a singer, a stillborn idea in her family's circles. Making dresses seemed less outrageous since it belonged to the realm of embroidery and fashion, acceptable activities for a woman, even though Mother could hardly sew a button. So she opted for fashion, just as her brother Paul Poiret did seventeen years earlier, though she never gave up her singing.

I can't say whether she sang well or not. To me, her voice was indecent, too shrill, and horrifyingly feminine, as were the voices of many women of that era. I would have preferred, if she absolutely insisted on singing, that she sang like the Swedish star Zarah Leander. When she started in with "It's Estelle and Véronique," "Monsieur, Do You," or "Push, Push the Swing," I cringed with embarrassment. Each time that she sang in public for her friends, to me it was worse than if she had appeared stark naked. Her repertoire of sailor's songs especially embarrassed me. At a banquet in Saint-Céré

in 1934 where she was invited by Pierre Benoit to celebrate his election to the Académie Française, she rose to
sing before the hundred or so celebrities gathered there
as dessert was being served: Roland Dorgelès, Francis
Carco, Pierre MacOrlan, Christian Bérard, and the others: *"Ah! Quelle triste vie que celle d'un marin / On y dort à la
dure, on y crève de faim . . ."*[25] Imagine the absolute horror!

But the listeners appeared transfixed and Father loved
it. For me, this terror stemmed from an incomprehen-
sible fixation toward one aspect of parental behavior. It's
impossible to reason with or overcome this fear, and it
remains one of those childhood phobias whose origins
could only be determined after five years of psychoanalysis. Since I was never analyzed, this phobia lasted my entire life, along with that wistfulness for the backyard we
never had. In order to get over it, I ended up with three
backyards! I just couldn't resist the desire to possess what
is charmingly called in French a plesure garden, which
means no vegetables, only flowers!

I acquired the first one in Brittany when I was over
thirty years old, when I considered myself definitively attached to Paul Guimard. A garden is also a lifelong commitment. None of them were large enough for me to plant
a sweet gum, a paulownia or a magnolia grandiflora since
the catalogs assured me that they would take up a third

of my small plot. However, I never would have found the time to write if I had the formal park or small grove of my dreams, a space for imagination. Four thousand square feet already seemed immense.

Providentially my grandfather Groult had a garden in front of the beach in Concarneau that surrounded the vast home where my grandmother Groult, who didn't really like anyone, felt compelled to invite the entire family—aunts, uncles, and cousins—during the yearly school vacation. For many women of that generation, only duty mattered. In any case no one worried about her particular inclinations, but merely looked forward to the date when she would take us all in.

My mother, as I said, didn't like Brittany or country houses at all and her appearances there were scandalously brief. During that season, she was usually preparing her winter collection.

Grandfather was a naturalist and he owned and operated the Maison Deyrolle, under the name of his spouse, on the rue du Bac in Paris.[26] The Sons of Émile Deyrolle spanned four fascinating and antiquated floors, populated with animal pelts, fossils, geological specimens, the skeletons of prehistoric species, insects, butterflies, and thousands of taxidermied animals. Pater, who had a degree in natural sciences and had worked at the journal *l'Acclimatation*, envisioned dedicating his life to these plants and animals. That is until Mother came along. Making the most of Lieutenant André Groult's internal disarray, with his Croix de Guerre military medal and three citations for bravery after he had been thrust back to civilian life in 1918, she tore him from this bestial universe and made him into an antiques dealer, and then an interior decorator who would become famous from 1925 to 1940.

Until I was twenty years old, when the defeat and then the Occupation kept the French from their own shores, I spent the happiest times of my childhood at Ty Bugalé,[27] Concarneau, and Finistère.[28]

There, my best friends were named *Lophius piscatorius* and *Maia verrucosa*, *Gadus merlangus* and *Gadus morhua*, *Zeus faber* and *Scomber scombrus*.[29] Each time I pulled one out of the sea, whether by line or trammel, Grandfather, who resembled the grandfatherly Victor Hugo with his thick white hair and mustache, lifted an index finger contorted by arthritis and yellowed by the corn paper of his Gitanes cigarettes, and said: "*Gadus merlangus*, a cousin of *Gadus morhua*." (If it wasn't a yellow pollock, then it would be *Gadus gadus*.)

At Ty Bugalé, we loved playing croquet (the children of the video-game generation must think that we were a bit simpleminded). We played bocce and tennis and this was where I learned to serve underhanded, just like all of my aunts. "Because of your breasts," they would say mysteriously. But my real sport was sea-fishing. We left each morning at six o'clock on Grandfather's cutter and came back around eleven, dragging a multitude of fish that would seem miraculous by today's standards.

Flora got seasick, which secretly made me happy, so I was able to win easily a reputation for being a real sea dog. She also couldn't stand the smell of the "chum," a mix of sardines' heads and flour which we ground out according to the day's needs in a crude meat grinder that you would find in any kitchen. Then we scattered the mixture over the ocean to "bring up" the fish.

I found myself surrounded mostly by men: Grandfather, master only after God, occasionally Pater, one or two visiting uncles, Flora when the sea was like glass, and my cousin Roland who complacently came to our aid throughout our adolescence, even revealing to us the anatomy of *Phallus miserabilis*. He was barely ten or twelve at the time and the mocking comments of his two cousins, Rosie and Flora, reduced what he had presented to us as something fearsome, to reassuring, if not pathetic, proportions.

During high tide, I skipped the boat and fished for

shrimp with my aunts and cousins. It was the women who fished for shrimp (*Palaemon serrata*), as all of the engravings from the period attest. It wasn't judged a virile sport. Yet lifting tons of kelp with scooped nets is much more tiring than line-fishing from on top of a seawall or seated in a dinghy. The acrobatic hunts in the rocks; the expeditions in the miraculous pools found only at a degree above ninety, but which guarantee a good haul of shellfish in five pulls of the net; the hikes across the sandbars that seemed to stretch out into the sun for eternity while two hours later it's as if they never were. The joy of hearing from the depth of the net the happy squeak which means that a fine mass of prawns has let itself be caught, the satisfaction of feeling the bucket's handle cut into your shoulder, a sign that the day's catch mounts—even today I would go to the ends of the earth to find these simple pleasures once more.

For that matter, I do. Every year for the last twenty, I go fishing at the edge of the western world, in Ireland. I go there to rediscover the joys of my youth, when Brittany's shores were crammed with an abundance of living treasures, where I fished for sea horses in the tide pools, goose barnacles (*Pollicipes cornucopia*) on the sides of boulders, crabs under each stone. At that time, even the smallest child equipped with a simple butterfly net could come back from the beach with a pail full of exciting bugs. Now even the butterflies have disappeared. In particular, the small blue ones, the size of a bluebell, have disappeared. Now, there is less than a one percent chance of discovering a tortoise when you turn over a rock. Though they're as useful today as a musket, the shrimp and butterfly nets are still sold in the tourist bazaars!

Each time that I station myself at a beachhead in Ireland, my eyes trained for the signs that will tell me that the sea is sufficiently low so that I can begin to fish, I become the little child, the young girl, the woman, of all of the tides that I experienced. Without any age except the age of the world at this precise instant, I watch for the magical moment when the sea submits and delivers to me her secrets from within. Against the wind and the tide, I protect myself with an oil-skin coat, a rain hat to guard me against whatever falls from the sky, waders to keep out whatever might creep up from the marine deep. The telephone doesn't ring. Bad news is out of reach. I let go of the whole world.

The smell of the seaweed, the silvery sounds of the water as it gently separates into a thousand rivulets, knowing that this joy will be limited to the hours listed in the *Breton Sailor's Almanac* and that you can't waste a single moment (showing subtle consideration, Nature has made it so that low tide in Ireland occurs at the same hour as it does in Concarneau)—all of these ingredients combine to create a miracle that I call happiness.

The rest becomes anecdote: returning, displaying the bunches of kilos on a waxed tarp, weighing, sorting out the clams, crabs, and sea urchins, drinking vodka and eating the warm shrimp, hearing the same story of those moments that fishing buffs always find so thrilling, discussing the calculations taken into account for the weather, for tomorrow's weather, for what the rest of the week should be like. And the next day, it all begins again, for two, three, four days, according to the rise and fall of the tide. Then suddenly, the sea gives you the cold shoulder and won't show you anything from her deep for weeks.

Pater never went to Ireland. He died in 1967, bringing Nicole with him three days later. People still fished a little bit in Finistère then, especially tourists like me and I thought that it would last longer than I would. But actually everything faded even faster than I did! Just as animals must migrate to find new grass, I had to change my marine pastures. I didn't expect to find a world so violent. The western region of Ireland has been whipped for centuries by an ocean that hasn't met with any obstacles since the American continent, and is marked by "upheavals which follow on the heels of each other without ceasing," as the *Guide Bleu* states. Its shores are torn to shreds, and are headed off by steep cliffs that forbid entrance to the country, attesting to the ongoing duel between land and sea. Located between two clashing areas, the western provinces of Donegal, Connemara, and Kerry know only brief and sublime lulls. In those moments, sand coves shine brilliantly and hundreds of little islands that the Atlantic has not managed to swallow up appear: tiny isles topped with a bit of grass where a dozen sheep graze or ferocious boulder heaps where no human could cross, the refuge of seagulls and cormorants. These islands always make me daydream, little spots whose beauty allow us to forgive the ocean for its terrifying aspects.

In Ireland, these moments of calm are nothing but gifts that the heavens soon regret. The land quickly returns to its demons and the fog comes back to enshroud the shoreline with its cloak pierced with pockets of light.

It's difficult to give up the smoothness of the Breton granite, the calmness of its coves, the reassuring neighboring ports and accept this savagery where solitude brings an added dimension of anguish. No one fishes along the coast in Ireland; no one collects anything from among the rocks, not even a periwinkle. You're left alone with a net, a harpoon, a clam digger, and a screwdriver for urchins amid acres of seaweed with all that getup making you look like a medieval knight.

I have always appreciated these differences but, recently, my troops betray me. I never had to watch out for this faithful servitor, my body, until now when I must remind it of its duties. Now I no longer jump without thinking about the rocks below. My automatic pilot refuses to function and I am forced to consider each step: Let's see, if I put my boot on this rock, I should be able to reach the neighboring one with a little jump without falling into this hole that's three feet deep. Is it safe? Nothing is still safe. The whole countryside has changed. From now on, you have to rest, evaluate your strength, try not to overdo it with this or that muscle that refuses to work overtime. You have to cheat it. Slow down. Stumble. Sometimes crawl along like Lucy, my ancestor. I used to be the boss and now it's as if suddenly my employees unionized and are delivering their new working conditions! Who knows, one day they may sequester me in my own body and I won't have another word to say about it.

One day, who knows, I might strain my back slipping on some algae with my boot stuck in a ditch or I'll fall into the water. I'll call in vain for help and I'll die in a pool which will rejoin the tide at the hour predicted by the *Breton Sailor's Almanac*. A fitting end for a fisherwoman!

CHAPTER 3

'43

It was 1943. I was twenty-three years old. The war waged on the outside and the Occupation's on the inside. Flora, who turned fifteen in 1939, never knew what a carefree adolescence was like. The prime years of our youth were slipping through our fingers.

Saint-François-Xavier, Chambre des Députés, and Solférino, what we thought of as "our" feeder arteries, together with thirty other Métro stations, were shut down, one after the other.

The Axis troops had occupied Toulon when the French fleet foundered. Saint-Nazaire and Lorient were in ruins and there was no longer any free zone. "The Bolshevik danger has been crippled, and the Communist threat has been definitively thrown out of Europe," Hitler declared. The Germans came and took Kharkov and Bielgorod. Von Paulus was wounded at Stalingrad, but the war wore on and France caved in on itself.

In Paris, there was still no coal. We brought our ski clothes down from the attic and went to bed early, reading in bed with a bonnet and wool gloves. Those French born between January 1912 and December 1921 (I would have been one, had I been a boy) had to enlist for the STO.[30] The reprieve given to students was over. The Germans forbade the making of bûche de Noël cakes for Christmas. In any case, it didn't really matter because there wasn't any cream or eggs . . . or logs of any sort.

As for me, I taught a class for young women at the Bossuet Institute, on the rue de Chabrol. The place was run by nuns who didn't wear the habit. I wouldn't have ended up there if I wasn't still sheltered, fed, and clothed at my parents' house. I gave my parents some of my salary. Nicole kept her fashion house alive by making capes for nurses. With her special allocations of thread and fabric, she was able to make a few gowns for the wealthy. Pater became more and more like a mad sculptor with a bonnet on his head, a cloak on his back, and a crazed look in his eye. Without anything but some oak to sculpt with, he spent his afternoons and Sundays in his studio, threatening to burn the pieces of furniture that he hadn't sold in order to keep warm, before trying to make others that he'd never sell anyway.

Even if you could earn a living, there was nowhere to spend your money except on the black market. No more skiing, no more traveling, and I still didn't know how to drive because we had no gas or cars. Ty Bugalé was requisitioned by the Germans and nonresidents were forbidden to go to the coast. The only distraction we had was to wait in line on the sidewalk in front of the shops in the 7th arrondissement. (Those shopkeepers whom we never really bothered knowing now looked down on us.) You always left the house with a string grocery bag, a folding stool, and a book, just in case there was an unexpected distribution.

There were no more parties because of the curfew and since all the boys left, there was no more romance.

Of course, I still wasn't married and in less than two years, I would crown the statue of Saint Catherine.[31] Everyone was talking about this in the fashion world. In Nicole Groult's two boutiques at 25, faubourg Saint-Honoré, the feast day for the Catherinettes was every November 25.

"Leave your daughter in peace," Pater said. "If she doesn't marry, she'll stay at home and take care of us. It will be wonderful."

The worst part about it was that I had just bungled a commendable opportunity with the son of a famous writer.[32]

B. was tall, not v. talkative, but seductive. Professor. Likes music, travel, film. Impeccable social and cultural pedigree, as the classified advertisements say.

I thought he was looking for a SF, excellent family, sweet, likes music, seeking a romantic relationship. Or more.

I had met him at the home of my old friend Yves Ciampi, who was in medical school, like B. Because he worked at the hospital, he opted out of military service to finish his studies in Paris. A doctor! It was the profession of my dreams that I didn't dare choose for myself. It took too long, it was too difficult for a woman, and, as everyone said, it repelled any potential suitors. Ancient languages were better because you weren't compelled to show off in parlor rooms that you knew Greek or Latin. Yet suitors were repelled all the same.

B. and I went every Sunday morning to the concerts held at the Conservatoire or to listen to the Hewitt quartet. He walked me home on foot across a glacial Paris, down the great boulevards to the rue de Bellechasse, all the while discussing with me the direction he hoped to take his life in, and how he needed a wife who understood him and his ideals by his side. He never asked any questions about my own ideals or aspirations. As he had warned me, he wasn't very effusive. But in front of the door to my building, he pressed me up against him for an instant and, across our two thick sheepskin jackets, I felt an electric current pass.

Mother frequented the most famous and the most expensive psychics in Paris. Stroking the glove that I managed to lift from B., they all foretold the same thing in prophetic tones: "Madame, I see that your oldest daughter will receive a marriage proposal. In the near future."

They couldn't all be wrong! My hopes grew each week and everyone watched over me tenderly. Until now I had only brought home the most impossible types: one was the son of peasants and he went to the Sorbonne on a scholarship, but still lived at home with his mother, a woman clad in an apron, in their little bungalow in Vanves (an unforgivable part of town). And then there was the young Jewish student whose mother sold *shmattes* in the market. However this fellow had opportunely disappeared and joined the Maquis. After a few other oddballs of this same ilk, I had finally pulled the golden ticket!

Paralyzed with love, I lived in the clouds until the day I got a letter from B. telling me that he had just gotten engaged to another girl and that he felt it was better not to see me anymore. A lead weight fell onto our household.

"Really, Zazate! You didn't notice anything? All winter long pining away, waiting for him to pop the question, writing him love letters. Don't think I didn't see the light on underneath your door. All of that to discover one fine morning that he's in love with someone else? If you spent less time with your nose stuck in a book, you might better understand human beings!"

"And when I think," Pater added, "that you gave him several jars of *my* chestnut butter, made by *my* hands, with *real* sugar!" (Only those who lived under the deprivations of the Occupation can understand the seriousness of my conduct.)

"You can't catch flies with vinegar," Flora offered, trying to explain my actions.

"Apparently, sugar doesn't work either," Mother retorted. "If only you had let me write those letters!"

And henceforth went Cyrano's shadow. However, I am not Christian and I was also sure that I hadn't failed when it came to the letter writing. The problem was that I froze the moment he appeared. Whenever he visited the rue de Bellechasse, being unsure of my feminine charms, I would slip him a jar of chestnut butter from the sacred reserve. We savored it in my room while listening to the *Variations symphoniques* or the *Dialogue du vent et de la mer* by Debussy, and he said to me, "Love is when two people contemplate the same direction." I didn't dare respond, because, for me, love was watching him and drowning in his green-gray eyes. He always had his mind somewhere else.

Should I add that I never even kissed him on his so-tempting lips? Being in love wasn't a big deal in those naive times. I could become aroused at the strike of a match. And I could keep it aflame. He must have well sensed that I was a bit idiotic sometimes and my shyness made things easy for him. His fiancée, whom he kept secret, was abroad and had only just come back home. I had helped him pass the time so he didn't have to go long without the sweet trappings of being loved.

This time, Pater abstained from saying *"Margaritas ante porcos."* I was fed up with being called a Marguerite! I would have preferred him to say *"Macte animo, generose puer!"* or "Cheer up, child!" That night I needed some comforting words. Instead under the watchful eye of Flora (who loved drama), Mother took me into her arms and I cried in front of the whole family.

"You'll see. He won't be happy with his little imbecile."

"She doesn't even have a high school degree," Father added gently.

B. did end up divorcing, but much later.

I did as well, but from someone else.

In the meantime, I had to make do with a few bores. You know the kind: these boys are always available, paralyzed by love. They help you get over the difficult humps and let you gather your strength for another love affair, a love which they themselves will never be the beneficiaries of. All young women have fellows of this type stockpiled somewhere.

My true problem was that I wasn't taking off professionally. I still hadn't written a tragedy, or a collection of poems, or even a short story. It pained me to meet the likes of literary types such as Paul Morand, Pierre Benoit, André Salmon, and Marcel Jouhandeau in our family's drawing room . . . Flora had been to see the artists Boussingault, Segonzac, Zadkine, Van Dongen . . . Ah well, but Flora was an artist, she drew. And I was exactly what Mother had feared for me: a little schoolmarm!

I hardly dared to say that I liked teaching, that I wasn't unhappy, that after all, the war was not over and we'd see later . . . I even kept a journal that several friends found worthwhile. I gave portions of it to Hélène, a close friend, and also to some fellows in the military. One brought my notebooks with him to Narvik. Another one, a spahi,[33] brought my pages back filled with desert sand. He compared me to Katherine Mansfield! I was going to be a writer one day—that was certain. I was sure of it. "Just don't wait until I'm dead," Mother said.

Terribly full of life, she took my education in hand each evening as we sat on the couch in the living room. How can you escape familial indoctrination when there aren't any parties or television? A whole generation, soon it will be two, can't imagine that we were able to live without television before the war, during the war, and following the war. We didn't even have a portable radio to listen to in our bedroom. For my readers born after 1945, for whom the avant-garde is at least fifty years old, it's completely unthinkable! We might as well be speaking of Clovis's era![34]

Without TV, we had to become our own entertainment. My soap opera was the "troika," the large divan in the living room where the three of us sat each night: Mother, Flora, and I, burrowing under a fur blanket after Pater had gone to bed. My mother was naturally the evening's host. There was always only one agenda: her own. I wonder if sociologists have measured the loss of influence that parents today have suffered due to the three hours on average that children spend each day watching television. We were continually exposed to this maternal discourse and could only escape it during vacations.

That summer, because we weren't allowed to travel any farther, I spent my vacation with Flora at Aunt Jeanne's house. She was one of my mother's sisters, eighteen years older, and she owned some property in Poissy on the outskirts of Paris.

The gentle boredom of the suburbs led me into one of

those mythical attics where the collective memory of an entire family resides, a throwback to the time when people held on to their family homes for a long time, accumulating in successive strata all that remained from previous generations. Next to the porcelain dolls, coiffed with real hair, and their delicate trousseaux that were better embroidered and sewn than the majority of our own wartime clothing, next to the wicker cradle with its big wheels where Uncle Paul Poiret slept, along with my aunt Jeanne and her sisters fifty years earlier, next to the cloak chests and the hat boxes that Jazz Age ladies carried on those dreamy ocean liners, there were some chests and an old armoire containing the complete collection of *l'Illustration* newspaper and hundreds of dusty books. These were books for young girls, and I found on one of the front pages, written in faded pencil, the names of the Poiret sisters: Jeanne, Germaine, and Marie (the future Nicole), for whom this pathetic literature was intended.

Most of these novels were written by women and were resoundingly successful, especially when they described scandalous young people who strayed from the standard model. After a few detours, the good heroines found fulfillment with a Saint-Cyrien,[35] or even better, with a Polytechnician,[36] whereupon they were soon made mothers many times over. The bad heroines, much more endearing in the beginning, became, without exception, after thirty-five years (thirty years in the most extreme instances) pitiful "old maids," either sickly or too horsey, devoted, tyrannical, or hysterical; dressed in shapeless sacks; struck down by early menopause; and left to end their days alone and miserable.

I tore through *Les Sévriennes* by Gabrielle Réval, *L'Institutrice de province* (The country teacher) by Léon Frapié, *L'Initiatrice aux mains vides* (*Burnt Offering*) by Jeanne Galzy, and *Ces Dames aux chapeaux verts* (Ladies in green hats) by Germaine Acremant. (An overwhelming success in 1922, this novel described the story of four old maids who were as mean as they were ugly. The youngest among them was only thirty-five years old but had already lost all hope of finding a husband.) And then I discovered Marcel Prévost's *Les Demi-vierges* (The half-virgins), Albert Cim's *Les Emancipées*, Marcelle Tinayre's *La Rançon* (The ransom) and *La Rebelle*, and finally, *Les Cervelines* by Colette Yver, which received the Prix Femina in 1907.

A jury of women, and women of letters at that, crowned precisely the novel that condemned the emancipated ones and the decadent society that had allowed such deviations to nature! It was proof that, even once they became professionals, the women of the Femina remained masochistic and mindful of tradition in order to condemn themselves, in the vain hope of making amends for their success.

Thanks to this huge public success, the word *cerveline* has come to mean any woman with a beard, those schemers who harbor the conceit of becoming a man of letters, a doctor, or any other learned profession in spite of the intellectual shortcomings that science has shown them to possess.

I had certainly read the classics: *Cousin Bette* and *An Old Maid*, in which Balzac reveals all of the horror that single women inspired in him.

Was it inevitable that being without a man condemned women to such odious caricatures and caused them to figure among the most unpleasant characters in literature?

I had also read Henry James, one of the most ruthless critics of a woman's single status. I hadn't been spared *The Turn of the Screw* or that *Third Person* who goes insane from unhappiness and ends up killing her mother before killing herself. Fate showed no mercy for these unfortunate women.

For the first time, I discovered the distilled poisons in these novels that had deluded the adolescence of so many naive young women. And suddenly, in that attic, I found the source of my mother's repulsion for the job of schoolmistress because the majority of these novels' heroines were just that—schoolteachers!

Poor Mother! In her eyes, being a teacher was a sure sign of becoming an old maid. The job itself demanded a sacrifice of femininity, which, at the very least, prevented a life of debauchery that concluded with the same fiasco. What was I in her eyes other than a *cerveline*, those girls whom Colette Yver mocked as "having let their lives ebb into their brains"?

Furthermore the statistics confirmed her fears: 70 percent of female schoolteachers and professors in the 1930s did not marry while the great majority of male teachers lived a normally married life.[37] In 1938, 64 percent of high school teachers were called *mademoiselle*. For women, teaching continued to be a sort of religious vocation requiring chastity. In the course of my secondary education, I knew only two married teachers. The first, Madame Ansermet, was a widow and therefore had been returned to the proper state. The other, Madame Espagne, my history and geography teacher (a more beautiful name could not have been invented), not only had a husband, but had the audacity to continue teaching while being seriously pregnant. Our upper grades were simultaneously exhilarated and scandalized by this fact. Did this mean that Madame Espagne made love? We had never dared to think such a thing of our other schoolmistresses.

I came back from Poissy deeply troubled. I had almost understood something. But I hadn't yet evaluated my situation from the outside and I didn't know that I was part of a sexual category that was more constrictive than a social class. One clear conclusion remained: I had chosen a profession without a future, especially given my lack of qualifications. Without having passed the *agrégation*, I wouldn't be promoted. Without a promotion, no pay raise. "In the end, perhaps you were made to play a supporting role," my mother said. Why should I insist otherwise?

Yet I glimpsed the first flicker of conscience from within myself. But I had to switch the channel. So when a family friend, an important member of the Resistance, suggested that I work at the Radio Française as secretary to Jean Marin,[38] who had just come back, gloriously, from London, I quit without any regrets my job at the Bossuet Institute. In November 1944, I became a secretary. I doubled my teacher's salary and felt like I had earned the medal of honor.

Nicole suggested to me, in vain, to set my sights on becoming a journalist. Just as I proved incapable of facing a camera five years earlier, I didn't think I had the strength to confront a microphone, or improvise, or even to read a text out loud. My political inertia during the war also began to make me feel ashamed when I found myself next to those men and women who were coming back from London or Africa where everyone had fought for the values that I shared but hadn't felt obligated to defend.

And once more, I couldn't hold my family responsible. A Gaullist from the beginning, motivated out of hatred for the "Krauts" and love of his country, my father ran more and more afoul of his Pétainist friends during the war. We religiously followed the news from London behind our darkened windows and we chanted, as if to exorcise, the proof of Free France, "Radio-Paris lies! Radio-Paris lies! Radio-Paris has German ties!"

"Hitler is mentally ill, like most Germans for that matter, and that's why they will end up losing the war," Pater repeated, even in the darkest days.

But the German defeat was slow in coming. We were still fighting in Alsace. In Paris, we witnessed the arrival of Leclerc's division with the American troops and saw the ranks swell with those fighters from the shadows who allowed us to reach victory. We congratulated ourselves for being on the right side in spite of everything and, if I didn't have anything to be proud of, I didn't think I had anything to reproach myself for either. Without exception, women weren't born to make history but were submitted to its forces. Nevertheless, as the deported returned and the first reports of the camps circulated, a vague shame began to envelope me, unearthing a memory that I had wanted to forget. My parents always lived at 44, rue de Bellechasse. Across from us, at number 35, the *Judische Geschäft* ("Jewish business") of the jeweler Markovitch hadn't reopened its doors.

"They will never come back," said those in the know.

And suddenly I saw the face of a girl of about thirteen or fourteen. I remember that she had chestnut brown hair and big pale cheeks. One evening she came and rang our bell. Her parents had just been detained and were being sent to an "unknown destination." Seals were then affixed over the apartment door and she didn't know where else to go. Since my parents had two daughters just a little older than she was, she probably thought that they would take pity on her and take her in, at least for a few days. But that was just it: they had two daughters and my father refused to endanger them for a stranger, and a Jewish one, at that. We held a family meeting.

"If someone denounces us, if they find her here, we will all be arrested," Pater said. "It's my duty to protect my family. If it were just me, it would be different."

It was undoubtedly true that, alone, he would have acted differently. We believed, as we had been told so many times (by the Germans particularly), that the Jews had played a large part in our defeat, especially Léon Blum,[39] who had not properly prepared us for war. But, at the same time, Father had been a Dreyfusard[40] (as he liked to brag). And it was true that he sent his tobacco rations for months to his friend Max Jacob before he was imprisoned at Drancy, where he died. It was easy to sympathize with each individual Jewish friend but somehow we accepted their collective punishment. That's how French anti-Semitism worked.

And so that's how I was anti-Semitic in my own way, despite boasting about being a humanist.

I saw the yellow star—that mark which sent them to their "unknown destination"—suddenly make an appearance on the chests of my classmates: Hélène Heller, Maurice Werther, Annette Birman. This formula mollified our sensibility and justified our lack of revolt. I saw them in the Métro, confined to the last car, and I thought I did my part by riding with them at the back of the train. But I didn't go any further: the Jews had their own fate that didn't concern me.

I can't remember anymore if I helped send the little Markovitch girl back out into the shadows outside. If I felt ashamed, I had forgotten. I know that she hadn't even gotten as far as our living room. She was like a lost animal: if we let it enter, it would be hopeless. It's better to be firm from the beginning. My parents knew this and avoided making a scene. We also knew not to look at her for too long, the little Markovitch girl.

After all, we weren't the guilty ones, and there needed to be a scapegoat for our crushing defeat. Pater performed heroically in 1914: he had been at the Battle of the Marne where he was wounded. No one could suspect him of cowardice today.

As for me, what had I done to exempt myself from heroism? Or courage? Or even thoughtfulness? What potion had I drunk that made me spend a quarter of my life in lethargy while the civilized world came crumbling down around me, without implicating me, if not in History, then at least in my own story? Why didn't I ever feel the urgent need to break open my chrysalis to become something other than a larva: a human being?

From out of murky depths and across this opaque and inert matter from which I, and so many other young women of my generation seemed to be made, these questions began to see the light of day. I was only beginning to make out this question, but I knew that the answer would be critical. I believe that there isn't anything more important and more vital for the millions of human beings belonging to the female gender.

"What's it called when, like today, the day breaks and everything is spoiled, everything is ruined, yet somehow the air breathes?" What is it called when youth passed you by and you realize that you haven't really understood any-thing and that you're poised on life's threshold, in a devas-tated country that has been ripped apart, and you haven't got much idea as to what the future holds?

Responding to Narsès' question after everything draws to a close in the tragedy of Electra, Giraudoux replies, "That has a beautiful name, Narsès. It's called the dawn."

CHAPTER 4

"A Wonderful Mother"

My mother was a self-made woman. She relied on her own moral code, which wasn't shared by those in her milieu. Because she had plenty of talent, courage, and spirit, Nicole Groult became someone in Parisian artistic circles. She owed this success to her ardent taste for life, something that she ultimately passed on to me (though I only became aware of it much later). She knew how to cultivate a rare relationship with her husband. He never stopped loving her and protected her despite being completely overwhelmed by the sort of woman she represented. He always gave her a hand with her career, even taking care of the financial side of her fashion line (all those numbers that my mother pretended to despise). As for the liberties that she took in her life, she knew to hide them from us. For who can claim to know the true nature of their parents' private lives?

Born in 1889, she had been raised to find a husband, like all of the young girls of her generation. Only Paul

Poiret, the oldest son, was allowed to pursue a career. She had already worried everyone with her desire to become a penny opera singer! And then the war came along in 1914. With wars, as with revolutions, women are freed . . . in the beginning. My mother was one of the rare ones who knew how to preserve this acquisition of freedom. From 1914 to 1918, she was alone in Paris, childless, by the side of her good friend Marie Laurencin, who was painting and spending time at the Bateau-Lavoir with Apollinaire and other artists. I imagine her, with Marie, discovering the complicity and pleasure between women that society seemed to tolerate surprisingly well at this time. This sort of love wasn't taken very seriously. And then Marie made the enormous mistake of marrying a German at the beginning of the war. He was a rich painter, a playboy, and she was forced to leave France and live exiled in Spain. To distract herself, my mother began making dresses for her friends and then she opened up a boutique. Her success took off. If she had left it up to her young husband on her wedding night in 1907, she would already have had four children by 1914, like her sister Jeanne, or three like her brother Paul Poiret, or two like her little sister Germaine and she wouldn't have any career or lovers to speak of! On leave from the war, André could have given her, in his enthusiasm, two more children and then it would have surely been over: Madame André Groult would never have become Nicole Groult.

As for me, I admired my mother on the whole, but the details made me cringe. I hated fashion, hats, dresses, clients. I hated parties and banquets. What's more, I wasn't an artist; I could barely make out the difference between the Sacred Heart at Saint Sulpice and Mantegna's Saint Sebastian.

"Rosie has the sensibility of an English governess," Mother lamented. Granted, I was raised by an Irish nanny until I was ten years old. I took refuge in writing, writing little silly things that I hid under my bed (or where I thought they were hidden). My mother, who rifled through everyone's things, decided that this nascent talent should be exploited and, at fifteen, I wrote a play to mark my debut. She ordered scenery and costumes and put me to work, after buying me a dictionary of rhymes. Because, naturally, I was going to write in verse. I took my inspiration from Joseph Pinchon's comic book protagonist Bécassine: a woodcutter, a fairy tale for small children. Uncle Paul offered to play the woodcutter. Flora was the elf and I was obviously the fairy. I held my magic stick like an umbrella. Uncle Paul hadn't bothered to learn his lines, the traitor! He improvised, which threw off the other poor actors (and it was actually Mother who wrote the majority of the dialogue). At the end, she announced to her guests that they had just witnessed the premiere of the first play written by Rosie Groult. I came forward to take a bow, feeling dread in my soul, for, instead of glory, I felt like a usurper, thrust face-to-face with more proof of my worthlessness. "There are some good things in the play," Uncle Paul told me, winking at my mother. "But you act like an amateur, my poor Rosie!" "Well, she spends her time tutoring those slow students in the 7th arrondissement," Mother said. "If that's her fate, what can you do?"

When my theatrical apprenticeship did not yield the hoped-for results, Nicole turned her attention to my sexual education since marriage would be, without a doubt, my one lifesaver. She quickly noticed my first anxieties on the subject when I came home one day from the Sorbonne with a button undone on my blouse (something which didn't escape her attention).

"Did you nurse a baby today?" she asked me at dinner in front of the whole family with an ironic smile.

Flora looked at me angrily and my father made a nose-dive into his plate, not daring to say "Leave your daughter in peace!"

This first boy was an Egyptian student who studied Latin and Greek with me at the Sorbonne. My mother soon warned me (she had been to Cairo several times to present her collections), "Be careful of Egyptians. I know how they are. They always have something up their sleeve. They are also obsessives who only think about one thing—*that*." She wasn't wrong. The Arab students, arriving in France and seeing the free young women, told themselves that these girls were obviously sluts. You could always sense their desire and their scorn at the same time. In any case, it was very difficult to fall in love when you were exposed to such maternal views: her suggestions for manipulating men horrified me.

"Don't believe what's written in novels," she said. "Sexual relations are generally an unpleasant moment to get through . . . it's very overdone!"

Was it to avoid these unpleasant moments that my mother always had her own room? She claimed to work at night designing her dresses and I did see the light under her door until late. We also had our own bedrooms, Flora and I.

"It's very important for your studies," Pater judged. "I have my studio."

So he slept in the dining room and never in my life did it occur to me to thank him for this!

To be a man in our home wasn't something with an intrinsic value of its own. It was reduced to several duties: bringing up the coal from the basement, fixing the outlets, driving the car, and looking under the hood when it broke down. Occasionally, from time to time, he served himself first at the table in order to say, *Ego primam tollo, quia nominor leo* ("I take the first portion because I am the lion"). Yet just like among the lions, the lioness was the most important. Even artistically, he didn't know how to measure his own worth, or how to sell himself. My mother earned more money than he did. Without her backing his projects and finding his clients, he would have certainly given up. As for his creative abilities, Nicole thought he was a genius and, until the war, he made a lot of money. Unfortunately the decorative style of the '30s fell out of fashion after the war and my father became discouraged. Not long before his death, in 1965, he sold his last pieces of furniture to Drouot. We didn't have any money, Paul and I, but I had really wanted to buy a shagreen piece that I had always seen in our living room. But my father kept me from bidding on it. "Don't even think about it. I want to see just how little anybody cares about what I do." And his pieces all went for pathetic prices. He sat there silently, savoring his defeat. He was a defeated man. I myself didn't truly realize his talent. It's easy to under-estimate those close to you. I didn't really appreciate his creations until ten years after he died. And he died so sadly, all the more so since his wife wasn't there to comfort him: she suffered from cerebral anemia. Today it's called Alzheimer's.

When I see, thirty years later, the insane prices that the furniture from 1925 to 1930 is fetching, particularly Pater's pieces, I just want to cry to think that he died poor, believing himself forgotten. I hope there is a heaven for artists somewhere where he's thrilled.

"Don't be defeatist like your father," Mother said to us. "I'm sure he's a genius. You'll see one day."

Perhaps because of his vanquished attitude, like my own, I bestowed a great daughterly affection upon him. I was his favorite daughter and we formed a team against Nicole and Flora's union. Yet, for years, I wondered if I was truly his. I had noticed several troubling signs: Why was I born in 1920 even though they had been married since 1907? Why didn't they sleep in the same bed even though they showed each other great affection day to day? How come we never caught them in the act of sharing an intimate gesture, or a suspect wink between them? I ended up questioning Nicole about her first encounter with love.

She told me that on the eve of her wedding, as she prepared the nuptial bed, her mother placed a mattress protector under the top sheet.

"That's for the blood, my sweet."

"What blood?" asked the future bride who was then still called Marie Poiret.

"You'll see soon enough, my little one," her mother told her.

Mademoiselle Poiret was horrified by this intimation of being sacrificed upon the marriage altar. And then even more horrified by the appearance, on the given night, of menacing and strange sexual organs that were completely unknown and baffling to her. Not wanting to be bled, she refused to perform her conjugal duty. My poor father, who was no rapist, had to clumsily insist, then beg, but he himself didn't know what a woman was made of, even though he had a degree in natural sciences! Virgins often married, those young things, before the Great War. In short, he got nothing and then he enlisted in 1914, leaving behind, from what I understand, a young virgin wife.

My mother promised to be examined by a gynecologist since she was convinced that there was something wrong with her. She went to see one with Marie Laurencin and the doctor told her, "Madame, you are completely normal and it must go in . . . here . . . where I will show you." Knowing her, I can't believe that she didn't ask several other practical questions so she could be truly prepared for her husband's return. Though she was married too young, she went out frequently during the war and made many friends. In retrospect, I even had a few suspicions about her friend Léon, who later became my godfather. He died when I was nine years old. But, for me, it was never about seeking paternity. André may not have been my father but he was my daddy! Many children often imagine that they were stolen by gypsies . . . I imagined that I had a mysterious father just like in a novel. I even had proof. I knew that my father had remarked once or twice, "Rosie has the exact same feet as Léon, with the big toe separated from the second one. Where did she get this Greek foot?" So he had had his doubts in the beginning too. Many women had cheated on their husbands during the war and plenty of children who had come from somewhere else were attributed to the legal father! In any case, Nicole also played this off successfully, convincing her husband that his suspicions didn't have any foundation. She was clever, as they said at the time. Anyway, I resembled Nicole enormously (except for the toes). There again, she must have been lucky.

I hope that my poor little mother experienced physical pleasure. With women she was never frightened and she didn't have any need to dominate. With women it was pleasure without the pain. I came to realize, much later, that she lived surrounded by several friends who were

obviously homosexual, women couples, who were often
the most beautiful, witty, and eccentric of her friends.
Two among them, Gaby and Tonia, were fairly well-known
antique dealers on the quai Voltaire who were so free in
their tone and manner that I was fascinated. I thought
they were sublime, much funnier than any of the wives!
They often came on vacation with us. Pater liked them a
lot. In artistic circles, during the Jazz Age right up until
the war, a surprising freedom prevailed among normal
customs. But, just as for Colette,[41] men remained the be-
all and end-all.

I remember that on her sixtieth birthday (she was an
Aries obviously) Mother came home triumphantly saying to
my sister and me (who were petrified): "I hope that you'll act
just like me, my little sugarplums, and make love on the day
you turn sixty! Let that be an example for you!"

Her lovers, generally writers or painters, always wrote
to her, dedicating poems to her, sending her flowers, gifts,
and drawings. I imagine that she knew how to playact at
love. So many women were frigid at this time because
of their lack of experience. But, in the end, men didn't
hate that. It was less worrisome for them than those who
were called "nymphomaniacs." The appetite and sexuality of women, especially among their better halves, often
frightened men of this era. They prized "conjugal duty" in

their wives. When it came to eroticism and pleasure, they went to houses of the same name.

In retrospect, I hold one main thing against my father: that he never defended me in front of my mother, that he let me believe that there is only one model of a young woman. As he lauded his wife, he led me to believe that I would be a failure if I didn't conform to this model. He never told me that I could please men just the way I was and that he could have loved a young girl like me. It's something that girls need to hear from their father, if they dare to confront boys with any confidence. Flora didn't have this problem. She knew how to seduce. It was innate and she effortlessly attained the rank her family desired. She was artistically gifted, studied drawing at la Grande Chaumière,[42] and designed plates for Christofle.[43] Then at the war's end, she met a young English officer who happened to be a rich banker, and she married him. She left to live in London and didn't work again until we decided to publish our *Diary in Duo* fifteen years later.

With my father, I experienced the most wonderful moments of my childhood, but I knew that they were intermissions, fleeting pleasures stolen from real life. When I returned to Paris, I fell back under the yoke of "real values," the things that led to success in Paris, not Concarneau. I felt like the rest was a sort of marvelous parenthesis, tied to the spirit of vacation. I know this seems hard to imagine with the backward steps and the following choices I made, but my personality had not yet begun to emerge. I'm surprised that even the war didn't serve as some sort of electroshock to my system. There was, without a doubt, a lack of courage. I was tough, but I wasn't brave. People ask me today, "Why weren't you in the Resistance?" It's easy to ask when you no longer fear anything. You didn't just enter the Resistance by pushing open a door. You had to have character, the ability to take on mortal danger, and a political orientation that I didn't have. When I learned later that Simone de Beauvoir hadn't done it either, nor had Sartre, I felt less shame.

My studies also served as an honorable alibi. And then, today everyone forgets just how much we all were overwhelmed by the tasks of survival: securing provisions, heeding the curfew, navigating the closed Métro stations, surviving the blackouts, the "hay boxes" that we put together to cook our food while conserving energy, the hours we spent trying to catch signals from the English radio stations. There were also one and a half million prisoners. We made packages, we knit scarves and socks, we sent them books. Young women weren't supposed to enter into History, but were there to take care of the warriors.

Since Flora was married and her older sister was still resting on her laurels at twenty-four years old, my mother began to worry. I wasn't going to win the lottery like Flora so she had to resign herself to my engagement with the sole suitor from the ranks, Pierre Heuyer. He was a medical student intern. He was also a poet and had written two plays inspired by French playwright Jean Anouilh. He was the son of a spectacularly Russian baroness, who was also a dramatic alcoholic, and of a professor of medicine, a neuropsychiatrist whose career was cut short because of his Communist sympathies. To my chagrin, my future father-in-law was very short, dressed terribly, and had very little money.

"Rosie is going to marry the son of a lush and a dwarf," Nicole told her friends. She had nicknamed him Professor Nimbus, a popular character from a comic book of the time—a tiny little dazed scientist with a mad tuft of hair on his bald head.

I didn't dare confess to her that we had fallen in love based on a case of mistaken identity straight out of Marivaux! I wasn't waiting for him that night in my tent at Ingrandes, on the banks of the Loire River where Flora and I had gone with a bunch of friends. I was hoping to find Jean Deniker, another medical student with whom I was madly in love. But he had become completely infatuated with another girl, who happened to possess much more allure than I did. And so, at midnight, he sent to my tent his friend Pierre Heuyer. I learned later that this little group of Incredibles,[44] as they called themselves, often employed such an exchange system to show their male solidarity in the face of the troop of females whose prattling and vague amorous attempts needed to be curtailed.

Deniker was tall, dark, and handsome. Heuyer was a small, blond, ironic type. But it was dark in my tent and I was aroused, finding myself alone with a man in such a confined space where something unplanned took place. Because it wasn't him, because it wasn't me.[45] And so Pierre and I fell in love in my sleeping bag!

Three months later, he hadn't dared tell the other Incredibles that he wanted to marry me. I hadn't dared to tell my parents that I loved a boy who wasn't finished with school, who was one year younger than I and barely a few inches taller, with no money and an outlandish mother who spoke four languages but was hardly presentable in our upper-crust circles.

To top it all off, three months later, the night before Pierre was supposed to leave with the Incredibles to join Leclerc's African division via a clandestine network in Spain, he suffered a hemoptysis. Though we were supposed to celebrate our engagement, and I was given a ring that I still wear faithfully sixty years later, Pierre (with death already in his soul and in his young twenty-three-year-old body) was sent to a sanatorium in Sancellemoz, on the Assy plain.

He spent eight months there in intensive treatment until they were able to declare him "negative," meaning that he was free from Koch bacteria. He was allowed to return to Paris to marry in June 1944. However it was just a remission. Before the discovery of the drug Rimifon, tuberculosis rarely spared its victims. The sick were very poorly cared for in the sanatoriums during the war. There was an overall lack of everything, even coal. Every week I sent him some Nestlé flour that I bought on the black market, with some eggs, usually one or two, which I took out of my family's ration. Trains weren't running then, so it was impossible to go and see him. We wrote to each other every day, waiting both hopefully and terror-stricken, for the Allies to arrive.

We were married on June 1, 1944. Instead of a honeymoon, we had to make do with a stay in the suburb of Villiers-Adam, at a friend's house. After a very brief life together, one of the follow-up X-rays revealed that Pierre's damned left lung had been newly infiltrated by the enemy and he had to return to Assy. At the end of several weeks, despite the pure air of the high altitude and the necessary rest, the spread of the bacteria had accelerated. Dr. Tobé, the chief surgeon, decided to try a last-resort operation: an extrapleural pneumothorax, which was an awful variation on the classic pneumo and as painful as thoracoplasty.

The surgery was successful, they told us, but there had been a mistake, which caused the long scar running down Pierre's back to open up over twelve centimeters, like a disgusting, wheezing, sagging mouth trying to breathe.

My young husband took forty days to die from an infection of the pleura, followed by septicemia while the Americans were arriving with the miraculous penicillin. They were just one week too late.

At the end, I was by his side in Sancellemoz. He died like a Russian, reciting for me the most heartrending poems which his father later published as *La Leçon des Ténèbres* (The lesson of the shadows). He laughed in the face of God when the sanatorium's chaplain came by his room each day, poking his head in. The priest smelled that death was imminent and thought Pierre would be sufficiently weakened and ready to accept the support of the Church.

In death, he returned to his origins, his facial features revealing the muzhik within, with his large cheekbones, silky blond hair and that look—half-childlike, half-ancient that the young dead sometimes possess. His face was at peace when he was no longer suffering, but I kept searching there for the simultaneously tender and sarcastic look that had seduced me on our very first night together.

When we are faced with the unbearable spectacle of the death of a young loved one, the craziest ideas come to the surface. I told this story using different names in *Diary in Duo*. I couldn't bring myself to admit that after such a short life together, everything was finished. Nor could I end the affectionate and esteemed relationship that I had with dear Professor Nimbus, whose generosity and avant-garde leftist ideas I admired so much. To prolong the story and to stay connected to this family, I saw only one way: I needed to have Pierre's posthumous child. Pierre's mother was from Saint Petersburg, that city that endured so much anguish and merited so much admiration during its two years of siege. I had always romantically dreamed of having a child with Russian blood and Philippe, Pierre's brother, bore a surprising resemblance to him. Against all expectations, their father immediately accepted my plan. He was seventy years old but still a man of great heart and it was the heart and the heart alone that led us to this crazy act. Out of our sadness, this idea helped some sort of hope grow. You have to remember the atmosphere as the war ended: the horror of the camps was being discovered, there was Oradour,[46] the bombing of Dresden with its 7,000 dead, French towns in the west had been completely razed to the ground. We were no longer living a normal life. There were no rules and my small individual act didn't weigh heavily in this context. It was nothing but a gesture toward life in the face of omnipresent death.

We had to act quickly if we wanted this child to pass for Pierre's. Philippe, who had been mobilized to Alsace, only had three days on leave to bury his brother and try to change my fate.

He came to my house the next day and we made love without uttering a word, as if it were a sacred duty. Leaving, the only thing he said to me was: "Stay in bed for an hour. That gives the spermatozoa the best odds." He also studied medicine.

I had the feeling that I was giving new life to my love for Pierre. And I knew that I was fertile because I had already conceived this child one year earlier, during our engagement. The growing embryo was discovered like all embryos in those crude times, without warning and without our consent. Pierre had just come back from six months of exile in the sanatorium and he had to return there for months in order to shore up his healing. How could I help him with this challenge if I was pregnant? We had to choose between the young living person of twenty-three years whom I loved and a few embryonic cells that had entered into our lives like thieves and were now planning on implanting in me against my wishes. I didn't hesitate one second. Pierre had studied for his boards with a reputable professor who accepted grudgingly, upon the insistence of my future father-in-law, to give us a fresh start, as long as I submitted to the curettage in silence, without a fuss during the monthly gynecological consultation that he held at his home on the boulevard Saint-Germain. It was too dangerous for him to operate at the hospital: abortion was still a crime in '44 and it could have ended his career. Since I was only four or five weeks pregnant, the procedure would only take about twenty minutes, without anesthesia of course (he wasn't set up for that). It took less than a half hour to become a real young woman again, one who could get married in white three weeks later at the Church of Sainte-Clotilde.

Fearful but determined, the two of us set out for the doctor's office on bicycles. Pierre waited for me on the terrace of a café on the other side of the street. I remember that it was one of those beautiful May days in Paris. He was more emotional than I was and his eyes never left the window behind which Doctor V. was working. I found courage by proudly showing Pierre that I chose him over the baby.

I also found courage in the tales of so many members of the Resistance who, under torture, endured solitude and panic, face-to-face with the hatred of their tormenters. What was my little curettage in a cozy doctor's office compared to what they went through? Twenty minutes of gritting my teeth and then I was offered a small glass of cognac by Doctor V. after his operation and the assurance that everything would be fine after a few days' rest at home with my family, who certainly knew nothing of this whole affair. Two days later I would be as good as new.

In my father's *Encyclopédie Quillet*, under the word *abortion* I read: "Used generally for female animals. Not used for women unless it is related to a criminal procedure."

Crimes are best not spoken of in families. Only Pierre's father knew about it. I pretended to have an upset stomach and my fiancé came to work beside me each day, on the rue de Bellechasse. He was still hoping to pass his boards, not knowing that a new hemoptysis would cause him to return to Sancellemoz three months after our marriage. And this time, he wouldn't come back.

Alas Philippe and I were unable to force our fate. Though I have been pregnant so often against my wishes, I had failed this time in my attempt. And, horror of horrors, the little brother Philippe, who had just turned twenty, got himself killed a few days later. It was as if Pierre died a second time. I will never forget the emotion of my father-in-law who took me into his arms the day of the burial of his second son and murmured into my ear, "You are perhaps carrying all that remains of my two children."

Life's a bitch and she refused me this gift. She doesn't like it if you take too many liberties. She made it clear that my love story was finished, definitively, this time. And I was in some way widowed twice.

My mother wanted me to come back home, but this move backward was just what I feared. France was in the midst of rediscovering her freedom and I wanted to find my own. I ended up living far from my parents in the 16th arrondissement and I worked at the radio station. General de Gaulle headed up the government, Paris was coming back to life, and I also wanted to be resuscitated. I had just spent a month face-to-face with death, the death of all those young people who inhabit the sanatoriums, especially Pierre's—that death which took forty days to pass over his young body, moving from fiber to fiber. I couldn't do anything else for him, or for his family, except to live.

It was the Liberation that saved me: the American presence in Paris, the duty to smile at the military men in the street, the sudden explosion of joy after five years living under the boot. I lived six months of a wild life. What I should have learned when I was eighteen years old, I devoured at twenty-five! You learn quickly at this age when you're no longer encumbered by your parents, morality, or any illusions. During this time, I truly became someone else, which allowed me to discover that we're not just one thing as I had thought. Rather we carry in ourselves different characters, who are unexpected, surprising and so thrilling to visit sometimes. My American apprenticeships[47] were a fountain of youth. I needed them in order to erase Miss Rosie Groult and Mrs. Heuyer the widow. In order to live the real life of a young woman, which, after all, I had never known.

CHAPTER 5

My American Apprenticeships

❧ The period of my life that coincides with the end
of the Second World War has remained for me a sort
of luminous parenthesis, a time when I played hooky and
started living again after a difficult adolescence and a marriage marked by illness. Pierre's death had created a huge
hole in my existence and France's Liberation, after five
years of war, opened wide the windows with such a gust
that it threw open the doors to the future. Since 1939, we
had lived life as if time were suspended and now real life
was beginning again. I had just started my radio job. I was
financially and romantically independent. I had my own
apartment, as well as the desire to forget, or rather, the desire
to live once more that youth that had completely eluded me.
These five or six months were my education. I wouldn't say
my sentimental education,[48] but I wouldn't call it an erotic
education either because after a war, eroticism isn't necessarily on your mind. We wanted to get our lives back, to find

reasons to laugh again, to take part in all sorts of pleasures all at once, even if it was just getting enough to eat of the foods that we had forgotten. I still associate Americans with concentrated milk, with chocolate, with Spam, with whiskey, with jazz, and with love of course! We were bingeing!

Like my sister Flora, I was lucky enough to speak English fluently and so we were able to become translators and welcome hostesses. Le Centre Franco-Allié and the American Red Cross were looking for young girls or young women who could speak English well in order to serve as volunteer guides to the Americans on leave. We were to take them around Paris to see the sights, and have them meet our French families. We signed ourselves up, as did many of our friends, for this cultural alibi. I even visited the Arc de Triomphe several times. Napoleon's victories were among the rare events from French history that the Americans could remember. I also climbed to the highest level of the Eiffel Tower for the first time in my life. I was seeing more of Paris than I ever had before while showing it to strangers!

But, let's be honest, culture served as a pretext. In reality, we went out to the clubs, not to fall in love, as you might believe, but to eat.

Our main activity was to attend every Saturday the dancing sessions at the Independence, an officer's club based at the Crillon Hotel. There was also the Rainbow Corner, a club reserved for GIs, and the Canadian Club, full of good-looking fellows with lumberjack shoulders, in a large requisitioned hotel on the avenue Montaigne. We would arrive around five o'clock and cast an appreciative eye at all the young men. They were well-fed and clad in their impeccable uniforms, a far cry from our poor privates who had survived the debacle.

Then "Shall we dance?" and the game had begun. But first you had to get there. By seven o'clock, you had to have won an entry ticket to the restaurant, which meant that you had to have been invited by an American. They were each allowed to bring one girl. In the dining rooms of the Independence Club, on the second floor of the Crillon, we knew that a feast awaited. As much concentrated milk as you wanted, Coca-Cola—an exotic drink to us—some white wine of course, as well as steaks (each one worth twenty of our ration tickets), cakes filled to the brim with cream, real coffee—all the things that we had dreamed of during our months of chewing rutabagas, sitting close to our sawdust stoves.

It was such a startling spectacle to see the daughters of upstanding families competing and soliciting these young men, freely exchanging almost bitchy remarks (since their partners hardly ever spoke French): "Oh, so you found one for yourself? So you'll be going up tonight?" all the while beatifically staring up at these guys who normally wouldn't even get a hello at a Parisian party. But no one wanted to be left rejected outside in the shadows. In other words, we didn't want to go home to our freezing apartments to snack on the three-and-a-half-ounce ration of corn bread and an omelet made from egg powder.

And so we rapidly learned the techniques of picking up men. I'm sure that this served me well later. As the hour grew late, we had to scale back our original intentions. By ten to seven, any oaf in uniform could serve as our Prince Charming. But, just like in the fairy tales, we were turned back into Cinderella well before midnight, and trucks took the place of the pumpkins. It must be understood that Virtue and Virginity were still thought very highly of back then. Most of the soldiers didn't have leave for the night, or they were stationed in barracks in the suburbs and had to be back in their trucks by ten o'clock. Meanwhile, so many of these hostesses still lived at home with Mommy and Daddy. In the end, they could play the flirt without having to do the deed—a real young girl's dream!

I lived in a tiny apartment on the rue Raynouard. It had a view of the rooftops of Paris. It was very Mimi Pinson and certainly conformed to the American stereotype.[49] That was what led to my downfall! Every time that I go to the Crillon now, which is where the Prix Femina[50] jury meets, I nostalgically remember that young widow who locked up her blue bicycle to the iron gates of the hotel, in front of the splendid Place de la Concorde, where there were hardly any cars in 1945. I think of that young woman who went along to these dancing teas like you might go to a market for men.

The best part about these men is that they never stayed long. You didn't have the time to get caught up in stormy trysts or to fall into the trap of a mad love in which so many innocent young women were engulfed, later believing that they could justify their lapses in judgment. It was better to admit the truth: we were, more or less, making love with perfect strangers—something most of us would never dare try again in our real lives.

I lived these months in a sort of egotistical joy. Pierre's death fell away into a chasm, along with France's defeat, the disappearance of so many friends, and my youth. (I cultivate oblivion willingly. It's a survival skill.) Plus, the Americans weren't men, they were our liberators. We were making love with our refound liberty . . . well, the instruments of this liberty. In the arms of these men, we celebrated the end of the Nazis, the regained territories, and the hope of universal peace. This lent a historical dimension to our . . . excesses.

Finally, it must be acknowledged that this sexual impunity gave us a carefree lightness unimaginable up until then because the Americans all used condoms. We didn't even talk about them; they just took them out of their pocket when the time was right. In the beginning, I saw them as some sort of cause for humiliation. I had never even seen a "French letter" (as they were called) up close before. Had someone told them that all French women had venereal diseases? But soon enough I came to appreciate the fact that I didn't need to fear the end of the month. This feeling of safety compensated largely for the condom's little snap as it was adjusted at a moment when you would have preferred to think of something else. In any case, this gave me entry to an insouciant pleasure, to lightness, to a taste for seduction that I never quite felt again afterward. Similarly I never found a French man to possess the touching admiration that so many American men had. They were in awe, finding themselves in Paris and struck by the allure and offhand manner of the Parisian women. France, and especially French women, reveled in real prestige during this time. They all thought of us as exceptionally skilled at making love with the most advanced techniques, as if we had all trained in the famous cabarets of Pigalle![51] But even more surely, none of this was of any importance in the end because they never stayed. It was man in his purest state, just under the guise of different faces, in an elementary relationship freed from social constraints and what others might say.

Their ignorance of Europe stupefied me. They hadn't the least inkling of what the Occupation had been like for the French. They hardly believed us when we told them we went without coal, wood, electricity, soap, butter, hot water. War, OK, but how can you go without soap? When Tex, or Red, or Bill came to have lunch at my parents' house, they brought all they could from their stores of reserves: cartons of eggs that had been laid in the United States fifteen days earlier, tins of pâté, chocolate, honey, cigarettes. Nicole didn't know what to think of my behavior. They wondered if I was turning into a harlot or a "courtesan," as Pater said.

"She's grieving," Flora explained. "Rosie never complains but I know she's suffering. The poor thing needs to let loose."

And so I let them say it and I certainly let loose!

A few of my friends had let loose to the point where they married Americans and went off to live in Wichita, or in Austin. We promised to write to each other and to see each other often. In reality, they were just as lost to me as young African women, forced to marry and leave the village where they were born to become transplanted into an unknown tribe where they had to learn to call a stranger Mother.

The thought of being gathered on a boat with other "war brides," like prisoners of war from older wars who were brought back in the luggage of victorious soldiers, the idea of crossing the Atlantic to meet the horrible American "Moms" who would be wondering what sort of spell these French women had cast to turn their little boys away from the perfectly lovely young women they had picked out for them, these thoughts made my blood run cold.

I did nevertheless fall in love with one of my liberators, a B-52 pilot. He was certainly quite skilled since he became one of Eisenhower's personal pilots. He wanted to marry me and bring me back to live in Blue Bell, a small town in Pennsylvania. He was Jewish, a butcher's son, and his family, having better prescience than others, fled Germany in 1928 when he was just twelve years old. He didn't really acquire any culture in any of his successive home countries. In his native German village, he was relegated to the back of the classroom because he was Jewish and the teacher never paid him any attention. In Philadelphia, he had had to work right away as an apprentice in a bakeshop. He never read a book. Though he traveled through many countries, he only knew their airports and was only interested in those flying fortresses, the B-52s. What would have become of me in Blue Bell, a poor little girl from Brittany far from her village, waiting for her pilot-husband to come and tell her all about his latest flying exploits?

He never understood why I refused to go live in America: I, the poor citizen of a vanquished and ruined France. Besides, I continued to see him for the rest of my life. We never quite succeeded in abating our love for one another. He was the inspiration for the hero in one of my best novels, *Salt on Our Skin*, though I turned him into a sailor and fisherman in the novel.

In 1945, the Peace Treaty was finally signed and the American troops left Paris. I found myself, like France, having to reconstruct my life. But I had been convinced, after this interlude, that I had become a seasoned woman who knew how to "go there" with men. Certainly with French men it would be harder, but I had plenty of confidence. I was just twenty-six years old and it was time to find a real companion and to have a real child. And here again we found ourselves victims of the way History catches up after five years of stagnation. We were tempted to do everything too quickly: make a home, have children, be successful at work, then be ridiculously happy—the hallmarks of any typical postwar syndrome.

I worked at Radiodiffusion with Georges de Caunes, a tall, sexy reporter. He was brilliant and was known as the live wire of the editorial staff. I thought that I'd have a lot of fun with him. I needed something light and stable at the same time, so we married in a hurry.

As for children, I also had them rather quickly: two in two years! Unfortunately the marriage itself went by rather quickly as well.

CHAPTER 6

Poor Zazate

It is often during the first days of marriage that the roles are assigned and that the one who loves the most will lower his or her guard for the rest of their life together.

From the first day of my marriage in March 1946, my mother formed her opinion as to the type of couple that my husband and I would become.

At lunch one day at a black market restaurant that the radio personalities and other press types went to, my young husband, Georges de Caunes, seized the occasion to show that he wasn't "married-married," as they say in Tahiti, and that, for him, his friends and his job came first. My doting, lovey-dovey ways, and my conviction that love was going to open up all of his secret passageways to me, made him bristle. I tried to take his hand. I thought he might make a few authoritative moves in my direction. At the very least, I tried to glimpse in his eyes some sign of conjugal complicity while, in order to underline his point, he simply avoided eye contact.

"Calm yourself down," he finished, pretending to be alarmed so as to make everyone laugh. "You would think that this is the first time you've been married!"

"And it's probably not the last, so you'd better watch out!" I should have gaily retorted.

But that idea hadn't even occurred to me. Instead I thought that I should be the first to laugh. Georges was really priceless; everyone thought so. But Mother, who was watching us, could already read the future in my submissive eyes. "It's over," she thought. "My poor little Zazate has started off on the wrong foot."

It seems that I hadn't retained anything from my American apprenticeships, from all those individual lessons where I had learned with delight how to carry myself as a free woman, well aware of her charms. With Paris liberated and the Americans gone, "poor Zazate" came back. What's more, I already suspected that I was pregnant and this secret child deprived me of the last snippet of freedom, the final chance of taking the plunge—the fantasy that lets you think that, right until you reach the church steps, you can still change your mind and escape, leaving behind all your astonished guests. This time the game was up.

Georges was tall and thin, with moss-colored eyes (which is just how they're described in romance novels for schoolgirls). He paraded about with a group of young journalists who were going to soon make names for themselves. His lithe way of walking, his offhand nature, the curly hairs that escaped from underneath his shirt-sleeves, his ironic little smiles, his awkwardness with women—to me, all of these things seemed the epitome of sexiness.

"Yes, he's a pretty boy," Mother had conceded. "But doesn't he seem a bit provincial? Don't you think, André?"

André remarked that, indeed, Georges was from Toulouse. But not everyone can be born in the 7th arrondissement. To be from the country was a handicap in my family's eyes and the fact that Georges was well on his way to becoming a brilliant journalist, known for his way with words and his caustic tone, hardly made up for his origins. The radio, just like the television that would come along a few years later, didn't impress artists or the bourgeoisie. In their eyes, Georges was nothing but a circus performer, barely better than a street hawker selling ties in the market on the strength of his smooth sales pitch. But I was, after all, twenty-six years old and Nicole began to lose hope. First with a "consumptive"—the word tuberculosis was avoided at the time—who died, and now with a clown who hadn't lost his southwestern accent, I had decidedly not shown any consideration for my family.

Since my first marriage, my actions were motivated by a desire to oppose familial principles. Georges became more worthy of being loved the more my parents put him down. The opportunity to land a particular apartment, the fear that my future husband had a mistress who might take my place, my desire to have a child—all of these things took the place of a more serious evaluation of our chances of being happy together. We made the mistake of marrying too quickly instead of living together in sin, not allowing ourselves the time to realize our error, which was so flagrant that we could have quickly discovered it had we been given the chance.

I never knew if Georges also felt trapped from the very beginning. He wasn't a man to share his secrets. Yet the sorry memory of our honeymoon trip makes me think that he was never any happier than I was.

We went skiing courtesy of the Tourism Bureau, which organized affordable excursions for those with meager salaries. I hadn't left France during the war years, nor had I been skiing in seven years (nor had I a supposedly loving man in radiant health all to myself). This time nothing was going to stop me from being happy and this certainty made me light up in such a way that he must have found obscene. Nicole always told me not to go overboard in displaying my enthusiasm, that I should make others want me before showing my own fervor. It's true that I had seen this type of tactic work well for Flora, for my friends, and in all the novels, but I didn't emulate it myself. To hell with tactics when you're in love. Giving my entire self, with no strings attached, seemed more honest to me. That was before I knew the true character of the stranger who had become my husband.

I learned my first lesson on the train. Crossing the border, especially into Germany or Austria, was still taken very seriously. Naturally my new "head of household" held on to our passports, our visas for Kitzbühel, and our third-class tickets. At the border station, he got out to go buy some sandwiches and to see about our authorization. The train started up again before Georges had returned to the compartment. I thought that he had mistakenly jumped into another wagon and would soon reappear, dashing, handsome, and so pleased to have given me a fright. He didn't come back until one hour later. At least it seemed to me to have been an hour. In addition to being frightened by the prospect of finding myself in a hostile country without a passport and a ticket, I was afraid that he had been stopped on the train platform. For the last five years, everyone thought in terms of arrest whenever someone was running late. I imagined all sorts of hypothetical explanations except the right one: namely that he had sauntered down the platform, then through the train, looking for a buddy who was supposed to be traveling as well. Just because we were married didn't mean that he needed to keep me informed of his every movement.

I reassured myself with the thought that he had never been married before, and hadn't learned in childhood how to be loved. I was ready to show him the pleasures of true intimacy. I didn't doubt that we'd get there. He was going to love it.

During the week we spent in Kitzbühel, I was constantly sick to my stomach and food made me nauseated. I was actually one month pregnant but my body was ailing elsewhere: my heart was sick.

Georges appeared panic-stricken whenever it was just the two of us. I was going to grill him, interrogate him about his past, his feelings—everything that he dreaded, without a single ally to come to his aid. I suspected that he may have tried to recruit one before leaving, his friend that he couldn't find on the train, for instance. During the trip, he resented me for being his wife and his disparaging comments accumulated. He sought to wound me, just enough so that I would get it. But I was one of those girls who pick themselves up smiling, without any hard feelings, desperately determined to be happy. Later, between us, there would be routine, the children, the reporting—he would go to the ends of the earth—but then during this honeymoon trip it was impossible to escape. Ecstasy and staring into each other's eyes were the order of the day. The horror!

He coped in his fashion by plunging into the newspapers. Fifty years later I can't picture myself a single time in his arms. I must have been, of course . . . but my recollection is of newspapers strewn across his twin bed in our room in Tyrol, with him taking cover behind them. *But!*, *Club*, *Sport-Dimanche*, *l'Équipe*, *Cheval-Pronostic*, *Paris Turf*— he read them all from the first line to the last. Naturally they were sports newspapers, and I never had anything to say about them.

"Let me read, sweetie. Can't you see that I'm busy!"

He also called his niece in Toulouse "sweetie." This was just one shade away from the difficult "my darling" and the unpronounceable "my love." Remembering the poems and love letters that Pierre wrote brought tears to my eyes. He called me "my I," I for idolized one.

At least I was happy to be skiing once again. Georges didn't really like it. I was better at it than he was. The whole world was upside down.

I quickly foresaw the fiasco: "Abandoned on her wedding night. . . . The vile seducer, just married reveals his true face . . ." In the end, I was no better than the pathetic heroines from the novels that I had read in Aunt Jeanne's attic, just another one of those silly ninnies who believe that they're marrying for love and then wake up next to a husband whom they don't understand at all. I couldn't resign myself to having made such a terrible mistake. I had only one choice: to transform the mistake into a victory. There was only one way to reach this goal. I would become the perfect wife, one he couldn't help but adore.

"I believe that in marrying, one of the two must renounce all thought of self, sacrificing not only will but opinion, accepting to see through the eyes of the other, to love what the other loves, etc. What torture and bitterness when you marry somebody you hate!" wrote George Sand. "But also what an inexhaustible source of happiness when one obeys the one one loves! Every privation becomes a new pleasure. One sacrifices both to God and married love, and one does one's duty while building one's happiness."[52]

That's what I believed in the beginning, like so many other women. It's exactly what Aurore, née Dupin, believed when she wrote those words in a letter to her dear friend from boarding school, Emilie de Wismes, in 1823 when she married Casimir Dudevant. Four or five years and two children later, Aurore divorced in order to become the famous George Sand so that she could live her life freely, throwing herself into politics, as well as into love, and writing over thirty novels. I didn't yet know that four years and two children later, I too would get divorced, take back my maiden name and contemplate eventually beginning to write.

Just how far can love compel us to forget ourselves completely? What percentage of opinions can be betrayed before you destroy yourself? What level of similitude can you reach? None of these questions occurred to me as I slogged away toward that perfect unity.

After about a year of marriage, Aurore too was intoxicated by her sacrifice and she wrote a letter to her Casimir. I would have only needed to change a few words if I had dared to write a similar letter to Georges.

She wrote, "I saw that you did not like music, so I stopped practicing, because the sound of the piano drove you away. You used to read to please me, but after a few pages, bored and drowsy, you would let the book fall from your hands. Above all when we talked about literature, poetry, or ethics, either you did not know the authors I spoke about or you called my ideas crazy, exalted, romantic sentiment. So I ceased to speak of them. I started to be truly grieved to think that there could never be any concert to our tastes. . . . Frightened at the thought of living alone, I decided to adopt your tastes."[53]

I made the same resolution. Boredom ensued since submitting to my husband's tastes first meant forgetting my own. There wasn't enough room for two value systems. I had to study the sports that I knew absolutely nothing about: rugby, boxing, bullfighting, and horse racing, and then had to read about it all in the Sunday papers. Fortunately Georges's desire to keep quiet how much he was losing from his bets saved me from going to Vincennes and Longchamp with him. But I attended, with seemingly great enthusiasm, rugby games without ever understanding what those pileups were all about. I just let myself admire their backsides and muscular calves. I followed Georges to boxing matches, closing my eyes in horror at each hard hit. I pretended to admire the beauty of the bullfighters and to ignore how all the blood made me sick. I set about laboriously commenting on all the news from the sports pages, and I submitted to the sacred schedule of our Sundays: in the morning, the predictions; in the evenings, the results. Finally I tried to take an interest in his friends, which quickly led to the thinning out, then the disappearance of my own (who tried grudgingly to remind my husband that I had had a life before him). Soon enough he wanted to see his friends without me because they usually came without their own wives. In the years after the war, men and women didn't yet know how to live together.

Males formed a vast club where war banners of virility flapped in the wind. They felt comfortable there, especially the men from the southwest, where a solid tradition of hunting, pétanque,[54] Basque pelota,[55] cocktails, PMU,[56] and other activities that left out women reigned supreme. Just like at the Rotary Club, women were only invited to birthday parties.

With even more seriousness, I forced myself to be critical on the points already raised by Georges, notably, my tendency to be a bluestocking. He seemed convinced that the requirements of marriage and motherhood would soon rescue me. Bluestockings, in his eyes, weren't true women, but a sorry attempt, always destined for failure, to copy men.

The sweet exhaustion and the animal pleasures caused by pregnancy (especially with the first one) helped me to abandon my personality. After all what did I have to lose since I was nothing but a little schoolteacher recently turned secretary?

Georges himself, no doubt, realized the mistake he made in marrying me, the poor thing! For a man, however, marriage is compatible with his ambitions and it even helps his day-to-day life. For a woman, it's the opposite and I felt trapped in a corner. Because I had been widowed after six months of marriage, I didn't want to become a divorcée just six months later! I had only one option: to take on the role of perfect wife and to share all my husband's likes and dislikes.

In my delirium to identify with him, I had plenty of excuses. This desperate quest to form just one being was long considered the ultimate form of love and it was highly desired behavior for a wife. This has been the case to the point where, one hundred and twenty years after Sand and close to fifty years after myself, one of my daughters agreed, just like us, to give up her own interests and to take a vow of obedience by marrying as the law incidentally prescribed.[57] For my daughter Lison, just twenty years old at the time, it was about linking herself with a handsome and rich young man who was also infinitely serious. He thought that poetry and the other bohemian tendencies of his fiancée were incompatible with the requirements for a young wife about to move to the Zurich suburbs. And rightly so, since they separated after two years of marriage.

"I, the undersigned, attest that once married and moved in, I will do my chores every morning: vacuuming, dusting, sweeping. The dishes will be done regularly, the trash taken out, the refrigerator stocked.

I will be a pearl once we're all moved in.

Lison de Caunes, May 29, 1970"

On the back of this little slip of engagement manuscript that she has allowed me to use (and which I didn't know existed until today), her future husband wrote in capital letters: TO KEEP UNTIL DEATH. And, a little lower, with a flash of lucidity, Lison added, "or just until exhaustion."

Women have always had the sad habit of translating their most fervent love into terms of domestic labor. Dusting, doing the dishes, vacuuming: this is how you prove your love, no doubt because husbands still hold these activities in high esteem. Any other sort of undertaking like "I swear to continue with my studies to the very end" or "In marrying, I promise not to renounce my literary (or artistic or political) ambitions" would be judged extremely suspicious.

I too reckoned that my greatest evidence of love for Georges would be to become a pearl. For as long as I remained in love, I succeeded in living happily—even if it was sometimes difficult devoting such a large part of my free time to what Proust has termed "the arts of nothingness," especially at a time when the phrase "sharing of tasks" had not even been coined. I muddled my way through by hoisting up each chore as yet another proof of my love. Apparently it was the future George Sand, the first between the two of us, who suspected that women always lost at this game.

"It remains only to be asked," she wrote again to Emilie, "whether man or woman should remake himself or herself on the model of the other. And since 'the bearded one is the all-powerful' and men are incapable of such attachment, then we are necessarily the ones who must bend in obedience. . . . One must love one's husband and love him enormously to accept this fate,"[58] she concluded insightfully.

For more than two years, I loved a great deal.

My mother knew well before me that my love wouldn't be equal to the task. I often noticed her desperate efforts to keep quiet when she found me submitting in flagrante delicto or when she caught Georges's utter indifference on display. I remained convinced that he couldn't be entirely uncaring. He just found showing his feelings in public to be incompatible with his manly dignity. He also decided that his beloved career took the upper hand over his private life.

Nicole didn't say a word when, though my first daughter was born just before Christmas, Georges agreed to spend Christmas Eve in the street interviewing Parisians as they went about their merrymaking. I read in his heavy silence that asking him to give a reason to justify leaving his wife alone their first Christmas together, on the first day of their first child's life, was ridiculous. In my room at the

Belvedere Clinic, I heard the young mothers on either side of me popping champagne corks and laughing with their husbands.

"It's an important program for me, but do you want me to not work that night?" Georges had asked me.

I wanted him to refuse without my having to ask him to do it. I wanted him to not have even imagined accepting.

For the birth of my second child, less than a year and a half later, Georges was in Greenland with the French Polar Expeditionary Forces. It was as simple as that.

"It's definitely a boy this time. Can you see me with two daughters?" he told me laughing before going, leaving me with only one masculine first name for the soon-to-be-born infant. His own mother had only produced sons, thank the Lord! The wonderful de Caunes family name was guaranteed survival thanks to my competent mother-in-law. It was now my turn to prove myself worthy. The poor Groult name had already become lost in the conjugal storm. None of my children would bear this name and I didn't give it a second thought.

Yet, I had a second daughter. "We will try again," Georges had told me, tenderly but firmly, when the oldest, Blandine, was born. I had disappointed him yet again and I needed to work twice as hard to become a pearl twice as large to make him forget this failure.

We must also recognize that we are all responsible for this desire of a boy. I don't know anyone, male or female, who wanted to have a daughter first in those times. Once you were legitimated by bringing a little man into this world, a minipenis finally slipping out of your womb, you could then intimate in a quiet tone, "It would also be nice to have a little girl." But not before. Mothers of boys seemed more worthy, more courageous, for they had best fulfilled their earthly duty.

Today, we're beginning to let go of this unrelenting preference for sons while just on the other side of the Mediterranean, quite close to us, a woman can be beaten because she had one girl too many.[59] Those blows then echo upon the stomach of all mothers of daughters. In their books, Gisèle Halimi,[60] Françoise Giroud,[61] and so many others have talked about their mourning for the hoped-for son, who would represent their own birth for their father. I felt just as guilty and helpless as the protagonists of these novels, Soraya or Fabiola.

So the telegram had to be sent to the humiliated father. Instead of the "Bravo, well done, Georges," that he anticipated, his buddies from the Expeditionary Forces gently patted him on the back, "Don't be upset, old man. Girls are cute too."

In addition to this disappointment caused by my performance, I had to face the anxiety of inventing a name for this baby that we certainly couldn't call Fabrice! Why not George, without the *s*? I didn't think of it and Georges certainly wouldn't have appreciated it. In the space of twenty-four hours, the poor thing was called all sorts of names: Violaine from Claudel, but her fate was too tragic; Félicité after the rose Félicité Perpétue, a favorite of my grandfather's; Delphine, after Germaine de Staël; Daphné after Apollo's beloved nymph; Marie, because, well, it was Marie. It was the name of Georges's mother as well as my mother (in the beginning). Yet we hesitated. "Choosing Marie is like decorating with white," Nicole said. "It's a nonchoice." All of a sudden Inès surged in the rankings. To our exhausted circle, the name seemed audacious, intriguing. As soon as Pater left for the mayor's office in Boulogne-Billancourt, we asked ourselves what sort of Spanish fly must have bitten us. André was then told by the civil employee that he had been called back for more consultation with the family. The baby herself wasn't happy; she spat up after each feeding.

As the period to declare the newborn's name drew to a close, we rallied around Marion, the name of my little sister who died. "Impossible," cut in the civil employee, who could already boast of refusing all the Breton names of the famous Le Goarnic family. (They finally ended up at the international court in La Haye in order to legitimate the names of their twelve children.)[62] "Impossible. I could accept Marie or Marinette, but not Marion."

Besieged by all the delays, Pater declared the name Marie, then Laurence, Lison, and Delphine per our instructions. Because Marie wasn't working, we called the baby Lorenzo while waiting for Georges, who in turn opted for Marie-Laurence when he came back. But she continued to spit up a bit after every feeding to express her disapproval. So we went to the third name and this was the right one. Lison was easy to say and to hear, for the child quickly stopped spitting up.

I learned that as soon as they slip out of you, children know how to take their mother hostage. Fathers, during the first years and sometimes for their entire lives, completely escape this emotional blackmail, which somehow always makes mothers feel guilty. Blandine wasn't going to be mad at Georges for bringing a sister that she hardly wanted into this world. I was the one who betrayed her. In her way Lison, I was sure of it, punished me for not having wanted her and for having refused to breast-feed her. I made this decision for Georges. I didn't want to ruin the breasts that I would offer to my husband when he came back.

From the beginning of our marriage, Georges only saw me as a female completely overwhelmed by her animal functions and this humiliated me. I was pregnant from the very first month of our life together, then nursing Blandine, my oldest, then tied twice daily to an electric pump when I had to begin working again. I was continually pregnant with embryos which were trying to implant themselves into our life against our will. With the fourth one, we gave up. We didn't really know where to get help. My mother's midwife friend, who had helped us with the first one, had retired to the other end of France. This was the first abortion that I had with Georges. I had succeeded in erasing the first one, the one with Pierre, from my memory for I knew well the importance of forgetting, especially if you want to keep making love without considering the measures you'll have to take in order to undo this act.

We all knew that four thousand convictions had taken place during the Vichy years for abortive procedures and that a laundress had been guillotined "as an example" in 1943. But we simply couldn't imagine having a child every single year.

So we turned to our friend Madame Rollières. Even though she was a midwife, she wasn't allowed to perform a curettage. She only agreed to insert a catheter. Then we had to "wait for things to happen." "Be careful on the road," she had told me as I got on my bicycle in Villiers-Adam to go back to Paris. "Especially no accidents! If anyone finds you with the catheter, say that you put it in yourself . . ."

In hindsight, I wonder to what extent our paths, our ordeals, and the risks that we took, we, the women who came before the Veil Law,[63] can seem crazy, disgusting, sometimes even incredible today. That was our everyday and we had to come to terms with it. Or become a nun. It was so routine that just three months later, I became pregnant again. In French we say *tomber enceinte*, which means to "fall" into pregnancy. Falling is the right word. With such a short span after my first cry for help, I didn't dare return to Madame Rollières whose affection and concern had been so dear to me.

So I had to make my way through clandestine networks, and I undertook some humiliating steps punctuated by anonymous telephone calls where the real meaning of things was never said. I ran up against some indignant refusals, and some hypocritical rejections until a friend one day pointed me to a shady connection. I was told of a caretaker woman who did "that" in her back room, on an oilcloth spread out on her kitchen table with the odor of stew simmering on the stove. It seemed like a good option but the cost was so high that I didn't dare tell Georges how much it was. He already reproached me enough for not knowing how to "figure it out." Injecting vinegar water mixed with increasing quantities of eau de cologne (it was supposed to kill off the cooties), and hurriedly getting up from the sweet embrace of lovemaking were parts of the sad and useless postsex routine.

The caretaker woman pocketed the money first and then inserted the catheter. She seemed to be honest. I was even allowed a second attempt if the first one didn't work. I didn't need it, but in the short time of allowing myself to be happy about it, three or four months later, it all began again. In the meantime, the backroom angel maker had been denounced and arrested. I learned this only when I found a police warning on the door of her apartment in the 19th arrondissement. I then pretended to go up the stairs just in case a trap had been left and someone was monitoring her door. Retrospectively terrified and overwhelmed by the thought of devoting another month's salary to this sinister need, I decided to take care of it myself. Selling catheters in the pharmacy was against the law. Informed sources recommended using aquarium tubing. I thought that the fishing line used to catch pollock, sold in fishing stores, could serve as a suitable substitute. Delinquents always remain a few steps ahead of their pursuers.

Knitting needles, those utterly feminine instruments, were also widely available.

After learning about the female anatomy and consulting diagrams of reproductive organs from a manual that Pierre had left to me, I shoved off on this voyage toward the unknown. First you had to thread rubber tubing about three centimeters in diameter over a metal needle that has been blunted beforehand, a size 3 if I remember correctly. When I tested my system in the open air it worked marvelously: the Vaselined line slipped easily over the length of the needle. However, once in the vaginal canal, I was working blindly. I couldn't guide it to pass through the cervix where I wasn't sure if it was located deep down or in the lining of the canal. After two hours, I was stiff from my acrobatic position and furious that love should lead to this distasteful gymnastics. I didn't let myself think about the dramas that were told under wraps between women, of those who had abortions—the perforations, hemorrhages, septicemia, sudden death caused by fainting spells. After two hours, I was finally able to put my device in place. The tube was coiled up inside the uterus and I could gently withdraw the needle. Now, all I had to do was "wait for something to happen."

Georges couldn't hide his disgust for these "women's issues," all these pregnancies, miscarriages, and abortions that seemed to be the daily lot of all my fellow creatures. And so I waited for him to leave for a few days on a reporting trip in order to carry out my guilty operation. I was just as disgusted by it as he was, but I felt more responsible and ashamed by my powerlessness. I hated this body that tried to impose its will over me. It was also crippling to have to act without any information or medical help; I was reduced to following the recipes of sorceresses and the remedies of good little women, some of them dating to antiquity for abortion has long been the most secret (but also an exceedingly common) act in the history of women. Scientific advances, the dawning of democracy, and the rights of man (so aptly named), as well as educational access for everyone, have done nothing to change the obscurantism that allows this practice to continue and the cruelty of a society that claims to remain ignorant of it.

Like before, everything went fine and I became a free woman once again, one who didn't remind her husband of the penalty of each sexual act. However, having waited too long this time before taking action, I had a fever for several days afterward and my obstetrician, the famous Dr. Lamaze, had to perform a curettage. "If you ever have to have one," Madame Rollières had told me before her procedure, "you don't have to explain anything to the doctor.

They know full well when it's not a natural miscarriage. There are over 500,000 clandestine abortions performed in France every year. Your Lamaze is a good man. He won't ask you anything."

"This pregnancy got off to a bad start," he told me, signaling that he wasn't stupid. "It's time I intervene. You should try not to become pregnant again for a little while." A recommendation that a gynecologist should suggest, and advice that a young woman should take, yet neither one of us possessed the least means of putting these wise words into practice.

The same causes produce the same effects and four months later, I found myself stuck in the pregnancy box once again in this game of chutes and ladders where you live your life every month by throwing the dice. I had returned to my job at the radio station. Blandine wasn't yet walking and the bathtub was permanently full of dirty diapers, the washboard balanced on the ledge. Our little one-bedroom already seemed too cramped. In these years after the war, there weren't any other available apartments, nor were there contraceptive methods, disposable diapers, store-bought baby food, or washing machines. I could only roll up my sleeves and go down to the mayor's office to fill out new paperwork declaring my pregnancy so that I could at least benefit from the supplementary food allowance.

Lison was born without any problems, except for her gender, Georges's absence, and my fears of winning the Cognacq Prize.[64] Pregnant five times within two years—I was on the right track.

After the birth, Lamaze thought that I should stay in the clinic for a while to rest in a horizontal position so that the internal organs, which had been rudely decompressed, could regain their shape. I appreciated this enforced repose of one week, which afforded me, in addition to the right to finally rest, the time to write to Georges. Because our only interaction was confined to short radio messages to Greenland once a week, I kept a daily diary for him, so that he wouldn't come back to his life like a stranger.

Blandine, who was seventeen months old at the time, came to see "the new one"—she was smuggled into the hospital hidden under Nicole's ample cloak (Nicole scoffed at the rule forbidding small children to enter the labor and delivery unit). "Doggie!" she had declared after taking a quick and disgusted look at the thing sleeping in its crib, before turning away from it entirely. This contempt did not suffice to make the intruder disappear. When it turned out that this new creature was going to move into her own room, Blandine fell into a "postpartum" depression. She wouldn't get out of her bed, where she slept with her head turned toward the wall. She refused to eat or to even look at the trespasser. Blandine had believed that the baby was just visiting and now she was becoming ingrained. In a game show on the radio several years later, she told the radio host, who had been expecting an endearing answer: "My sister? My sister's dead!"

The pediatrician advised us to separate her for a while from the family and the object that caused her suffering. She was sent to spend several weeks with her godmother in Toulouse, the other "sweetie." Until her teenage years, she could not get over this new baby.

Post coïtum, animal triste ("after sex, any animal is sad") is perhaps true. But *post parturium*, any female animal is even sadder. During my week of enforced rest, I happily received a daily visit from a certain fellow named Paul who was himself recovering from a long illness. Or in the midst of a long sick vacation, as he liked to put it. He didn't live far from the Belvedere Clinic where I was convalescing with my daughter. And so he came every afternoon to my bedside.

It was a beautiful May and my window opened onto trees with brand-new leaves. Like his good friend Georges, Paul was a journalist at the radio. I liked Paul's wife, who had a little boy the same age as Blandine. Paul had been the best man at our wedding and was then the godfather of our first daughter. The previous summer, we had rented the same villa in Port Manech. Finally, we lived on the same street in Paris. We were two couples at high risk. For the first time, we found ourselves alone with each other, Paul and I, and we discovered that we liked the same poets, a detail that should have forewarned us because poets have strange powers.

But our time had not yet come. I was still very much in love with Georges and I hadn't yet found out that "it's the spirit and not the body that allows marriages to last," if we're to believe Publius Syrius.[65]

Besides, I wasn't especially attracted to this Paul: he was too skinny, too pale, too unathletic, too much of a whiskey drinker, and too funny for me. Moreover his reputation as a ladies' man put me off. I have always hated ladies' men. I don't know how I managed to live for over fifty years with one of them. He was big—both in his height and as a seducer, given the number of girls that I saw gravitating around him at the radio station and elsewhere. He was so thin and so white that my mother said to me when I married him three years later, "To think that you managed to find yourself another consumptive!"

At that moment, we were a thousand leagues from thinking that he might one day decide to take back his freedom and end his marriage (a bond that seemed to only slightly keep him from living according to his liking). Or, for my part, that I would have enough clairvoyance to notice the inanity of my efforts and the insufficiency of those of Georges toward establishing a harmonious relationship between us. Husbands only fight for their marriage after it has been lost. Georges thought he had done enough by allowing me to bear his name and children, and trusting me to mind his household. He was the one who would earn our living. It was the standard agreement. Love was included and didn't need to be brought into question every day.

"You can clearly see that I love you because I come back! Women read too many novels and they make too much of a big deal about love," he said. "It's in their nature to complain and moan."

I impatiently counted the days that kept me from his return. Only thirty days, he had let me know. As for myself, I thought: thirty more days! The *Strength*, the Polar Expeditionary Forces boat, had to first reach Godthåb in southeastern Greenland, in an ice-floe-infested sea. Then from there, Georges would wait for a boat headed to Denmark. In Copenhagen, he would visit Elsinore of course (one can't miss this important place).[66] Then he would skip over to Malmö, in Sweden, to cover a story. From there, he would take the train to Paris. One forgets that connections via airplane didn't exist then. It would be a several-day affair and it was important for him: I had to understand that a few extra days wouldn't make much of a difference.

Of course. I understood this even more now that this long separation had beneficial aspects: no longer torturing myself over the harshness of Georges's nature, I had forgotten my disappointments and I recreated, bit by bit, the partner of my dreams. Nothing belied this revised and corrected version because Georges could not write or telephone from his ice floe. Reduced to telegrams, only pure love remained. His first messages, entrusted to his friends who were returning home to Europe, cast a shadow over my idyllic picture:

"I'm working a lot. I am gathering experiences to write a book later. You will be proud of your Parzouf." Certainly I wanted to be proud of my Parzouf. But how could I make him proud of me? This question was never broached.

"I just had an extraordinary life experience. I will tell you everything and I hope that you'll help me accomplish all that I want and can accomplish."

Certainly I wanted to help him, but did he realize that with two children and my full-time work at the radio station I was the one who needed help, preferably and quite simply, help around the house. My own "life experience" seemed meaningless because it was shared by millions of women, who were all going through, at every second, the same motions I was, in millions of similar households.

"You know, dear Namour, that it's my job to leave and I have to earn our living. But one day when we're rich, we're going to get away and I'll write novels that will make your husband one of the great men of his time."

And for me, dear Namour, I'll still be a housewife, but a rich, secluded one?

"If you really would help me, I think I could write excellent things about whale-fishing and the life of the Eskimos."

I did want what he wanted but having never seen a whale or an Eskimo, it was clear that my help would be reduced to filing his papers and typing his manuscripts, an honorable activity that conformed to the stock image of conjugal productivity. A great number of couples had worked in this manner in the past. Why couldn't I ever be satisfied? I chastised myself for not perking up before this glorious future.

Not able to respond to letters because he was at sea, I didn't know how to make him sense that what he didn't say hurt me more than his loving protestations made me feel good. The letter never arrived that would have lifted my spirits by saying: "Thank you Benoîte [not honey or sweetie]. Thank you for taking care of our two children.

In spite of your work, thank you for providing them with your precious presence that allows me to leave and pursue what I believe is my destiny with my mind at ease. One day it will be your turn and then I will help you. You'll see."

I'd have signed on for another ten years, if he had said such things to me.

As for Georges, saturated with his grandiose landscapes, his solitude, his adventures and bingeing on male camaraderie, he could finally be moved by the three females who constituted his familial cocoon. He never loved me more than when he left me. "I'm miserable without you," he wrote to me every time and it was true. He forgot that he was even more miserable with me. Family life didn't hold any appeal for him unless he was in a state of regret or hope. He was inept in the present.

"You'll see, we're going to be happy."

"When I get back, we'll go out as much as you want."

"I promise not to leave all the time. It makes you too unhappy."

I wanted to believe in his promises, as much as he believed in them himself because he, too, thanks to the long distance between us, had recreated the ideal woman that he could finally make happy.

"When I get back, I would like to teach you how to love bullfighting, to share in my hobbies."

But you can only really share what you already have. Why didn't he choose a woman who already liked bull-fighting? We truly ask the impossible from marriage.

As the absence waned, with each letter received, the Georges of my dreams thinned like a fog, allowing the jagged outlines of my true husband to emerge. His last letter dissipated the final misty veil, "I can't wait to be home, sweetheart. I hope to find the house spick-and-span and the children nice and clean. And you too— beautiful, thin, and elegantly able to welcome home your lawful husband. Poor Georges is tired indeed. He has trouble sleeping, and you will have to spoil him. You surely have plenty of things to tell me and I promise to listen closely as you prattle on . . ." (*Even if you didn't have the time to fix everything, even if Lison cries at night, even if you haven't lost all the baby weight, I'm just waiting for the moment when I will hold you in my arms.*) No, I never received those words. It was the Georges veiled in mist who wrote them to me. The other one, the real one, brought me back down to earth.

"When I return, knowing the desire that I have for you, my dear, there are certain dangers that we already know all too well. You should take precautions to avoid another accident."

He was right, but what precautions could I take other than the same old remedies that had already failed? It's only today that I can see the extent of his selfishness, and of my fatalism. How could we have not considered condoms? Even worse, how to explain that no obstetrician or internist ever advised us to avoid such "accidents"? I was even more unpardonable since I had known rubbers in situ. So, why choose abortion? Yes, why? I suppose that to abort was one of the fatalities of the feminine condition, a norm in some ways. Condoms were reserved for prostitutes and those with venereal diseases . . . in sum, for Evil and Sin. An honest couple didn't have to "protect themselves." An honest couple didn't even talk about sex in 1950. There were certain words that Georges and I never uttered, zones of our bodies and our souls that we never touched. We lived in the dark, just like how we made love.

I ask myself today how we could have "preferred" repeated abortions instead of seeking out condoms. But I know that this question doesn't make sense. It wasn't framed in this way and wasn't asked in any sense at all. It would be like asking a reckless driver, "So you would rather die than slow down?" He would reply that he prefers not to slow down and not to have any accidents. I preferred to continue to make love *and* not to become pregnant. Anyway that wasn't what killed us, Georges and me.

This stupefying inconsistency, shared by all the women of my generation and by so many who came after me, didn't have any explanation, other than the fact that sexuality has always worked outside of any logic, prevision, or morals. Sexuality is the madwoman dwelling in the attic.[67]

Georges didn't feel responsible for our failure. Not making your wife happy has never been considered a problem for a husband. Perhaps it's a little negligent but that's life. Don't most women have everything they need in order to be happy? They've got running water, which their mothers never had, as well as a modern kitchen with all the working appliances, updated at each birthday, and then a big baby of a man to pamper (which is not always convenient but deep down women love it). The problem is that they ask for too much. They let themselves get overwhelmed by housework, in addition to their professional work, because, most of the time, they have decided to do both. But they don't know how to stay organized. A man would know better how to plan his time.

"I don't know how you never manage to have any time to yourself!" Any logical response would have seemed like an insult. "Maybe you could help me?" would not even reach the threshold of my consciousness. The division of household tasks remained frozen in the 1940s and even afterward. Nothing troubled the tranquil waters of households. Men had just come back from the war, right? That guaranteed them a respite when it came to questioning their roles.

"Can't you make dinner tonight, dear? I feel like writing down a fleeting poem." If I had said that, there would have been an earthquake. Georges didn't know how to cook a potato, much less peel one. This would come back to bite him later when he decided to spend six months on a deserted island in the Pacific. I only knew one man from this period who did the cooking: my father. But he did it as an artist. It was different. He served us fish cooked in puff pastry with fins sketched onto the dough and glass marbles for their eyes. A man was a grand chef or he didn't cook at all.

Sweetie didn't even think of asking her husband for a little bit of help. But often, her life seemed so onerous. She didn't understand why—she did have running water after all!

Parzouf had tried to teach her about life as seen from a woman's perspective. Marriage wasn't fusion, the act of sublime sharing that she had naively imagined. Marriage was the fair division of the conjugal space. Georges didn't ask her to summarize the day's news with him. She needed to learn to do without him at home, especially in the kitchen and the broom closet. He had given her the first lesson, from the beginning, on the train that took them to Austria. He had to react quickly before becoming stuck in the sentimental sludge that young women know how to secrete.

The trouble was that she continually questioned everything. She didn't discuss things, she quibbled, and she contradicted him, even in public. She had forgotten the first lesson that he had given her during their honeymoon. The second lesson rang out on its own. He hadn't wanted to do it, but it got away from him, that slap.

It wasn't even over a personal disagreement but, as usual, a difference of opinion expressed in front of their friends. The slap was just an unforeseen reaction that didn't originate out of anger or the desire to do her harm, but from his rightful need to show who was the boss. The scene happened in Port Manech, at the "Pauls'" house, during a dinner bringing together about a dozen friends. Georges had been back from Greenland for about a month and he had forgotten just how irritating his wife could be when she thought she was right. They were talking about Caligula's horse, or some other trivial fact about a Roman emperor. She was showing off her historical knowledge just a little too much.

"Please don't be a bluestocking while we're on vacation," Georges, on edge, had warned her.

Instead of piping down, she flew off the handle. Georges did too. He rose up from the table and dealt her a real slap, in front of the astonished guests. At the time she didn't react, hesitating between a nervous laugh, tears, or an insult. Before she could decide, he left the table without a word, ruled by an anger taken over, little by little, by shame, which distorted his face.

He came back in the middle of the night, at the hour when gestures replace words. The next day you don't dare invoke the incident. You are too afraid that, by pulling one thread, you might unravel a whole marriage.

I ask myself today, my poor Zazate, how this slap, at the time, closed your mouth, but didn't open your eyes? How did you remain pinned at the heart, with just your will to be happy so that this unfortunate act wouldn't phase you? How did this terrible action not suffice to disconcert you? The body doesn't give up its sweet habits in one day: the scents remain familiar, the same words are said, carried along by the tide. Time must go by before the gestures and the words that make up a couple's everyday become obsolete. Time passes. I'm not at all spiteful.

But a slight crack
Pierces the crystal each day
With an invisible and sure gait

These verses from Sully Prudhomme's poem "The Broken Vase," which every girl had learned by heart before the war, suddenly came back to me. It's one of poetry's secret powers, for even the most anodyne lines will suddenly well up on your lips from deep within the dark when it resonates with an event from your own life.

What would you have thought, my Zazate, if you had known that your precious George Sand, whose life so resembled your own, had also been slapped by her young husband and for the same reason: disobedience! A serious reason for, as Creon tells Antigone, "Disobedience is the worst curse." "We must not tolerate, in any way, that a woman should teach us a lesson. They must remain women and they are not to exercise their four desires." George was still called Aurore and she was only twenty when this scene, which she will later tell in *Story of My Life*, took place. It was the moment that ended her marriage. She was "acting like a madwoman"—those are her own words, in her yard in Nohant, with some friends' children who came to spend the summer there. A little sand fell into the glass of one of Casimir's friends and he ordered his wife to stop her childish games. She didn't do anything and merely frolicked about all the more. And so he got out of his chair, walked over to her, and slapped her in front of her son and all their friends. "From this day I no longer loved him at all and everything went from bad to worse," Aurore wrote.

Certainly Georges was more attractive than fat Casimir, but I, my Zazate, was less brazen than the fiery George Sand. However the "slight crack" worked its way toward definitively breaking up our marriage.

I didn't dare write, even in a diary, because it was an activity considered unhealthy for a married woman. I ended up taking the photos of Pierre off the wall because Georges had a jealous and possessive nature. He gave me more proof of jealousy than of love. I couldn't receive a box of chocolates without Georges threatening to "beat up" the sender. I was embarrassed by such idiotic lines like "Come out here, if you're a man." He said this sort of thing to my friend Noguera, a radio technician with whom I worked. Georges was a real man, right? I long believed that he didn't love me enough and that in desperately trying to do so, he would end up trusting me. Our friends remained persuaded that we were happy. Georges was such a charmer in public and so brilliant! The problem was that I wasn't part of his audience once we were married. You don't waste your gifts at home. And when you take your wife out, it's not to take care of her. One didn't go out to rediscover one's wife, but rather to discover new faces. In sum I was unhappy without him and unhappy with him. What a poor little goat all the same!

But eventually it's the wolf that gets eaten in the morning.

Nevertheless Georges was so sure that I couldn't live without him that the day I proposed a trial separation for a few months, he agreed to go stay with a friend in Montmartre for a while. "In three months you will have reconsidered and we will start again together. We can still be happy; you'll see."

He didn't understand that I had never been happy! From the second he left the house, I knew that I could never again live with him. While on the contrary, he wanted to win me back. We never made love so passionately as during those brief nights when he would come by the house to see our two little girls. Now that I could no longer hear them, he finally said all the loving words that I had longed for during the previous four years. And now, whenever he traveled for work, he wrote to me what he thought were love letters. Was I already contaminated by the urge to write and by a taste for style? "Your husband thinks about you," "I embrace you with all my love," and others like "I can't stop thinking about you"—in my eyes, these lines didn't equal the "my I" that Pierre said to me. It seemed to me that the more you loved someone, the better able you should be to put it into words.

"It's blood, not ink, running in my veins," he replied.

Everything fell apart quickly between us during our hurtful conversations. As soon as I dared to become myself again and the fear of losing him ceased, I no longer became worn down as I had in the past. We had to resign ourselves to begin that vile procedure known at the time as "no fault divorce with mutual consent." Constructed of false witnesses and letters of invented wrongs, it soon led to real insults and the inevitable blackmail, culminating in the fragmentary reenactment of the past.

My mother wasn't unhappy that I was leaving the man who, according to her, paralyzed my development and would inevitably cripple my children. She took my oldest, Blandine, to stay for a little while at her house to help me with my reconversion. This gave me the opportunity to discover just how much a husband adds an extra burden to one's daily life. Suddenly time was given back to me, the days were longer, life was easier. I listened to the music that I liked and didn't care about horse racing or the defeat of the Parisian soccer team. I reconnected with friends who had been lost because Georges didn't like them.

It had yet to be determined what poor Zazate was made of. Would I become once more Madame Groult? Or Widow Heuyer? Or even Madame ex–de Caunes? Professionally no one asked me under what name I was going to continue my modest career. Too many names means not having any name at all.

You began to discover, my dear Rosie, that a woman's identity is a concept that fluctuates a great deal.

CHAPTER 7

Dear Paul

"It's completely useless for women to write about their silly ideas. It only serves to cloud the more important things."

—*Johan Strindberg*

I was thirty years old and I wasn't writing anything silly, my dear Strindberg. I didn't even dream of it. However I had picked up the bad habit of keeping a journal again. I wrote down everything, saying to myself that perhaps one day . . .

For the moment, I savored my freedom. Finally! A freedom embellished with two little girls, who were one and two and a half years old. A blonde and a brunette. This freedom was limited by my job at Radiodiffusion: for six hours a day I wrote up the hourly news bulletins broadcast over Paris-Inter (a rather cushy job).

Once again I lived alone in my little apartment on rue Raynouard where I put Pierre's portraits back up on the wall in my alcove. I kept a photo of Georges in the library, for my daughters—at least that's what I told myself, but really it was because I was still attracted to him. Each time that we saw each other through the years, I was tempted in the first few minutes to fall back in love. How could it be that we didn't succeed in being happy together? Whose fault was it? I hope, my dear Georges, that you found happiness in your next marriage, or in your third, but I don't really know. You never gave me the slightest inkling of your personality . . . or if you had, I didn't know what to do with it.

Nevertheless I can only really reproach you for being a man like all the rest. My marriage didn't seem like a prison; it resembled the majority of marriages in those times. In the '50s divorce was rare and, when it did occur, it was frowned upon. Most of my contemporaries, unhappy or not, gave themselves reasons to be happy in their roles as mothers. Because I was influenced by my precious Nicole, I couldn't resign myself to this common lot.

In addition to my two husbands, I also hung up another photo in my alcove: one of Kurt in his Air Force uniform, the American lieutenant looking ridiculously handsome with his Colgate smile. He had cast a spell over me one night that lasted for the rest of my life, when he asked me to dance to "Only You-ou-ou." But I knew that "for life" didn't mean "every day" and so I had refused to follow my handsome pilot to Philadelphia. We had both cried a good deal as we said goodbye, but I felt that I couldn't put down roots anywhere other than France. Knowing that I had remarried, he also married and had two children. But we continued to write to each other, unable to forget the wild surge of fate that had brought us together, and left us quietly convinced that we would find each other again one day. Which did indeed happen, but that's another story.[68]

For my first vacation of this newfound freedom, I knew where I should go: Brittany, specifically the coast, which had been forbidden to us during the five years of the German Occupation. So I accepted the invitation of our best friends, "the Pauls," who had just rented a fishing house and a motor boat in Port Manech.

Georges Heuyer, whom I have always loved like a father, had offered to take me in for two weeks at his villa in Saint-Cast with my two daughters, who were the same age as the children that he had with his second wife. I spent one week with them before taking off, an unfettered young woman greatly in need of spending time with friends after all those difficult years. I was glad to see more of Paul, who happened to be Georges de Caunes's best friend, and Paul's wife and boy.

You have to watch out for the "best friend" among couples. It's a risky post for anyone and especially for friends.
I never really felt attracted to this Paul Guimard. Although
I, along with all his friends, certainly enjoyed his humor,
intelligence, and culture and his knack for living. Physically I found him to have many faults: too thin, his skin
was too white, his mouth was too delicate, he had no muscles or body hair. His voice was a bit too soft, he was too
touchy-feely with too many women, and his gait was too
nonchalant, almost sluggish. Over the course of the fifty-
four years that we were going to spend together, I never
saw him run, or even walk quickly! He didn't chase after
success or money either; everything seemed to fall into
his hands without any effort and he pretended to scorn effort, hard work, and conscientiousness.

Over the course of those fifty-four years that we managed to live together, I feel like I never saw him "hustle."
Honestly never. In some ways I held this amateurism
against him because I was such a hardworking student
who swore by effort, pain, and in a word, sacrifice.

Since I found myself there (Paul never "ran" after
women either; they just fell into his arms) and since, after
a few years of use, his current wife was found to be in-
adequate, we discovered each other with an unexpected
pleasure. Port Manech is no Saint-Tropez and I wasn't

bothered by any female competition! Moreover I had finally found a man who appreciated my "bluestocking" nature. I could talk about politics with someone on the same side and poetry with someone who quoted the same poets.

I didn't watch out for the other addiction that we shared: a passion for the sea, for fishing, and for sailing. Navigating together each morning, setting up the trammel, discovering the small ports of south Finistère, Merrien, Brigneau, Doëlan, Trévignon, united us more surely than a sexual fling. He would become an excellent sailor and write beautifully about the sea, but he lacked the physical bravery and the taste for suffering that defines the true sea dog. As for me, on the other hand, I didn't balk at seamanship. I liked the various duties: untangling the nets, mending them, skinning the fish, hoisting the heavy triangular sail, bailing out, splicing rope. Paul only enjoyed being at the helm, dreamily consulting maps and setting off toward the islands by gauging the depths where he knew every reef. Between the two of us, we made one excellent sailor, each with his specific job: he was happy as the navigator while I took exquisite pleasure in maintaining the equipment so that it could hold up during bad weather. This is what we succeeded in doing, in spite of our differences, over the course of the fifty-four years that we would confront together.

The first kiss, the one that led to all the others, was at sea. We exchanged this kiss without having planned it; in fact, it was the sea that we kissed on each other's lips. The weather was splendidly rough that day and the rain, mixing with salty sea foam, gave it such a beautiful bitterness that we really had nothing else to do but to drink it off each other's lips, keeping one eye on the ocean, which just waits for a distraction in order to swallow you up.

Coming back to shore that night, I naively believed that I had reached an intimate milestone with Paul, but this kiss seemed of little consequence to him. I quickly saw that with him, the normal codes of conduct didn't apply.

Our kiss? What kiss?

There wasn't any other that summer. But when we returned to Paris, since I lived alone and we were neighbors on the same street, rue Chanez, Paul got in the habit of stopping by the house to borrow a book, to take me to the movies, or to read me a poem. Weeks slipped by and he continued to navigate back and forth, from my company to his wife's, without giving the slightest sign of regret or impatience, to the extent that I never knew where my position ended and hers began.

Then, in just as surprising a manner as our first kiss at sea, one evening like so many others, we came back on foot from the ORTF,[69] where every day Paul hosted *The*

Paris Tribune, a political program, and he came upstairs for a drink. When I went to show him out, I froze in my tracks: Paul remained in the middle of the living room and nonchalantly took off his shirt and pants before getting into my bed tucked within the alcove as if it were his own, without a word of warning or excuse! I stood at the door, my arms dangling, as frightened as a virgin.

I was a little bit in love, but only moderately. Who wouldn't be when you're thirty years old and a young man comes to read you poems? I was certainly interested to learn how this strange fellow would behave in bed, but from here to there. . . .

There hadn't been any discussion or any preliminaries, not one misplaced gesture. . . . This situation hadn't been predicted in my playbook and since Paul never told me about himself, I didn't know if he found me sexy or merely available to fill in some recently vacant gaps in his life.

He looked at me ironically from the center of *my* bed and the only thing left for me to do was undress myself out of respect. You can't keep your skirt and blouse on in front of a completely naked man. It was too late to say, I'm not who you think I am. Evidently I *was*. Even if I didn't yet know that he would become the man I wanted. Not at that moment. He was even more white, more smooth, and

more soft than I had feared, completely lacking that smid-
gen of simian qualities that had been essential to my definition of virility.

I can't remember how that first night unfurled. I love
preliminaries, the work of the approach, the hesitations;
these were all tossed aside and I found myself naked, completely lost in front of this man whom I hadn't wanted—I
never would have chosen him from a catalog. I don't know
anymore if it was with words or caresses that he set forth;
I only remember a certain emotional climate and the moment when Paul asked me "Are you crying?" as he held
me tightly against him. I would not have been able to say
where these tears came from, surely from deep within, as
if I had finally reached a shared country with a man and
had a fundamental reconciliation with myself. Reconciliation can be so difficult sometimes for it's easy to forget
just how tormented the relationship was between a young
girl, even a young woman, and her sexuality up to the '70s.
We have forgotten how hard it was for us to accept our own
genitalia, those strangers in the house. We have forgotten
that we all felt ashamed of our bodies, "down there," as my
Irish nanny said.

"Don't forget to wash yourself down there, Rosie," she
reminded me every day in English with what seemed to
me to be an imperceptible curl of disgust on her face.

How could we trust this body that had betrayed us the
first moment it left childhood behind by subjecting us to
the bloody ritual of our periods, inflicted on us in our stu-
por and without any explanation, ceaselessly returning
and leaving us terror-stricken. It threatened to reveal to
the boys what we hid every month in those shameful sanitary napkins while they moved so effortlessly from childhood to manhood without undergoing this humiliating
ordeal.

How to approach the first overtures with the opposite sex
under these conditions? How could we engage our chastised
organs in an act meant to be trusting and relaxed? In short,
how could we forgive ourselves for being women?

I had tried various methods. With the passionate mo-
mentum of my first love affair, I forced myself to conform
to Pierre's expectations. He was only twenty-two years
old, but he was a doctor, which impressed me, especially
because I knew zero about my own body. No one had ever
spoken to me about the clitoris, even though my famil-
iarization with it landed me, at ten years old, in a stitched,
brushed cotton nightshirt that tied at the feet. I remember that it had been bought in the little girls' section of
Bon Marché, which was, in the 1930s, a department store
popular with the neighborhood religious communities.
As for the word "cunnilingus," which I could guess the

meaning of (I was a Latin teacher after all), its barbaric connotations made the thing unthinkable. Sometimes I gave in, masturbating in shame, like someone climbing the steps to the guillotine.

Because Pierre got sick so soon, we weren't in a position to deal with anything complicated and his ardor, which was exacerbated by his approaching end, created such an intense feeling between us that we were transported beyond ourselves. With him it was no longer about pleasure, but defying death.

Those heroic days were over.

With Georges, I fell back down to earth, ready to laugh at everything: our beauty, our health, our future, which nothing could threaten.

The landing had been rough. Georges decided that there were certain things that you just don't do with your lawfully wedded wife. Other than missionary, we didn't try any other positions. Was this out of respect? Or out of timidity? The fear of being rebuffed? Without a doubt, it was all these things. Here again we should have found something, read something, invented the right words to talk about it, but a profound silence covered all these questions. We made love in the dark, literally and figuratively. Georges didn't begin to show me that he enjoyed it until four years later, when we were in the process of a divorce. He would have deemed it too indiscreet to ask me about my own feelings and I was too shaken up to explain what I didn't even dare confess to myself.

One day someone told me that Georges had really loved me. I had never noticed this. He didn't either, in my opinion. Poor us!

Someone else told me later that he was a marvelous lover. My jaw dropped. Apparently we weren't talking about the same man.

It took me years to realize that each of us contains multiple characters, and some may never see the light of day. This is especially true for women because tradition and morals are confined in the most restrained spaces, spaces that are barely open to the world's diversity.

What a waste that so many of these lives are not lived! What misery for those women who are deprived of experiences and moments of resilience.

I was only thirty years old and I was already at the start of my third life. That was not counting other moments of playing hooky that sometimes teach you more about your preferences and your abilities than a long journey. If I was crying quiet tears in Paul's arms, it wasn't just because of my first encounter with this man, but also with the woman that he was coaxing out of me, the woman who finally resembled my self.

Paul confided to me later that he had been very moved by my tears. But he wasn't a man to say "I love you" for so little. He tread peacefully between his wife and other women, between his career as a journalist and his writing, between his dream of traveling around the world and his congenital carelessness, and finally, his need to flee and his desire to be taken care of. Marriage served as a comfortable alibi, which prevented him from committing himself anywhere else.

While he so hated the thought of putting another leash around his neck (even if it was a golden chain), I was more stubborn and conformist. Living together was still frowned upon in those days, and risky enough to cause me to lose custody of my children. For the first time, I felt not only a growing attraction to the way this man took me into his arms and the netting of his words, but also a desire to experience a male/female relationship that wouldn't be strained by any presupposition linked to one's gender nor any other principle that might go against our need for freedom. His need for freedom, I discovered, was staggering. In the end, I was proud enough, or naive enough, to take up this sort of challenge.

I had always thought that in order to survive living together, you have to agree not on the virtues of fidelity, which are fleeting and change easily into a prison, but on the fundamentals: ethics, morals (or the absence of morals), religious beliefs (or the absence of religion), political opinions, not to mention culinary tastes (we eat two or three times a day after all). Then it's also important to laugh at the same things, to like the same people and the same sports. Paul didn't play any, other than sitting at the helm and pressing a button to start the diesel engine, which was easy enough.

However, months passed, with their fair share of delightful evenings, stolen weekends, and conversations that led nowhere—to the satisfaction of at least one of us. I feared that the situation was becoming permanent. But Moïra, God love her, came to my rescue with her own turn of events.

Paul and I were in my bed one afternoon, doing what people are supposed to be doing when in bed at this time of day, when my pearl necklace broke. I often wear my necklace when I am undressed: on tanned and bare skin, pearls can be striking. It was a necklace with small, fine pearls, without any knots between each pearl. My godfather gave me this necklace on my tenth birthday, just a little while before he died, this monsieur named Léon, who had possibly also bequeathed me his Greek foot that so tormented my father. I was quite fond of it for all of these reasons, so we got down on all fours to find each of the pearls scattered on the carpet and underneath the bed.

We ended the evening by going out to have oysters at the neighborhood brasserie and Paul went home around ten o'clock. His wife was already in bed and while he was undressing, he carefully explained to her why he had been held up so late at the studio. Suddenly, she pointed her index finger with vengeance in the direction of her husband's pubic area: "Paul, can you tell me what I see there?"

Paul looked down: a small pearl was nestled in his pubic hair. In spite of his imagination and his art for evasion, he could only respond after a quick glance down:

"Well it seems to be a pearl."

"And can you explain to me how it got there?"

Paul had refused to tell me the rest of the conversation. I was dying to know what line of defense could have been deployed by this man who never let himself be thrown by anything. He merely gave me back the small pearl and I restrung my necklace just as it had been before.

But, dear godfather, I am indebted, without a doubt, to this tiny pearl for it was the one that eventually allowed me to marry Paul, that relieved me of having to conduct myself badly. What could "bad" mean when I was certain that I had found the man who fulfilled all of my senses, even the sixth sense, even the sense of my life? Without Paul's knowing it, given his commitment to take on whatever might be thrown his way, I had decided to become his anchor of mercy, which he would need one day, even though he never worried about throwing it down in case of bad weather. He was happy enough to float elegantly wherever the wind took him.

For me, I only had Mount Himalaya left to climb: seduce Paul to the point where he would decide to divorce and then, once divorced, coax him into remarriage. He didn't see the correlation.

Then once Paul became my husband, I wanted to have a child with him. Once again he didn't see the correlation. Because he had lost his little two-year-old son a year earlier, I thought it was indecent to give him as dowry two young daughters who weren't his, but whom he had to love and raise. He never mentioned Gilles's death. Paul never voluntarily talked about his feelings. Yet I imagined that a new little boy might ease his pain a bit.

The majority of women of my generation had four or five children: after all, it was the postwar baby boom. Two seemed enough for me, though I dreamed of having a son before the famous "alarm signal of the ovaries," as Sylvie Caster so aptly calls it, tolled. I had changed my husband and I thought it was normal to fabricate a new child who would bear the Guimard name. It wasn't an attempt to perpetuate the last name, rather to make its presence visible to the following generation. To only have de Caunes when I was no longer a de Caunes myself seemed strange. And I certainly knew how to make them without too much trouble.

I had never heard of painful periods or periodic migraines in my family and had been told even less about menopause. My mother appeared invulnerable and she insisted that our bodies were forged out of stainless steel, ready to obey us without flinching.

"Only do it if you really want to," Paul said to me with concern, not wanting to weigh in on a decision that was fraught with so much consequence. "I'm not crazy about children; you know that." I really wanted one, especially to have a little Breton boy with curly red hair like his grandfather. Another aspect that entered into my consideration was the desire to recreate the close relationship that my sister Flora and I had woven with Nicole. I wanted my daughters to find the irreplaceable feeling of sisterly complicity, which is even more precious than fraternity, no matter what anyone says. Boys already have the benefit of so many places and people of all different types to welcome them and bring them together: Boy Scouts, the VFW, soccer clubs, the automobile club (where women

were never allowed), bowling leagues, the whole of political parties, and business dinners. Women didn't have
any meeting place available to them since the disappearance of the communal washhouse, and young ladies' clubs
where they could laugh and cry together, tell their stories
and complain about men, while continuing to keep up
with their housework, of course, just like the Tricoteuses
of the French Revolution.[70]

Finally I had the benefit of one favorable circumstance:
for the first time, my "suitor" didn't displease my mother,
even though he was from Nantes and had recently "come
up" from the provinces when he was twenty years old. Paul
was without an accent, as Nantes is located in the Gallic
part of the country where they don't speak Breton. Paul
pleased her because he liked women, not woman per se,
but all sorts of women (and oh how many!).

"He's a Casanova," Nicole decreed. "He loves them all
too much to be happy with just one. You aren't fit to keep
him, I'm afraid, because you're too unassuming. But I
hope that he will convince you to write. There again you're
too unassuming. Still you need someone to push you, my
Zazate. I didn't quite succeed."

Paul did succeed in pushing me a few years later, but
I had something else to do beforehand. First, in 1953, I
had a third child, with curly red hair, but his name was

Constance! Then I worked on a popular radio program called *Rendez-vous à cinq heures* (Five o'clock meeting), which was aimed at "women in the home." For this show, I reviewed films, played clips, and interviewed the actors. I had the opportunity later on to listen to a recording and I was appalled: was that really me, that awkward host who spoke like a timid schoolgirl? I was thirty-three years old and I still hadn't managed to find the lively and bubbly tone that was necessary for "speaking in the line of fire."

I realized that during all of my schooling, at secondary and university levels, I had learned how to write, to add, and to conjugate, but never how to speak. That was the case for many women, even the ones who seemed the most sure of themselves. In an interview with *Figaro Magazine* in October 1996, Ségolène Royal, who was running for president, declared: "Until 1984, I was incapable of speaking in public. . . . Even during dinner parties, I didn't say a word." This confession comforted me. Today it's difficult, but I know that we can cure this infirmity. It took me twenty years of trying in order to begin to feel at ease, after 1968 and then after 1975 and *Ainsi soit-elle*.[71] I was already fifty-five years old! And I know some women who still haven't succeeded in doing this.

Once again, one detail is always forgotten for women: whatever their profession or their social origins, they are required to carry out simultaneously, day and night, their standard career as housewife and mother.

I remember something that seems hardly believable to the pretty young things of today: in the '50s, disposable diapers and store-bought baby food didn't exist! Neither did the washing machine or the dryer! Moulinex hadn't yet liberated women.[72] I will remember for the rest of my life the old zinc washboiler on the corner of the stove where the diapers were perpetually in the process of being boiled. There also weren't, my dear girls, disposable "sanitary napkins," much less "tampons," which would have required, oh the horror!, touching yourself *down there* (this act was considered so terrible that American Tampax will provide little sticks to avoid any such contact).

Three little girls under the age of seven in a cramped apartment makes for a lot of noise, mixed with the presence of a man who was born in 1921, which meant that it never would have occurred to him that he could change the baby or even wipe down the kitchen countertop. I didn't think about it either: it was quite simply unimaginable and even a little indecent.

Then somehow I recklessly decided to take on a second home. Ever since my childhood spent in Concarneau, I dreamed of putting down roots in Brittany, where Paul had also spent his childhood. His parents still lived in Saint-Mars-la-Jaille, in the department of the Loire-Atlantique. With a loan, we were able to buy two dilapidated thatched cottages in a tiny village close to Raguenès. I still remember the price: five thousand francs for three thousand two hundred square feet of a little presbytery garden. It had no running water, no electricity. Aside from the new thatching, made from real rye straw and not the reeds that they use today, I did the rest practically all by myself. The beams were polished with linseed oil, the ceiling with boat varnish; we put V33 red on the cement floor to imitate the tiles that we couldn't afford. The shutters and doors were painted blue, and the terrace made from flat stones that were gathered one by one from the low-lying walls in the vicinity and that were brought up by wheelbarrow at night.

Every improvement, every step toward comfort—the first year that we didn't have to draw well water, the first overhead shower (we hoisted the bucket up with a pulley and operated the plug-shaped showerhead with a string), the first time we used gas heat, replacing the butane that made water drip down the walls—every advancement signified a financial tour de force and a personal victory. No other house was more damp, more inconvenient, more often flooded (we were at the foot of a muddy road), more determined to return to its vocation as a cattle barn, more full of smoke (the magnificent granite chimney always refused to draw), and ultimately more painful to the skulls of those visitors who were taller than 5'3". (Bretons are small and the stone lintels of the doors were placed very low.) Yet no other house gave me more pride and joy.

The last thing we needed to fulfill our dreams was to buy a boat. Our first of a very long line was an old fishing vessel, the *Flower of Ajonc*, which was immediately rechristened *Potemkine* and painted black with red trim. It only lasted three months! We didn't yet know that you should never play around with the christened names of ships, no matter what they are. Our boat from Morbihan, which measured about sixteen feet, didn't like bearing the name of a battleship from the Russian armada and she caught on fire three months later, apparently after a careless mechanic filled up her gas reserves.

With the next boat, bought from a fisherman in Lorient, we kept its name, *Kenavo*, and it did its duty for ten years, like a trusted mare.

The inaugural weekend we spent at our cottage was to celebrate Paul's birthday on March 3, as well as two years of marriage.

"It seems like a miracle but I also want to celebrate two years of being faithful," Paul announced as he uncorked a bottle of Gros Plant. "I never thought I could do it, but I lift my glass to this miracle, for which you are responsible, my love!"

"We overestimate ourselves all the time, you see. . . . We think we're Don Juan and then—"

"You will admit that it's silly not to be able to go one hour without missing your wife! I don't know what happened to me with you," he added with a tender look in which I believed I also detected a serious amount of nostalgia.

"Don't worry, my big, bad wolf, if there's anything certain in this world, you'll certainly be cured of this illness!"

On the other side of our granite walls, the timid spring crept in between the trees. Our first *Camellia imbricata* opened its pink and white flowers wide, keeping its promise, and we ate langoustines, followed by monkfish with a crab coulis, inspired by the shrimp coulis from Nantua. I gazed at Paul's handsome face and his curls, like those of a Greek shepherd, which were heightened by the Breton climate, asking myself what he plotted behind this granitelike face. Was he sorry to have set sail with a woman who didn't allow him to be completely himself? Had he been better off with the former? He was afraid of being understood, studied, dissected. While toasting our love, I knew that I mourned a certain other love that couldn't last.

The following year, when we celebrated our three years of life together, he didn't say a word on this subject and I didn't dare ask him anything, for I had a premonition that his nature had taken the upper hand. Paul seemed happier without a doubt. Maybe he even loved me more, because he no longer betrayed the young man that he had been.

Neither one of us had taken the other for a traitor. We agreed entirely on our definition of an honorable marriage: never extinguish the fires of adventure, never say goodbye to the unexpected, and never close the lid on youth, or draw the iron curtain over hope. In short we asked the impossible. But why not? It had been difficult at times, for both of us. We each "experimented," in our time and in our fashion. But I never stopped thinking that that's what living was all about and you can't scrimp and then save on suffering.

Finally, to us, it was the pact between Sartre and Beauvoir that seemed the least destructive way of alienating each other's freedom. I had sensed that Georges felt trapped by the institution of marriage and so I refused to watch Paul discover that any life together meant having to give up a part of himself. His need for freedom was, simultaneously, his best quality and his principal fault and I didn't want to see him suffer. He was too fragile for unhappiness. I didn't want him to run into La Fontaine's[73] wolf, who would say to him one evening in the corner of the woods: "You don't eat where you want to?"

"Not always, but what does it matter?" he would reply to the wolf.

"It matters because I wouldn't want any of your meals," the wolf would conclude.

I could have well accumulated meals, but I knew that they weren't as important as Paul's fickleness. With him, you had to take the imponderable elements seriously.

Nothing specifically alarmed me: Paul lived with panache and, from my perspective, I willingly turned a blind eye. With willingly, there is always a will.

Paul never cheated on me because he never cheated himself. He was a Pisces, with a split personality, and that's an understatement. He had five personalities, or even more, and I got to know, little by little, all of the Pauls that I had married: from the dilettante to the diplomat, from the political official to the poet, from the explorer of the ends of the earth to the ingenious chef, from the editor to the one being edited, from my lover to someone whom I suspected of having other liaisons, to the writer who never wrote a single letter (out of prudence, he said).

I always put up a happy front, knowing in advance that living with all of the personalities named Paul Guimard would require a certain acrobatics. But he had been faithful his entire life, if not to me, to our partnership. He was a faithful man in his own way: loyal to his single malt whiskey and his fine wines, to cigarettes, the pipe and the cigar, to the Atlantic and Pacific oceans, to all the unconditionals of the high seas, to the sailors Eric Tabarly, Olivier de Kersauson, Fauconnier, and Alain Colas. Because he was faithful to such different men and inspired by so many true passions, one penetrating question struck me deep down: when, and with whom, had he been truly happy? He was clearly not a happy man, but a man of many pleasures. While, in spite of my various misfortunes, I had been a happy woman.

We had the sea as our ally, the sea that we had worked together as a crew in Brittany, in the Caribbean, and then in Ireland until we were in our eighties, well beyond all reason. There, we created a union with our life, a team that didn't need words in order to be understood. I often dreamed that it would be lovely to capsize on a Celtic reef, sinking together into "the green seaweed"[74] from the weight of our waders. A beautiful death for two novelists . . .

But that didn't happen. Paul let himself slip away quietly, too quietly, into the depthless ocean of old age. For me, the problem remains in its entirety.

But in the '50s, I was just living out my new birth: happily in love, with a new child, and writing. Like an underground river finally finding its outlet one fine day, writing appeared. It had always irrigated my life beneath the surface—in my private diaries, in the letters that I wrote to one or two friends, with the boys that I could have loved, or wanted to love, or ended up loving, and with my daughters as well. We solved all of our problems through the mail. All of this correspondence piles up in the big school binders from my youth. I loved those binders: the bigger they were, the happier I was. Back then, only boys carried them on their back. I remember trying to balance mine on my left thigh. I belong to the last generation that will have written instead of telephoning.

So it wasn't writing that I missed, but the idea that it could be acknowledged. Meanwhile I helped with Paul's literary productivity. In 1956 he published *Les Faux frères* (Traitors), which won the Prix de l'Humour and then, in 1957, *Rue du Havre* (*The House of Happiness*), which received the Prix Interallié. This was when I began to gauge the inequality inherent in creativity. We lived at 6, rue du Havre, in a two-bedroom apartment (both rooms were tiny!) and we didn't have a corner to work in, other than a desk in our bedroom where the mail, taxes, social security paperwork, my notes for the radio show, and the homework that the girls needed help with all piled up. Paul had to go stay at a hotel to see his novels to completion. This was unimaginable behavior for a woman with three children at home. Furthermore a wife has "a husband to attend to," while a man has a wife to attend to him—a crucial difference.

Gauguin didn't leave to paint in Tahiti, abandoning his young wife and his four children, because he was a genius: he didn't know anything about his genius yet. He left because he was a man and he could desert his family without being followed, jailed, and condemned by society.

I never would have spoken about this unfair destiny, the squandered talent, in my case. I am only trying to explain the sacrifice of so many women, who perhaps had something to say, to create, and weren't able to express it. "How should it be otherwise? For women have sat indoors all these millions of years, so that by this time the very walls are permeated by their creative force," wrote Virginia Woolf in *A Room of One's Own*.

In my case I needed completely magical circumstances in order to finally envision publishing something: Paul was invited by some millionaires, a couple we didn't even know fifteen days before we left, to tour the world by boat. It was the sort of miracle that happened to Paul, which he considered his due. Josette Day, the actress who played Belle in Cocteau's film *La Belle et la Bête*, and her husband, Maurice Solvay, a descendant of the creator of the "Solvay process,"[75] which I had heard about in chemistry class, sought people, preferably writers, to distract them from their usual company, and to leave for a six month trip with them. (Josette was adored by many notable writers—Cocteau,

Paul Morand, and Marcel Pagnol in succession.) A mutual friend, Christian Millau, had suggested Paul to them, as he had just been awarded the Prix Interallié. It was still the era when writers enjoyed incredible prestige, almost equal to that of an American actor today. In three weeks, stunned by the exceptional offer, we had packed our bags, wrapped up our work, and made arrangements for our children. The oldest went to stay with her father, who had since married Jacqueline Joubert, a television presenter. The second one went to a couple that we were friends with, Marie-Claire and Jean Duhamel, and the third went to her grandparents, the Guimards, in Nantes. We set sail in December 1958 from Cannes, on the *Shemara*, a 230-foot boat with a thirty-five-man crew, including personal staff.

I was away for only five months—out of a feeling of maternal duty!—and I went home to see to Easter vacation, leaving Paul to continue on with our friends to the Marquesas and Galapagos islands and the Panama Canal. During these five months, I sat down to dinner never knowing what I was going to eat, nor what had been bought, or how it would be cooked, a rare luxury for a woman. During these five months, I didn't rinse out a glass, make my bed, iron a shirt, or touch a broom. There weren't even any sailing duties to perform on board because the crew of this English destroyer-turned-pleasure-boat took care of everything for its nine passengers. Between the fabulous ports of call—Piraeus, Port Said, the Hanish Islands, Aden, Bombay, Kochi, Hong Kong, Singapore, Nouméa, Cairns in Australia, Tonga, Tahiti—we continued on interminable journeys at an average speed of twelve knots: the Mediterranean, the Suez Canal, the Indian Ocean, and then the misnamed Pacific Ocean. This laziness forced me to write: first a daily journal, which aided me ten years later in my novel, *La Part des choses* (Things in perspective), and then, for Editions Denoël, I tackled translating the American short stories of Dorothy Parker, a collection where each one is a chef d'oeuvre.

Years later, flipping through my book for a stage adaption by Andréas Voûtsinas, I was amazed to see that it had been signed Benoîte Guimard! In 1960, neither Paul nor I found it odd that I should make my entrance into literature bearing my husband's name.

Born Groult in 1920, I went by Heuyer when I was twenty-five, de Caunes at twenty-six, and Guimard at thirty! At forty, I still sailed under my husband's flag. In 1959, after returning from our world tour, Paul suggested that I write a daily column with him. We lived in an exciting environment, full of filmmakers, journalists, and writers. Since I had kept a diary all my life, it wasn't very hard for me to do this. Then, after a few months went by,

Paul confessed that he didn't really enjoy writing as a columnist and he had chosen this method to "bait me" in some fashion. Through a happy coincidence, Flora had moved at the same moment and we found dozens of black moleskin notebooks, with the red trim and rubber band that were popular at the time, in wicker trunks. Every evening we had consigned in these our daily life under the Occupation and the dreams of two dutiful daughters between 1939 and 1945.

Twenty years later and thanks to this historic context, our intertwined lives were thrown into high relief and took on an unexpected charm. It was initially to amuse ourselves that we decided to make a book from them. Flora had also never imagined publishing what she wrote. During her return to France with her husband, who directed the Parisian branch of Barclays Bank, she assisted our mother at her fashion house in the Saint-Honoré district. This type of work in the family business didn't bring in a salary or pension, or even any respect. "She helps her mother," people said as if it didn't constitute a career or a way to earn a living and was more akin to filial devotion. It should be understood that this sort of unpaid activity was reserved exclusively for daughters.

Paul, who had since become a literary director, set about getting us published and so we got to work happily, recovering the silly laughter and the arguments of our adolescence, as if all they needed was one word to come alive again. One year later, in 1962, the *Diary in Duo*, retouched and dusted off, was ready to live again, under the names we had as young women. This time we needed to set aside our husbands, Pringle and Guimard, in order to become once again the Groult sisters after a twenty-year interruption.

At the time of the first publication, in 1962, I had thought that "my" young girl was a bit pathetic. She was fed, housed, and cared for by her parents whose intellectual beliefs overwhelmed her, and she was unable to escape their grip. But it was exactly this authenticity and this innocence that readers of our diary enjoyed.

"An original and brilliant work, often profound, this is a precious document about a difficult time, and about young women from any time." So read the conclusion from a long review by the celebrated French novelist and Académie Française member André Maurois, which appeared in *Vogue*. It was followed by reviews from Pierre de Boisdeffre, Matthieu Galey, and François Nourissier, which all ensured the book's success, and our "taking off" into literary life.

We then continued to write as a pair *Le Féminin pluriel* (The feminine plural) and *Il était deux fois* (Once upon two times). This literary concubinage protected us from the critical misogyny that is difficult to imagine today and which we discovered with astonishment. For, after Maurois's fancy for our first work, journalists, with amused indulgence, put us back in our true place, that enclave reserved for "women writers," a term not unlike "handicapped athletes."

There is an association for handicapped painters who paint with their mouth or their feet. We were also handicapped because, amputated of the phallus, we were condemned to write with our ovaries a literature that was intended for readers also endowed with ovaries. At bookfairs, men told us, convinced that it would make us happy: "My wife loves your books!" as if it were out of the question that our scribbling should interest the husbands. Often critics didn't treat our novels in the pages devoted to literature, but in the rubric marked "For Ladies," placed between a recipe and a beauty tip, under headlines that always reminded us of our place: "The Groult sisters have given birth to a novel!" or "When women exchange the feather duster for the quill." Sure, the feather duster was fine, but when it came to the plume—hands off! Unless it was for your ass like Zizi Jeanmaire and the Paris Casino dancers!

To make matters worse, I wrote for *Elle*, *Marie-Claire*, and other women's magazines, which guaranteed a sense of futility, and didn't confer any sort of authority in the literary world.

Flora and I wrote three books together, but I believe that we wouldn't have succeeded in becoming our own authors in spite of the books' success with the public, and we wouldn't have found the courage to split up. Geography came to our aid: Flora, divorced from her first husband, married an English diplomat who was shortly named an ambassador to Finland. She then left to live in Helsinki and we each discovered the famous writerly solitude. The desire to write stayed with us: I published *La Part des choses* (Things in perspective) in 1972 on my own. Flora wrote *Maxime ou la déchirure* (Maxime: the rift) and then a lovely novel with a Chekhovian title: *Un seul ennui, les jours raccourcissent* (The only problem is that the days grow shorter).

Then in 1970, to my great surprise, I had a midlife crisis, which was compounded by the commotion of '68. I suddenly felt the need to take stock of the sparse snippets of feminism in my novels and in the articles that I published in various magazines. I had been so clearly boxed into the women's literature category that I was hardly considered a feminist. I wasn't even asked to sign the pro-choice declaration known as the "Manifesto of the 343 Sluts." I would regret this for the rest of my life. When I see the names of the signers—Simone de Beauvoir, Delphine Seyrig, Christiane Rochefort, Colette Audry, Ariane Mnouchkine, Marina Vlady, Marguerite Duras, Dominique Desanti, and so many others—I tell myself that my name should have been there among these women whom I admired so much!

But it was because of a phenomenon that I still can't explain: I wasn't considered a true feminist or a true novelist (at least not before *Ainsi soit-elle*).

I wasn't a true feminist because I didn't belong to the university ghetto, which was the only place to gain notoriety and the attention of one's colleagues: women like Hélène Cixous (who had her doctorate in literature), Luce Irigaray (philosophy), Julia Kristeva (she was a semiotician before becoming a psychoanalyst), Andrée Michel (the director[76] of the CNRS[77]), Marie-Josée Chombart de Lauwe (an associate professor), and assistant professors such as African anthropologist Françoise Héritier (the second woman professor named to the Collège de France and director of the Social Anthropology Laboratory). Or others like author of *The Children of Athena*, Nicole Loraux, who specialized in Greek thought and women's studies and who also called herself *directeur* of the School for Advanced Studies in the Social Sciences;[78] or Véronique Nahoum-Grappe, a sociologist and author of *Le Féminin*; and *L'Identité masculine en crise* (The crisis of masculine identity) author, Annelise

Maugue, PhD; or linguists like Claudine Herrmann, the author of *Les Voleuses de langue* (*The Tongue Snatchers*).

I wasn't edited by Antoinette Fouque, a figure from the feminist avant-garde who, in 1974, created the publishing house Des Femmes, which was quite a closed secret society, making and launching its own celebrities. Even Evelyne Sullerot, a successful essayist, published "with the support of the CNRS." All of these women had grandiloquent, masculine titles, and this masculinity gave them an additional grandiloquence and provided them with a stamp of approval and credibility. What did you have to do to be under the patronage of the CNRS and prefaced by Levi-Strauss or Beauvoir? Or to be called a semiotician? Even though I also held degrees, they didn't equal anything like the ones these university professors had after their names, so I didn't dare use their vocabulary, which was so often hermetic.

Without a doubt, unbeknownst to me, there was still a little bit of Henriette, from Molière's *Les Femmes savantes*, in me: "Learned discussions aren't any of my business!" I hadn't managed to emancipate myself from all of these clichés. I felt like one of those "thieves of language," as Claudine Herrmann says. I remained crushed by this vast score of female characters who had irrigated French literature, from Rousseau to Barbey d'Aurevilly, from Baudelaire to Montherlant, to name only a few. Paul was judged and critiqued as an individual with his own flaws and strengths, but I always felt that I was the tributary of my genital organs, which I should be ashamed of, as everyone ceaselessly reminded me. Pascal Jardin, in the erotic-chic magazine *Lui*, evoked Kate Millet, Annie Leclerc, Marie Cardinal, and others (myself included) when he wrote: "All these sinister descendents of Simone de Beauvoir are nothing but one lugubrious cohort of poorly fucked, poorly dressed suffragettes, who devour men with their terrifying incisors, and brandish, in a moral fashion, their monstrous clitorises. . . . They are nothing but nightmarish ovary-owners or union activists for menopause." In this one sentence, all of the Freudian neuroses come together: the vagina dentata, the hypertrophic clitoris, and the old woman who becomes a witch!

There was a second instance of this type of "critique," if we dare to use that term. Maurice Clavel, in *Le Nouvel Observateur*, also described me as "poorly fucked"! As if fucking depended on feminine skill! It hurts and you feel ashamed when this sort of critique comes from admired authors, like Clavel, who write these things in magazines that all your friends read. You never recover from these low blows, even if everyone agrees that they're degrading for the authors themselves.

It was in the hope of acquiring a little more legitimacy that I wanted to write an essay or pamphlet about women. Articles that appear here and there are frustrating in the long run. A book remains and witnesses.

When I discussed this project with Jean-Claude Fasquelle, my dear editor and friend, he seemed disconcerted: "What a strange idea! Your novels work well. With this, you risk . . . annoying everyone."

I talked about it with people around me without finding the least enthusiasm even though it was the Year of the Woman in 1975. People only warned me:

"Definitely don't talk about the clitoris!"

"If you try to proselytize, you'll have the world on your back, both men and women!"

"But everyone agrees about equality now. It's a given. It has even resulted in a crisis for men. Is that what you feminists want? To destroy society?"

The general consensus was, You're better than that, implying that feminism as a whole wasn't worth anything and that I had everything to lose if I got myself mixed up in it.

All of that furiously excited me, as one might say in Sade! So I went to the National Library on the rue de Richelieu where I stupidly began by searching for "woman" in the catalog. At that time, it was still the card catalog, composed of small cards made of beige stock with their corners all manhandled, impeccably handwritten and organized in long sliding drawers. All of the world's knowledge was there, collated by humble scribes; all you needed to know was how to read in order to possess it for yourself. Today a whole technological training is necessary before you can access a virtual book where you can't even turn the pages.

Fate willed that I discover *Woman, Why Do You Weep? Circumcision and Its Consequences* (1982) by Asma El Dareer, *Le Drame sexuel de la femme dans l'Orient arabe* (The sexual drama of women in the Arab Middle East) (1962) by Youssef El Masri, *La Cité magique* (The magical city) (1972) by Jacques Lantier, and the three volumes of *La Fonction erotique* (Erotic function) (1982) by Dr. Gérard Zwang.[79] Thanks to these works, I uncovered "the world's most well-kept secret."

It is estimated (the figures from GAMS[80] cited in *Le Nouvel Observateur* in 1992 and by *L'Express* in 1996) that one hundred million women today live with a mutilated sexual organ in about thirty countries. Even in France, twenty-five thousand little girls, the daughters of African immigrants, are circumcised or are about to be. Meanwhile, in 1985, after much hesitation, the World Health Organization finally took sides definitively against circumcision and infibulations, which are "catastrophic for health, for fertility, and for human dignity." Several countries declared them illegal.[81] But traditions, like illiteracy and fundamentalism, interfere with the application of official directives.

The discovery of this practice, unimaginable in your worst nightmare, served as a sort of electroshock for me. In fifteen days I left behind the state of western bourgeois resignation where sexual inequality seemed like a universal truth. I left behind the ability to live in agreement with the other sex, smilingly accepting the hackneyed macho jokes as any other respectable lady would, merely shrugging my shoulders at the "nightmarish ovary-owners or union activists for menopause." I left behind my ability to shake the hands (instead of spitting in the faces) of those old prostates who so often hold court at the Académie Française and who wrote in the best newspapers of both the right and the left. In short I went from the underdevelopment that was so adroitly warped by our Lords and Masters to a revolt that would only grow and amplify itself in the great outpouring of May '68, a revolt that would never leave me.

How could I have survived fifty years of such flagrant discrimination? Why didn't we dare proclaim that feminism was just a form of humanism that finally liberated the other half of humanity from its thousand-year-old slavery?

The answer was already evident to Paul. In the end he was more feminist than I was.

"I have the feeling that you're ready to write an essay about women," Paul said to me. "*The Second Sex* is already twenty-five years old! Things haven't really changed but right now, things are fluid. It's the right time. . . . Besides listening to you this whole time, the idea for a title just came to me: what do you think of *Ainsi soit-elle*?"

"Paul, do you realize? That's the most beautiful title that anyone could ever give to a feminist essay . . . after *The Second Sex* of course! It's as if this book were already written, it's that evident, that luminous. And do you recall that it was Jacques-Laurent Bost who had found the title for Simone de Beauvoir?"

I had tears in my eyes from emotion. What more precious gift could one writer give to another? What more magnificent diamond could a husband give to his wife? A beautiful title is so much more than a few words. It's the locomotive that will pull along the entire book.

"That being said," Paul added, "I'm not really the person that you should discuss this with. You should perhaps approach certain aspects of this question with another woman, preferably a journalist, and someone from another generation. But especially not an avowed feminist!

One is enough for one book. Otherwise you might not be read, if you want my opinion."

It was a piece of advice that I would remember much later. In 1972 I had already written plenty with four hands and I didn't have any more desire to make another "women's work," as all the critics said. The desire to witness and to take my place on the battlefield of feminism spurred me on. It was the Year of the Woman, the springtime of feminism, and every editor had his or her stable of young writers who were tackling, without any precaution or any modesty, the hottest subjects. I had never before written with such zeal. And so, in such a way that no one could have predicted, *Ainsi soit-elle* became the best-selling book in France of my whole career! And it still hasn't become outdated thirty years later—not as long as women's rights still encounter obstacles, as long as they still don't belong to the Rights of Man, and as long as these rights are still constantly questioned across the world for various reasons.

However, in 1990, when I wanted to understand why I escaped so late from my condition, I needed help flushing out the reasons for this lethargy. I needed to be jostled out of my intellectual comfort. I needed help for the essay that I wanted to undertake; I wanted someone to shine the spotlight on it. I needed someone with a perspective different from my own in order to avoid the sense of complacency and self-satisfaction that such work could have.

I thought of Josyane Savigneau[82] to help me with this, because I had admired her biographies of Marguerite Yourcenar and Carson McCullers. I knew her independence and critical spirit well.

"You had a strange beginning for a feminist," she said to me at the outset. "You were pushed to write by your partner—the third (you're a bit of a repeat offender when it comes to marriage). Then you were supported in writing by your little sister, Flora, and finally, published by Paul Guimard, your husband, who was then the literary director for Editions Denoël!"

That was exactly what I had expected from her. We got off to a good start.

CHAPTER 8

Feminist at last!

Josyane Savigneau: Benoîte, I would like to know, were you already a feminist when you began to write Ainsi soit-elle? *In short, at what age did you realize that you were a feminist?*

Benoîte Groult: Horribly late. When I began *Ainsi soit-elle*, I didn't yet know that it would be a feminist manifesto. But, as you know, Beauvoir didn't claim to be a feminist either when she wrote *The Second Sex*. The word was never uttered. She naively thought that with the rise of socialism, male/female equality would automatically take hold. We always underestimate the extent of misogyny—and the determination of men to keep things from changing.

—As do you. You always underestimate yourself as far as I'm concerned. From the 1960s, your feminist affiliation was clear. In addition to your work with the small weekly review Pénéla,

your articles that appeared in Elle *left no doubt as to your determination. There was your "Open Letter to a Gentleman" in response to Jean Lartéguy's "Open Letter to Ladies," and your reply in* Le Point *in '74 under the title "New French Women and Old Misogynists," where you commented on Jean Dutourd's article that thought it prudent to give women an age limit for having a lover. "Will we ever get out of this?" you asked in the beginning of the article. "One day, will a woman, even if she's a grandmother, be able to make love with the man of her choice, even if he happens to be young, without her character being called into question, without her social and moral status plummeting, without being called a 'bohemian, a clown, or insane.'" Your question, "Will we ever get out of this?" has not, unfortunately, been answered affirmatively today.*

Then there were your editorials for Marie-Claire *for two years, and your column on the back page of* F Magazine. *Even though all this takes place after* Ainsi soit-elle, *a period when everyone knows that you are a feminist, it's worth revisiting because you were already calling for the importance of using feminine equivalents for nouns related to professions if women wanted to truly exist as women in these careers. For instance, you advocated for "la" minister, "une" secretary of state. In November 1978, you predicted that the first woman elected to the Académie Française would be "Madame" Académicien.*[83] *You*

*were right about this, as the first was Marguerite Yourcenar.
But it held true for the second, then the third! Who knows who
will break this ridiculous trend? Worst still, in their acceptance
speech, new members of the Académie are supposed to begin by
addressing their peers as "Messieurs." This has continued even
though women are now members of the Académie. Jean-Denis
Bredin, elected to Marguerite Yourcenar's chair, shocked everyone when he began with "Madame" (addressing Jacqueline de
Romilly), then "Messieurs."*

—And when he was elected to the Académie in 1997, Hector Bianciotti was not allowed to follow this "bad" example and he was required to address the forty members
of the Académie as "Messieurs," even though there were
two Académiciennes seated right in front of him![84] Two
women who didn't bat an eye. It would have been better if
they had left the room!

—*You anticipated all of this and you have made clear that,
far from being mere details, these instances signal a symbolic
blockage, a refusal of the feminine. But I want to go back to the
shock that you experienced—which was felt by everyone who
discovered this for the first time in* Ainsi soit-elle—*when you
learned of sexual mutilation in Africa. It was this extreme,*

definitive aspect of women's oppression that acted as a sort of detonator for you, and it forced you to serve as a witness. In writing the chapter that caused such a scandal and such incredulity, did you have the feeling that this book liberated you?

—And how! Being born as a feminist is a bit like being born for the first time. I was in some ways the first "victim" of what I was writing. After so many individual battles, which were lost from the start, I became convinced that the emancipation of women, all over the world, should be our century's fight . . . and on into the following century. I finally gathered in one place all that I had never dared to formulate during my first fifty years. Fifty years before waking up—it's terrible! I wasn't a citizen until I was twenty-five and got the right to vote and I became a conscious feminist at fifty!

—*Was* Ainsi soit-elle *first and foremost your own aspiration, a book for yourself?*

—In some ways. But in the measure that it was for me, it was also for many others. I had received so many letters after my novels came out that I felt a sort of obligation for solidarity. I have always had a militant streak. I had the growing impression that I could open doors, help other women.

—Yet you didn't take the situation of these women who wrote to you, or your own, as your starting point, rather the tragedy experienced by women in other societies who are abused under the name of tradition and the continuation of civilization. Why?

—Be careful—tradition and civilization should not be confused. Mutilations are the result of a cultural phenomenon that varies according to the political regime or the weight of a particular religion. This is proven by the fact that it is practiced in a number of different Muslim countries but also among Christian Copts, and Animists from sub-Saharan Africa. In fact, I wanted to explore this problem because for women in Africa and in Arab countries, it was, and is, a world of silence. There were, scattered here and there, stories from journalists or "explorers" who wrote on what they deemed a "picturesque custom." But the suffering, the moral and physical enslavement that this practice represents, has always happened in silence.

I remember reading in a glossy *Air France Magazine* a description of one of these "initiation ceremonies" in the Upper Volta (which wasn't yet called Burkina Faso) that seriously claimed that the purpose of the procedure was "to fulfill the femininity of adolescents." Basically femininity is achieved by destroying an organ intrinsically feminine!

In the following article, the same journalist was outraged by the numbers of poor dogs abandoned each summer in France. No one questioned the scandal of mutilated children because no one wants to touch a subject so disturbing and . . . so indecent!

It's not quite right to say that journalists and anthropologists were indifferent. It's worse: they were afraid. If they didn't stand up to compassionately denounce all instances of this custom, it's because men everywhere are afraid to touch male/female relations. Over there it's under the pretext of respecting customs; here it's because they haven't quite sorted out their own contentions with women. So many scandalous facts then remain unknown, thanks to an enormous conspiracy of silence. Rape is another example—its existence has been denied for so long that responsibility for it has been placed upon the victim. Incest, battered women, pedophilia are other examples. "Silence is the most civilized form of genocide," Régis Debray wrote in *Teachers, Writers, Celebrities: The Intellectuals of Modern France*.[85]

The arguments of anthropologists who were called as witnesses before the French courts in cases where excision caused the death of children were more subtle and more damaging still. Their reasons—respect for local traditions, the right to cultural differences—led the judges, in the beginning, to acquit the accused. However, this reasoning prides itself on respecting ethnicities, but leads to troubling slippage. The idea that human rights could vary according to one's sex, race, or religion is, like apartheid, a form of racism. This celebrated *right* to be different was, for mutilated women, a *requirement* of difference, the opposite of freedom. If little African girls are considered equal to our own, they must be equally protected, no matter their color, against any attack to their bodily integrity and against all forms of torture (Article 3 of the European Convention on Human Rights).

Moreover this false respect for African traditions, for even the most harmful ones, didn't cause any qualms when it came to imposing less humanist "values" on the African peoples, "values" like promoting a for-profit economy or excessive urbanization.

Through a remnant of old colonial guilt, what Pascal Bruckner calls "the white man's tears," certain sociologists, some so-called ones, went even further. "Genital excision," they said without batting an eye, could serve a purpose. Robert Arnaud wrote, "The child from a civilized country, not knowing whether he or she is progressing, seems to have trouble overcoming the different stages of his or her development. Far from alienating an individual, initiation thus helps him or her reach the phases of their evolution without any conflict or repression."

That's news to our therapists: clitoridectomies can contribute to sound mental health! It should be made clear that for these hundred thousand women and little girls who have been mutilated, in close to a quarter of the cases, excision is coupled with an additional guarantee: infibulation or "pharaonic circumcision."[86] This means wrenching away the small and large lips and then completely suturing the sexual organ, creating an anatomical monstrosity—a smooth space marked by a hard, scarred strip, leaving only one miniscule orifice for expelling urine and menstrual blood. Imagine the pain as the scar heals. The legs are tied together for three weeks to ensure that the genitals are welded together. Imagine the pain during menstruation and during penetration by one's husband on the wedding night. Then there's the pain during birth, which requires reopening the vulva and then a new suture in order to guarantee a "clean" sexual organ to the husband. I have witnessed this terrible intervention, with Micheline Pelletier-Lattès, when we covered a story in Djibouti for *F Magazine*. The woefully young spouse—she was only fifteen—had just given birth for the first time and she begged the obstetrician to stitch her back up "nice and tight" afterward in accordance with her husband's wishes. The doctor at the hospital in Djibouti, a Frenchman, resigned himself to this fastening-up, knowing all too well that polygamy, poor treatment, and repudiation were the punishment for any insubordination.

The entire sexual life of so many women unfolds in this way, marked by the sign of the scissors or the razor blade. The "absurd clitoris," that organ that was thought to be useless for reproduction and doesn't present any increase in the husband's enjoyment, has been erased. This is not a visible "social initiation" but a demented masculine fixation on the female sex organ that he seeks to reduce to its simplest expression.

Side effects from the operation, like hemorrhages, septicemia, tetanus, and fistulas, which join the ureter with the rectum, transforming the victim into a cripple for life, aren't that rare. But they don't amount to anything in light of the desired effect: "to calm the temperaments of our Negresses," said Yambo Ouologuem (from Mali, with an advanced degree in philosophy and the author of *Bound to Violence*). It's true that this practice is often declared illegal today, but it has been endorsed, as soon as a country becomes independent, in a number of countries. For instance, when he took power, Jomo Kenyatta reestablished it on the same day as Kenya's independence.

—You summed up in a paragraph of Ainsi soit-elle *all of the horror you felt when you discovered this torture: "You're sick to your stomach when you read it. Your whole being is sick; you're sick just thinking about their dignity as human beings, sick for all of these women who are just like us and who are destroyed. You're also sick for those imbecilic young men who believe themselves to be superior in everything, men who have chosen the most degrading solution for the two sexes: to belittle the other." How can you explain why women haven't denounced and fought against a custom so destructive and so widespread?*

—Once more it's all about the great conspiracy of silence that we mentioned earlier. Everything happens as if the oppression of women didn't belong to the more global problem of exploitation of the weak, as if it only shows the way different people put "their" women in the place that has been chosen for them. In fact, patriarchal society— and they all are—considers each woman to be the property of each man, his "genital field," as the Koran says. Napoleon didn't say it any differently in his civil code. If this custom has persisted for so many centuries, it's because no one talks about it.[87] Everyone who knew chose to silence themselves. What can a slave do if she congenitally believes herself born to be a slave?

*—Simone de Beauvoir said that speech in itself is a subversive
act, the first stage of liberation.*

—Definitively, for as soon as this practice came to light,
the situation, which had been completely stalled, began to
evolve.

The most optimistic people predicted that it would take
another generation or two to make this custom disappear.
I am more pessimistic, knowing the weight of politics and
religion. But the idea that a book like *Ainsi soit-elle* could
have contributed even just a little and have woken up people's consciousness about the seriousness of this problem
is a source of great happiness to me. Another source of
happiness is the fact that feminists are at the origins of
this liberation. The little girls and the women who are, or
will be, delivered from this curse owe it to the determined
and united actions of women in Europe and America, who
could investigate since they had direct access to the intimate habits of African women—which was forbidden to
men—and who could convince the WHO that it was a fundamental health problem and not a sexual gimmick. Mutilated women couldn't have done anything without us, for
they were forbidden to speak and deprived of any power.
They remained convinced that women the entire world
over had to submit to this "genital rectification."[88]

—After the success of your book—one million copies were sold in the paperback edition and there were a number of translations, including into Japanese—why didn't you become one of the high priestesses of feminism?

—I suppose I was unfit for the role.

—Yet—and this is why we're still able to discuss Ainsi soit-elle *today, thirty years later—your book's strength is how it mixed your individual experience with your research on other women from other societies that are even more bullied than the Western ones.* Ainsi soit-elle *is still read today because you reflect without trying to guess or calculate the effect that it was going to produce on such-and-such a group or such-and-such a movement. You never say at any point, which was frequent at the time, "I place myself on the side of this feminism . . . for feminist psychology and political theory or against Choice."[89] You were careful not to reference any such feminist ideologies.*

—I refused to have to choose between churches—I was going to say between different sects.

—But in '68, did you participate in the ferment?[90]

—I was definitely too old in '68 to join up with the students. And by then I had already moved away, out to the country-side, for about a year. In the end I had trouble identifying with all those spontaneous movements, so often disorga-nized and completely utopist. They often led to grandi-osity: for example, Françoise d'Eaubonne and her group Ecology and Feminism, which claimed "to rip the planet from the grip of today's males to give the planet back to the humanity of tomorrow. Then the feminized Earth will grow verdantly for everyone again!" I couldn't take seri-ously rhetoric in the spirit of "revolutionary feminism," which called for the "total destruction of the patriarchal order." A nice dream, sure, but it made me think of one kid saying to another, "We'll have fun once we get rid of the parents!"

That said, I admire the militants and the founders of all these women's movements. I admire Élisabeth Bad-inter, even if I don't share all of her ideas. I feel kinship for Antoinette Fouque and for Gisèle Halimi and I'm a member of the Choice party. But I confess that I get lost a bit between Monique Wittig and Christine Delphy's "ma-terialist feminism" and the so-called French feminism, which is only known in America. It's reduced to a holy, unshakable trinity, incarnated in Hélène Cixous, Julia

Kristeva, and Luce Irigaray, whose theories are based on masculine philosophers like Lacan, Foucault, and Derrida. Historians or philosophers like Annie Leclerc, Michèle Le Doeuff, Séverine Auffret, Michèle Perrot, and so many others bring so much more to the debate! But I felt discouraged by all of the different schools. I preferred to remain on the outside where I could write in total freedom.

—That is what allowed Ainsi soit-elle *to reflect without weighing the results that it was going to produce on whatever different trend. But I want to emphasize that it's in large part thanks to your humor that your message has been heard so widely. Your success with the public was immediate and massive, but how did the critics and old-guard misogynists react?*

—You know, 1975 was the Year of the Woman for the first time. And during one year, all of the old-guard misogynists toned it down and my reviews made me happy: reviews from Romain Gary, Claude Roy, Jean-François Josselin in *Le Nouvel Observateur*, from Reverend Roger Parmentier, who wrote in *La Croix*, "Here is a feminist book that men must devour." I was stunned to read that in *La Croix*, from the pen of a Protestant. And then I received thousands of letters; each one gave me a lasting confidence in myself. But the one that moved me the most came from Gaston Defferre, whom I didn't yet know personally: "I loved everything in *Ainsi soit-elle*," he wrote in a long letter of six pages. "The style, the thought, the violence sometimes, the documentation, the strength of your argument and, between the lines throughout the entire book, I appreciated your humor."

—*You rightly call attention to the problematic relationship that women have with humor: "Since 1758, the date of the creation of the first periodical for a female audience, not one single humoristic feminine magazine has been created. We don't know how to laugh, we don't know how to play, and no one encourages us to do so." Do you believe that this has changed or that women still have this same difficulty when it comes to humor?*

—You need to have a certain amount of freedom in order to laugh—at yourself, and at others. This threshold must be crossed by a few so that laughter, humor, as well as jokes and gags, and even a certain vulgarity—vulgarity is also important!—are available to everyone. Among these few, I would say that Claire Bretecher leads the way.[91] She has cured women of this terrible seriousness that they thought they had to cultivate. I also recognize the comediennes of café-theatre, from the three Jeannes to Josiane Balasko, to Charlotte de Turckheim, without forgetting Zouc and the feminine humorists, from Claude Sarraute to Isabelle Alonso. The cream of the crop and those who were less so. All these women were needed to help pave the way. Professional misogynists continue to cash in on the traditional horrific images, treating women like monkeys or crows— the whole menagerie files by. The biggest difference is that the monkeys have changed and their humor defuses the old discourses, making them ineffectual. I profoundly believe that a deep wave was created that cannot surge backward. But women are in a poor position to lead an effective fight: when the "oppressor" is your lover and the father of your children and often the principal purveyor of the funds, freedom becomes a complex and risky undertaking. So much so that many women prefer security, even under supervision, to the hazards of freedom.

At least in private life, thanks to financial independence and to contraception, the two teats of our freedom, the power structures within a traditional couple have been shaken up. Statistics show that more women seek divorce today than men. They have realized that marriage penalizes them. The expression "deserted man"[92] has been coined and single-parent households are households of women, with or without companions, who take responsibility for themselves. It's incredibly new.

—Two bastions (to avoid saying bastilles!) remain that men defend ferociously because they deal with the sacred: the Church and political power. Will fighting on these two fronts get bloody?

—It already is, if you consider that, in spite of the lack of priests, the Catholic Church still won't resign itself to treating women like human beings. There are women rabbis, women pastors, but not one woman abbess like there were in the Middle Ages. Misogyny is still just as virulent. And I am convinced that it factored more than everyone says it did in Ségolène Royal's defeat in the second round of the presidential election. As they went to place their ballots in the box, so many women must have said to themselves, It's more comforting to vote for a "normal" candidate and a "normal" candidate is obviously a man. A woman is never considered as capable or as competent.

—Listening to you now, Benoîte, I ask myself why you never got involved in politics. With all of your views, it's clear to see just how much you want to convince others, to share your ideas. Why didn't you enter into the political arena?

—It's not because I was afraid of others—I don't fear punches—but it was out of fear for myself. I didn't have a confident voice, I didn't know how to get attention, I never learned how to talk. I spent five years at the Sorbonne without ever doing an oral presentation. It was only after '68, especially after 1975, in meetings for women, that I spoke up for the first time. It took me a long time before I dared to speak in front of a male audience. So how could I possibly keep an electoral meeting under control? I was afraid of being heckled, afraid of being booed off the stage!

—*That said, do you belong to a political party?*

—I'm not registered with the Socialist Party but I have always been a fellow traveler (albeit a silent one). I wonder if men ever find themselves afraid of the opposite sex? Young women today have gotten over this handicap. I believe that this fear has disappeared. You can see it on TV when high schoolers protest. The girls aren't afraid to be at the front of the line.

—*This is perhaps true for the next generation but in the working world, I think that women find themselves very much alone. In certain masculine circles where I am sometimes the only woman, I realize that my voice doesn't matter. The men protect each other and come to an agreement with each other in order to exclude me. If, suddenly, I interject, they dismiss me as the black sheep.*

—This is one instance where parity is the only solution. When half of the sheep are black, there's no longer a norm, therefore no more intimidation.

—*I read recently, in the review* L'Infini, *an interview between Julia Kristeva and Danièle Sallenave. They began with literature but the conversation quickly turned to the question of women. Kristeva said something that really struck me because it resonates with what I feel in my own work environment: "Today it's easier to be a woman by not being a woman. Merging with the normalizing order rewards those who bend themselves in this fashion."*

—It's upsetting to be required to distance yourself from your femininity in order to enter the workplace. For this reason, parity is crucial for us, at every level. According to studies carried out in the United States, women need to be at thirty percent or above within a group in order to have a noticeable influence. It's a decisive threshold. Below it, women are useless, other than to provide exemplary models to other women (which is no small feat). But, without thirty percent, women become alibis, mere hostages, who cannot change the norms in any way.

—*In an article in* Le Monde, *Élisabeth Badinter claims to be "deeply humiliated by the idea of quotas."*

—Well, for me, if I'm deeply humiliated, it's because we are last among democracies in Europe in terms of female representation in our assemblies. Worse, ninety-five countries, from among the one hundred and seventy-six that have a parliament, have a higher percentage of women than our national assembly in France. And then I admit to being thrilled when I see those deputies about to be tossed out—up against female candidates who claim the honor, since Olympe de Gouges, to participate in the running of the state, candidates[93] who have been regularly sent back to their kitchens, or else to prison, or even the guillotine.

—*But would you go so far as to say that elected women would make for better politics?*

—They wouldn't necessarily make for "better" politics; that's not the question. Rather they would make for a more complete politics, more respectful of the interests of the two constituents of the human species. The first sex is protected in all its diversity and particularities, not the second sex. There are deputies from agricultural regions to defend the grain growers and the cattle breeders, elected officials from maritime provinces who argue in the name of all those who live off the sea, etc. Because there are practically no women in the Assembly, the problems and specific needs of women are never judged a priority. We have an urgent need for deputies to reverse the priorities.

—*Yet women who have held positions of extreme power like Golda Meir, Indira Gandhi, and Margaret Thatcher have done nothing for women.*

—At the highest level, a woman must conform and even give additional proof of her conformity. We must look to other levels of power where women could inflect the choices, through the condition of being more numerous.

—*But—and here I'm playing devil's advocate—in requiring the parties to meet a certain quota of twenty-five or thirty percent of women, wouldn't that also encourage other categories— Muslims, homosexuals, the disabled—to claim their share of elected officials' posts?*

—It's mind-boggling to put these types of arguments into circulation! Women are Muslims, homosexuals, or handicapped. We aren't a category because we are represented in all categories. We remain lamentably underrepresented in France. I could hope for proactive actions, like nudges or eventually even kicks in the ass, when the situation is stalled. But we don't have the Gray Panthers like in the United States, or the Big Mouths in Italy. It's proven that politeness, patience, and supplication don't lead to anything. The circumstances were exactly the same for our right to vote, regularly voted overwhelmingly in our favor by the deputies between 1915 to 1939, and then just as regularly rejected by the Senate. After twenty-five years of polite claims, the end result was nothing!

History repeats itself when it comes to keeping the fairer sex under supervision.

Men in the Resistance hoped to send women back to their kitchens after victory, exactly as men in politics did in 1918. Without General de Gaulle in 1945, a Lucie Aubrac[94] or a Germaine Tillon[95] would not have had the right to vote! General de Gaulle decided to avoid this parliamentary farce by granting women the right to vote in 1945 by decree, an unusual procedure to avoid any debate.

This is why I refuse to let myself be moved by anyone who talks about universalism with tears in their eyes. The universalism of 1789 was the most distinctive and communitarian of its kind, but when universalism creates such an exclusion, a corrective must be found. This corrective already exists: it's what the Scandinavian countries have put into practice, turning them into the most egalitarian countries in the world.

—*As long as men are in control of the political parties and will make the decisions, they will shoot down a law on parity. But I sometimes ask myself the question: If the two sexes are too different to work together, how can they govern together?*

—Personally I don't believe that at all. People in power, whether they are men or women, have something in common. That's clear. Whether they have breasts or balls. Masculine mannerisms in a woman have been so thoroughly stifled or derided that you don't really see them in evidence today and the reverse is also true. When everyone becomes less trapped by their gender, the gap between these two groups will be bridged.

—*But to your point, don't you think that women have let themselves be boxed into thinking that they're different? Isn't differentialism a trap?*

—I would ban this word. Differentialism is a trap for idiots. Everyone has the right to their own destiny, not just those for whom their sex enables them or their gender allows them. The one thing that all individuals have in common—it's exactly our differences, our right to be unique.

—*Danièle Sallenave writes that the right to difference leads to different rights.*

—A lovely way of putting it! And, in my opinion, it's in the name of this right that certain feminists have gotten bogged down and have bogged women down in lanes without any way out.

We'll never get out of this unless we replace the word "difference" with "diversity." As long as we consider individuals in terms of difference instead of diversity, or worse complementarity (this applies for the color of your skin as well as for gender), we will keep coming up against the equation of "equality with difference."

—*I want to ask you a question, Benoîte. Did you send* Ainsi soit-elle *to Simone de Beauvoir?*

—Of course. I had so hoped to meet her. But I didn't hear from her. Nevertheless I would have been completely ecstatic if she had enjoyed my book.

—You don't need an authority to comfort you, in any case.

—At that time I did. And hers—it was more than authority; it was mythic. It would have placed me in a long line of historic feminists.

—Shortly afterward, you created F Magazine *with Claude Servan-Schreiber?*

—Yes, in '78. *Ainsi soit-elle* had had such a great success that, commercially, I became a bargaining chip for Jean-Louis Servan-Schreiber whose wife, Claude, dreamed of creating a true feminist magazine, written specifically for women, by women. To the advertisers it was important that I didn't look like a banshee (their preferred way of imagining most feminists). I seemed to be an approachable woman. I didn't wear ripped jeans, I had clean fingernails, and I didn't say "shit," so they asked me to accompany them on their promotional campaign as they sought out financial backers. I thought for a moment that they liked my books, my personality. But when they decided two years later that feminism was out of style and that our magazine, which had started strong, had begun to go downhill, I realized that I was nothing but a pawn and *F Magazine* was just an anomaly, a small miracle in the history of women's publishing. Claude Servan-Schreiber was tossed out, the editorial team was changed, and *F Magazine* was rechristened *Le Nouveau F*! An ironic title because they went back to the oldest tricks in the book. And so we saw the return of things like Sylvie Vartan's memoirs, Dalida's secrets,[96] and articles by men like Bernard-Henri Lévy, Philippe Sollers, Gonzague Saint-Bris, and others who criticize all womankind.

—Feminism was no longer fashionable! People returned to the traditional formulas that made magazines like Cosmopolitan *and* Biba *successful.*

—Alas! We really had tried to do something different, with women who wanted to talk about subjects other than orgasms, tricks for trapping a husband, wrinkles, asses, flabby thighs, and lipo. When, thirty years later, I leaf through an issue of this magazine, or when I see the cover of the first issue with the big photo of Claire Bretecher, her naked shoulder showing one of her cartoon characters, one of the Frustrated, drawn on the skin, I remember the humor, the dynamism, and the intelligence of that whole operation. Intelligence! Not a word that we normally associate with women's publishing; it's reserved for masculine publications like

Les Temps modernes and *Tel Quel*. There were intelligent articles on the cinema, for instance, and the roles reserved for women; on the meaning of stiletto heels in masculine fantasies; articles on women older than sixty, or even seventy years old—oh the horror!—with beautiful faces and not just old skin, what a relief! We really responded to the true desires of our female readers. We printed 200,000 copies and had many subscribers, including some who signed up for two years at a time!

—The magazine was beautifully conceived on the page— handsome paper, gorgeous photos, not at all like one of those small newspapers printed on recycled paper like so many feminist reviews from the era.

—Exactly. It was expensive to produce and the advertisers, whose hands had been forced to give us a huge budget, found their misogynistic, or more precisely their anti-feminist, reflexes once again. So they ended by strangling us. What good is it to wax poetic about shampoo to women who don't wash their hair? The ads came back as soon as cooking, fashion, and beauty became once more the unique concern of *Nouveau F.*

—You sensed that the wind was changing?

—Yes, and it blew away all our illusions. Editors dropped their Woman series. They all used to have one: Denoël, Stock, Laffont. The press no longer reported on feminist protests. We went back into the shadows.

—*Laws were voted into existence, sure, but behaviors aren't changed by decree. Laws, in general, come before habits. Behaviors stay the same, unless they get worse. In the microcosm of my company, there is one thing that stands out. When men argue with each other, even if they raise their voices, they never use the same words or even the same irritated tone that they use when they are angry with a woman. That's very characteristic of men from my generation. Because men from the preceding generation never even dared to get angry with a woman.*

—Only because they basked in the patriarchal code of conduct. You didn't frighten them. Young men are panicked because you are a rival and they no longer have inborn authority.

—*Perhaps, but all the same when I came to this newspaper, I was nothing within the hierarchy. With men like Jacques Fauvet, Bernard Lauzanne, and André Fontaine, who truly were from a different generation, I never felt as despised as I feel today by guys of my own age.*

—It's a defense mechanism. When animals are afraid, they bite. Men today are experiencing an identity crisis and they don't know how to act around young women just as competent as they are and who use the same weapons but with a different type of ammunition and a different way of pulling the trigger. It leads to panic, sometimes to hate.

—So what do we do?

—Well, that was one generation.

—My generation—sacrificed? Thanks a lot!

—You were on the front lines, someone who emerged from the trenches and found yourself in no-man's-land. We were all sheltered: given help, protection, and then, all of a sudden, we are exposed. There will be necessary losses. It's hard to admit that from my comfortable position in my little corner. I belong to the generation that was afraid; we didn't make others afraid! My only enemy is the blank page. You, you're headlong in the battle, in a career that symbolizes power and influence. Everything must be learned on the ground: how to fight, how to be cunning, how to become desensitized to insults, to blows, and to never undermine the cause of a group of women because of the failure of just one.

—*That's perhaps the comforting part about it: women don't let themselves be intimidated. There are losses, as you say, but overall we continue on in spite of the machine-gun fire.*

In terms of advancement, I want to broach a subject that doesn't draw unanimous agreement among women. Some find it to be a futile endeavor, while you place great importance on this front. You served as president for the Commission of Terminology for the feminization of nouns related to career, rank, and duties from 1984 to 1986. You call yourself an "écrivaine."[97] I'll admit to you that, in the beginning, I asked myself if this was really an important battle.

—Listen, Josyane, we recently honored the "fundamentals" in our primary schools and Hamon's good old grammar textbook makes it perfectly clear: "The common noun generally changes its form according to its gender. It should be masculine for male beings and feminine for female beings. The feminine form is denoted most often by a final silent *e.* Nouns in French have lost the neuter gender, which was frequently used in Latin." It's cut-and-dried, no?

—The Académie has believed for three centuries that it had the capacity to represent both sexes! You, for example, Benoîte, are you always able to refer to yourself as "écrivaine"?

—Sometimes it draws a few pitying smiles, "Poor thing, she's obsessed with her feminism!" But I find it grotesque that the standard word for novelist is feminine [*une romancière*], while writer [*un écrivain*] is masculine. We have both forms for the owner of a manor [*un châtelain* or *une châtelaine*], as well as for sovereign [*un souverain* or *une souveraine*]. "*Écrivaine*" is grammatically correct so I'll hold my ground. I admit that I falter when it comes to tax inspectors. When I fill out my income-tax form, under profession, I write "*écrivain*" just in case I should run into a misogynist (male or female)!

—What troubles me, I have to confess, is my own behavior. I am convinced that what doesn't have a name doesn't exist although I agree about the symbolic reach of your struggle. But I just can't get myself fired up for this cause. All the same, on my business cards, I have put "Head Editor [Rédactrice].*"*[98] *But why not*

just let things evolve on their own? Why have such a frenzied desire to correct everything?

—Because when it comes to women, nothing evolves on its own. As for the importance of this battle, if you gauge the violence of the reactions that we have experienced, you would conclude that we were engaging in acts of verbal terrorism! This violence confirms the fact that language touches something profound and visceral within us all. It's not just a simple tool for communicating, but it reflects our prejudices and mirrors our relationships and our unconscious desires. How women talk, how people talk to women, and about women, all play an essential role in the image they project and what they make of themselves. Keeping the progress of women invisible as they attain new roles and careers is a way of denying it. Men are able to adapt to changes in language more easily than the few lacunae in vocabulary that concern them would suggest. For example, there are no self-designated "midhusbands" among male midwives in France. Instead they have chosen the pompous title of *maïeuticien*.[99]

—*If, as you say, it's the usage that counts, what purpose does it serve to legislate for changes? Why do you think that a law, unaccepted and not integrated socially, will change usage?*

—What do you think a grammar textbook does? It tells us the right and wrong usage. And let me remind you that the Académie Française tried desperately to legislate! At the very least, it's important to counter their misogynist views.

So we claim that language evolves on its own and that it's useless to make recommendations. But this is totally false, especially in our country. Since the time of grammarian and original Académie Française member Vaugelas, the French language hasn't ceased being codified, rectified, and called to order! The French have a very particular, and very passionate, relationship with their language. This love affair began with the famous Ordinance of Villers-Cotterêts in 1539 when François I decided that French should replace Latin and all of the other territorial dialects in official and administrative texts. He founded what would become our Collège de France, where, going up against the influence of the Latin-speaking Church, the masters taught in French. There are poignant coincidences along the way: King François I lent credibility to this new language, calling it *François* after himself, which was the way we used to spell French.

Then there was *The Defense and Illustration of the French Language* by Joachim du Bellay in 1549 and after that, grammars began to multiply. Language became the business of the state. Richelieu created the Académie Française to draw up a dictionary under the authority of Vaugelas. Then Furetière, who didn't agree, drew up his own, breaking with the Académie's rigid principles. So soon! Then in 1660 there was the grammar created by Port-Royal. France was weighed down with all its dictionaries and grammar books. Our country has published the most edicts, directives, and manuals of correct usage in the world. Our country respects its language so much that we feel guilty if we change one iota of it! Even if we don't speak it well ourselves, we are all lovers of "proper French."

Another subject that shocks foreigners: the respect that we have for our spelling, even though it's sometimes aberrant. We have long had—the only people in the world— our crusaders and our martyrs for dictation, shepherded by journalist Bernard Pivot on TV. In order for a word to enter into use, acceptable words must first be forged. That's what was done in the '80s with a good number of terminology commissions in order to adapt medical, technological, and philosophical vocabulary to new realities.

The work of commissions, composed of linguists and specialists from each discipline, was unappreciated. Yet thanks to them we escaped a massive invasion of "franglais":[100] pacemaker, computer, hardware, software, walkman, etc., (with the tortured French pronunciations that you can imagine) were replaced with *stimulateur cardiaque*, *ordinateur*, *logiciel*, *informatique*, *baladeur*, etc. It's the usage that counts, in the end, but first, new words have to be offered. It's not the public who invented *logiciel* for software or *ordinateur* for computer. Of course some words just don't take: *ciné-parc* instead of "drive-in," or *commanditer* to stand in for the terrible *sponsoriser* [to sponsor]. As for *baladeur*, it's a shame that young people didn't adopt it. It's much more lyrical than walkman! My commission didn't have anything to invent. We simply wanted to make language work, forming feminine versions of words as had been done in the past. In the Middle Ages, words were feminized without agonizing over it; people said "seamstress," "abbesse," "deaconess," "fisherwoman." But our commission, because it was in charge of language as it affected women, was greeted in 1984 with outright laughter.

"What? The ridiculous *précieuses*[101] are going to natter on about our beautiful French language over a cup of tea?" Bruno Frappat cracked ironically in *Le Monde* (your own newspaper, dear Josyane!).

Everyone got their two cents in, even Mr. Weather in *Libération*: "A heavy delirium is setting in," Alain Gillot-Pétré wrote. "Benoîte Groult has perhaps won her crusade to become an *écrivaine*. But I must ask the question: what is the masculine form of the expression 'to have a real stick up your ass'?"

Figaro Magazine applauded our "commission of futility whose intent was to put a petticoat around our vocabulary."

"Pity poor Madame Groult and her fantasies," Georges Dumézil, one our best philosophers, wrote in an article for the *Nouvel Obs*. "These women who attack our vocabulary are profoundly lacking in their knowledge of Indo-European languages."

"Here's the clitocracy to the rescue," Jean Dutourd shot off in a column on the first page of *France-Soir*.

When I saw this string of potshots, I understood why Yvette Roudy had asked me to preside over this commission. I was already in the media at this point in time: *Ainsi soit-elle* had come out not too long before and she thought that I could easily find a platform from which I could respond to our detractors. At least more easily than a linguist could, even a brilliant one, who teaches in a university somewhere in the suburbs. Because I was convinced of the necessity of doing something, I took on this sentence of hard labor. And it truly was. I was delighted because this adventure confirmed that misogynist behaviors had not changed, even if they were expressed in a more subtle manner, which only justified all of the misgivings that I harbored against men in general and particularly men in power. They were the same; we didn't have any illusions. These powerful men would never, *never* embrace women's progress.

—The outburst of bawdy and imbecilic misogyny that you describe shows that we are truly involved in a struggle whose symbolic import reaches far. What I would like to understand is why so many women, beginning with myself, didn't perceive the importance of this symbolism and why certain women lined up on the same side as the ones laughing at them. In short why did women, once again, let this happen?

—That's the big question. It has been asked before. Women who protest feminization today are the rightful daughters of women who opposed women's right to vote yesterday. With men we understand it, they're defending their piece of the pie. But when women march against this cause, it's crippling.

—Do you believe that it's because they want to go in the same direction as men, that it's one more way of consenting to men's desires or, worse, is it an act of aggression against other women?

—No, I believe quite simply that women privilege their relationships with men. French women always favor men. As a result, we don't have the same war of the sexes that you find in America, for example. Male/female relations remain civilized, marked by the vestiges of "French gallantry." But this is at the price of our own pugnacity. That said I believe in the vitality of language and I am convinced that ten years from now we will find ridiculous the *précieuses* who continue to use the formula *Madame le* . . .

—Do you think that it's right to be so optimistic?

—I'm already seeing it happen. In the press, you see more and more often *la juge* [judge]. Or at least when they're talking about juvenile court, it's *la juge*. In the left-wing press, *la ministre* [minister], and *la secrétaire d'état* [secretary of state] are routinely used. In Jospin's administration, all of the women had a feminine title: Guigou,[102] Aubry,[103] and the others. Only *Le Figaro* still subscribes to the horrible *Madame le*!

—If French women decide to refuse to be called "Madame le ministre," they will gain the upper hand. So this is about their own passivity, their own refusal?

—Some women have already gotten the upper hand. Yvette Roudy, for instance, is the *première ministre* of women's rights and the *deputée-maire* of Lisieux, for good measure.

I wrote to Panafieu,[104] Ockrent[105] and all the others beginning in 1986 when our ordinance, signed by then-prime minister Fabius, was published in the *Journal Officiel*.[106] They never responded to me and, in their eyes, I must have seemed like a famous nuisance, crossed with a ninny.

Ségolène Royal was the only one who wrote back to me on her stationery with "la" Minister of Environment printed at the top. Not one of her colleagues apparently knew how to read! If a woman of great prestige like Simone Veil had decided to be designated as *la présidente du Parlement Européen* [president of the European Parliament], then that would have been a decisive shock.

—What did Simone Veil think of your platform?

—I went to see her to gain her support, which I had assumed was a given. Naively. She did not want to risk being taken for the wife of the president![107] She sent me packing. "This is not of the slightest importance and I'm not going to fight for this sort of thing. As for you, calling yourself an *écrivaine*, it's terrible, simply a horrible word." I told her that the word's beauty or perceived ugliness had never been one of the criteria. You have to use *écrivaine*, just as we say *souveraine* or *contemporaine* [female contemporary] without asking ourselves if they're ugly or nice words. If this were the case, the word *institutrice* [female school-teacher] should have been rejected. It's difficult to pronounce, especially for children. Yet the important thing is that it is linguistically correct.

—*So she wasn't won over?*

—Not in the least. At the end of our commission's term, Bernard Pivot devoted one of his shows to the question of feminization. He had invited me, along with Thérèse Moreau, the Swiss linguist who had just published a masculine/feminine dictionary that the Swiss government was using. The discussion was going to be held between qualified people. Should we put an *e* at the end of *proviseur* [principal], *docteur* [doctor], *ingénieur* [engineer]? Should we say *la cheffe*, as they do in Switzerland, or *la chef*,[108] as we advised for use in France? I planned on reminding everyone that the standard feminine form for *chef* should be *chève*, if we followed the example of [the adjective] *bref/brève*. Which is unthinkable. In some cases, trying to find the correct feminine form throws us for a loop and it's exciting to try and find the best solution. And who do you think Pivot had chosen to discuss linguistics with us? Guy Bedos! We knew each other slightly and he politely warned me beforehand: "It's going to be hard for me not to make fun of you two." That's exactly what he had been invited to do! And so he tossed off comments like this: "Will you suggest the term *enseignette de vaisselle* now that women are in the navy? And of course you'll use *major-dame*?"[109] What can you say to that? We laughed stupidly and the real discussion was shot down. And then, the final blow, an ad was aired in which Michèle Gendreau-Massaloux declared, "I am *recteur* [rector] of the university and I'll stay this way. While there are two million unemployed in France, to debate whether we should say *recteur* or *rectrice* is inappropriate." And so, the whole thing was finished. But what more could she do, "Madame *le recteur*," than I, for the unemployed?

Or I can cite Marc Fumaroli, a professor at the Collège de France, who, in an article for *Le Figaro*, suggested several feminine alternatives at our expense: for women *recteurs*, he suggested Madame *la rectale*! That's not even funny, but the sort of humor you might expect from a rug rat laughing at potty jokes.

Alas, intelligence has never warded off misogyny!

—How did you deal with all of these sarcastic remarks? What did you think when serious people were tempted to mock you, when an eminent historian evoked "poor Madame Groult and her fantasies"?

—I grew a thick skin. I find that it's men, whether eminent or not, who are victims of their own fantasies, chief among them the fantasy of the superiority of the phallus. And I'm reassured by the opinion of *all* the well-known grammarians—Brunot, Dauzat, Hanse—who have denounced, for years, the impasse that exists, not at the level of vocabulary but in people's mentalities. Already as early as 1922, Ferdinand Brunot deplored "the awful *Madame le* that spoils all our texts." Maurice Chaplan, who wrote under the name Aristide in *Le Figaro*, ended one of his columns with: "Long live *la ministre, la deputée, la préfète* [headmistress], *l'ingénieure, la professeure.* . ."

—*But, in spite of these "eminent" specialists weighing in, why is it that nothing changes?*

—I think that refusing to feminize nouns stems from a group strategy that is more or less consciously trying to delay the surge of women's access to power. That means to delay their access to all powers, even the power of naming things. It's clear that feminine versions of nouns become rarer as you climb higher in the social order. The capacity for a noun to have a feminine version is inversely proportional to the prestige of that profession. You can be a female *boulangère* [breadmaker], *opératrice* [machine operator], or *concierge* [superintendent]. If you rise in the ranks of professions, suddenly there are all sorts of pretend linguistic and philosophical reasons to deny a feminine equivalent. Someone is *la doyenne* when she's one hundred years old, but it's *Madame le doyen* at the university.[110] Calling yourself a museum *conservatrice* [curator], which is perfectly and grammatically correct, remains an act of insubordination in the twenty-first century. But, it seems to me that these women should then go all the way and call themselves *monsieur*!

—Do you interpret this as a reflex motivated out of fear?

—It's a lack of confidence with women. But with men it seems to me that it's a genuine fear when they're confronted by these female rivals who are entering into the enclaves that used to be exclusively for men. The anomaly in language underlines the anomaly in society. Language forges the identity of those who speak it, whether this identity is national, cultural, or sexual.

Wanting to be comfortable in your own language is not capricious. It's a vital need, a means of social integration. But women fear the risk of being discredited, which can often happen for those who pass as feminists, just by calling themselves a museum *conservatrice* or *directrice*. It's a ridiculous formulation, but it happens.

—*So your law didn't amount to anything?*

—What law? It was just an "ordinance" in the *Journal Officiel*. It was completely forgotten in the heady first days of Chirac's new government, which didn't concern itself at all with broaching another quarrel about language. It was clear that the French would react passionately. Remember the reform about spelling! The various ministers (Youth and Sports, National Education) would have had to make the new words acceptable in all of their administrations, with all of the bureaucrats, in order to guarantee a following with our work, as was done in the United States. There, today, they say "chairperson" instead of "chairman" and so on. I won't even mention Quebec, where the French language is attempting to survive in the face of the Anglo-Saxon world that surrounds it. In Quebec, French is alive and well and it has figured out how to evolve. For some time now, they have used *la docteure*, *la professeure*, *la ministre*. Louise Beaudouin, who was Quebec's longtime general delegate to France (a little bit like an ambassador), was horrified to arrive in Paris and see her name and position written at the Quai d'Orsay as *Madame le délégué*. She was truly the first one to really get it and Laurent Fabius, when he bestowed the Legion of Honor upon her, was impressed and told her, "I name you *chevalière*."[111]

I didn't get this from François Mitterand—even though using *chevalier* for a woman is ridiculous!

The French Canadians have also decided to replace "the Rights of Man" with "the Rights of the Person" or "Human Rights," following the American model that Eleanor Roosevelt called for. In France, we hang onto the ambiguous expression the "Rights of Man" that comes from the French Revolution, which cast women aside as citizens. Everything is connected.

It seems to me that the tide is changing thanks to Francophone Europe. Already in February 1990, the European Council published a bill "on the elimination of sexism in language," recommending that all member states "adopt a vocabulary with an autonomy for both sexes, the basic principle being that the activities of each are equally visible." They weren't a bastion of feminists. No one suspected the European Council of being a den of feminist hell-raisers. Nevertheless France continued to refuse any change. The press didn't mention this bill at all because its language reminded us once again that "interaction exists between words and behavior" and noted that "the use of the masculine gender to designate people of both sexes generates occasionally uncomfortable uncertainties."

If I'm optimistic today, in spite of the Académie Française, it's because, ten years after our decree in the *Journal Officiel*, dictionaries are beginning to recommend the feminization of career nouns.

In 1996 a good number of feminine career nouns appeared in *Le Petit Larousse*. For the first time, you could find *la juge*, *la ministre*, *la sculptrice* [sculptor], *la baroudeuse* [fighter], and a few others. Let me also remind you that *factrice* [mail carrier] and *inspectrice* [female inspector] were in the *Littré* dictionary since 1967 and *agricultrice* [female farmer] since 1982.

These restrictions that match the access to the post of female judges or ministers speak volumes about the extent of the prejudices that they had to overcome.

The main point is that we have entered the Noble Book, even if it was through the back door. Just as you can find "*instituteur, -trice,* noun," we will soon read "*sculpteur, -trice,* noun" in the place of "*sculpteur,* masculine noun. Feminine: woman sculptor." Female sculptors and composers will then find themselves more comfortable in their own skin. Remember that Madame Claudel said to her daughter Camille: "You can't embark upon a career that doesn't have a feminine equivalent."[112] There needs to be a courageous woman one day, in an important position, to make the distinction that *le* signals the masculine and *la* the feminine. It's elementary, my dear Ms. Watson! And why not Ségolène Royal if she becomes president of the Republic? She would do it and all of the prejudices would fall away in one fell swoop. All it takes is one well-said sentence, at the right time and at the right moment.

And last but not least, my sister Flora and I have appeared as *écrivaines* in the Larousse dictionary this year! They phoned us and said, "Benoîte and Flora Groult, you will be happy to discover that in our last issue, you have won your feminist battle: we have agreed to call you and your sister *écrivaines*. You have triumphed at last!"

CHAPTER 9

Paul's Fan Club

Getting older, sure, I had been warned. It was part of the program. But when it came to my own children, no one said anything about that. I realized that watching *them* grow older is what's unbearable. The first wrinkle that appears on your oldest daughter causes an uproar that affects you personally. The first time that fatigue leaves its trace on her face, you suddenly realize what she will look like when she's your age, and then you, yourself, suddenly age about twenty years.

The day when your oldest begins to squint her eyes and to hold the newspaper at arm's length in order to read it, or the day when your second-oldest has to have sclerosis for a varicose vein in her leg, or the day when your third (she was always "the baby"! What right does she have to no longer be "the baby"?) tells you that she's got psoriasis—these things sting you like a string of insults.

Look, Blandine, I provided you with impeccable eyes

not too long ago. What have you done to ruin them? You read too much.

Look, Lison, I don't have any varicose veins myself. What right do you have to strain a blood vessel in your leg? You stand too much in your studio and you go to bed too late at night.

Look, Constance, how on earth did you get psoriasis? You're not careful. But of course, you never were.

With a bit of effort, they could have never gotten any older. That's for sure and it's briefly reassuring to reproach them. Stand up straight, dear! You'll see, you'll start to look like my mother, you say to the one whose back slouches a bit at times. But you didn't realize that the apple fell even closer to the tree: it's you she's starting to take after! It's true that we'll try anything to cheat our own looks. We somehow manage never to see ourselves in profile or from behind. It's only when someone else takes a photo that you realize you have a belly, or a hunched back, or that you stoop. Or all three of these things. Where did our insolent grace go, the unbridled youth of our twenties? The grace is still there, holed away in our heads, where it will last a long time against the untimely reminders. The accusatory photos will be quickly swept into a drawer. But you can't get rid of your own children and you appraise them with a despairing eye. You brought these brand-spanking-new organisms into the world, made from impeccable materials, and it's simply not acceptable that they should break down in front of your very eyes. It discredits the mother company.

Rolls-Royce stands behind the quality of their automobiles to the extent that they agree to repair them, no matter where they are in the world. I would be ready to do the same for my daughters, but I've just learned that organ donations aren't accepted if you're over fifty-five years old. Am I full of nothing but spoiled organs? People are crazy! In response I say that I'm still using a good portion of these organs, which have some mileage left. But people are obsessed with age and expiration dates. As for myself I methodically finish a fair number of the medicines that I find in my drawer even though they have supposedly expired and they manage to serve me quite well, in spite of the label's warning. Fortunately for my daughters, their problem is not currently any defective parts. They've simply slacked off.

"Just a dozen days, Mom, it would go by quickly. I really need to take some time for myself, and have a change of scenery. Do you think that you could take Violette and Clémentine for Easter in Brittany?"

"And what about Pauline?" I ask in a stricken voice.

"Don't worry, I know that she's still too young, with the rocks and the ocean in front of your house. We'll put her with her grandma Paula and then we could go to Egypt with some friends."

I know that the conditionals here are nothing but pure politeness. Everything has already been decided, the tickets perhaps already bought. But how could I refuse my own children who happen to be the three women I love most in the world? Three women who need to take some time to themselves and explore the pyramids in high style. The other grandmother is on board and now I'm called to duty as well. I almost didn't dare tell them that I had a presentation to prepare on "myth, culture, and sexuality," for April 15. I was told that two children are easier than one to take care of, in the end, because they'll play together and that I should manage to find the time to work.

It was true that Lison seemed worn out this winter. She certainly looked the part of the modern woman, meaning that she was one part loving wife, another part full-time mom who tries hard not to compromise in her duties, another part intellectual who enjoys books and the theater, another part diligent housekeeper, and another part passable athlete. Never before in the past have so many different characters, pursuing such diverse and contradictory activities, been gathered under the skin of the same woman, with each one devouring its share of her flesh, time, and energy. The resulting product was this overburdened woman, who spends long hours in her studio, polishing shagreen or hand pasting straw for her marquetry; who goes and picks up her oldest daughter every day at elementary school and her youngest at day care; who gets upset when she misses the latest Finnish or Turkish film that's playing at the other end of Paris but which was so highly recommended by *Le Nouvel Obs*; who keeps an open table with her husband for their many friends; who takes one daughter to horseback riding, another to dance, both of them to piano; who meets with their teachers, takes them to the pediatrician, the orthodontist to retighten the retainer each week and the oldest to the orthopedist for her arches and knock knees while the youngest goes to the ophthalmologist for her eyes, all the while thanking the heavens that neither one of them needs to see the speech therapist, and without forgetting to take care of the cat. On Sundays it's important to amuse the children, take them to the pool, or the museum, or the flea markets, or to see *101 Dalmatians* for the fourth time, then find some time to read or watch television and to complain to her husband that there's never a spare moment for romance.

Because of this situation I found myself, one sunny Monday in April, at the airport in Lann Bihoué, trying to pick out the two girls who were destined for me from among the herd of children with name tags getting off the airplane: Violette, the oldest who would soon be thirteen, with her hair styled like Louise Brooks, and Clémentine, eight years old, whose golden brown hair fell in curls just to her waist. They recognized me first and their faces lit up. They run toward me; I open up my arms. I think they're just wonderful. I hug them together against my chest; I almost have tears in my eyes. I am stupidly proud to be a grandmother. It's a lovely moment, the loveliest, along with the one when I will bring them back to Lann Bihoué (but this I don't know quite yet).

"You'll see, Paul, they're older now. Everything will be much better. I will teach them how to scull this year. They already swim well and they can amuse themselves with the boat in the harbor. I won't be after them all the time."

I sincerely believe this. Each time they come to stay, I'm full of the same illusions about the authority of grown-ups and the respect of grandchildren. I believe in my ability to make them obey me and their desire to make me happy. I dream of little heads bent under the lamp-light, pouring over their coloring or decalcomanias while I write in my room, just within earshot, as the odor of potato leek soup emanates from the stove where it gently flickers on a low flame. I forget that they don't like soup, that decalcomanias only amuse me, and they aren't interested in nautical sports at all. I dream of watching them play around in the rowboat just like the woman next door's little grandkid, who is barely seven years old, or stationing themselves, at half-tide, on the garden wall, surveying the sea for mullets for hours at a time, like my friend C's son did last year. I bought a fishing rod, a reel, some hooks, all ready to go. I refuse to believe that girls prefer parlor games or dolls.

The first day is so full of promise. We go down the forty-six steps that lead to the coastal road and I glimpse the small fishing boats between the oak tree branches which lean over the water, marveling to myself yet again that I live practically in the sea itself yet under the protection of these powerful trees that grow between the rocks.

"Paul, we're here," we cry out to no one in particular, reaching the terrace that overhangs onto the harbor below by a few granite steps, which are covered in wild grass and where the stubborn blue periwinkles are already in bloom. Preemptively and in order to keep his distance, Paul had retired to our bedroom and didn't waste any time telling us that he had important work to do. That was his right, not mine.

"Poor Paul, he's always working," said Clémentine, who still believes what people tell her. I cast her a baleful eye. My own work was waiting for me in a folder opened onto the first page where the beginning lines of my presentation were written: "I am honored to find myself here among you, ladies, gentlemen, dear friends, in front of this audience of doctors and scientists though I am no scientist myself." Indeed, what was I other than a poor grandmother?

At the moment, my work was unpacking and organizing the children's things and this wasn't work because, as everyone says, being a grandmother is just sheer joy. Violette had dragged an enormous book bag, full of books, notebooks, and her beloved teen magazines from which she endlessly cut out silhouettes of schmaltzy Adonises and she arranged them on posters in ascending order of their sex appeal. She tirelessly adjusted this hierarchy according to new arrivals, and I was called upon to give my opinion daily. I tried to find the signs of a budding documentarian in this obsession, rather than a nymphomaniac. In their lumpy duffel bags (the suitcases that I asked them to use were declared to be too fuddy-duddy, especially the ones with wheels, which are too old lady), I didn't see any sign of the anorak for one of them or the bathrobe for the other one. However I did find bottles full of soapy blue bubble water, loaves of modeling clay stuck between two mohair sweaters, sneakers without laces, and old boots, each one weighing about five pounds, intended for tramping around in the marshy field.

"Where are the moccasins that I bought for you to wear here?"

"Moccasins?" Violette retorts, the word itself seemingly turning her mouth inside out. "No one wears moccasins, Bounoute!"

"Oh yes they do, well-brought-up girls do," I say *in pectore*. "Girls who don't question the choices of their parents." I still bitterly remember the first pair of high heels that my mother insisted that I wear for my sixteenth birthday. We bought them at the Hannan Shoe Company, which quickly changed ownership and became Aurèle, on the rue Royale in Paris. I have never forgotten this cursed store window where I longingly eyed my dream shoes, beige buckskins with a crepe sole, while Nicole pointed her finger at the cruel pumps that she had picked out for me. I offer up a pitying smile for poor Zazate every time I pass by the rue Royale.

I unpack jackets, shirts, pants—everything uniformly a shade of gray, black, or brown. Why not any red? Or light blue? Or green? No, Bounoute, colors are superstupid.

While I am putting things away, the two cousins are taking things out, spreading the contents of the toy chest onto the floor. I had bought a Trivial Pursuit, two Chinese kites, rackets, a ball, all of which they don't even look at.

They're after the old totems in the trunk to remake their familiar territory: a tiny insect on wheels that flaps its wings with a little noise that goes "gling!" that they had played with when they were learning to walk; the tin frog that used to hop but can now only pull off a dying somersault when they wind it up (but I've been forbidden to throw it out); a one-eyed doll with dislocated joints that is brought out a few weeks every year in its role as the cherished baby. In the bottom of the trunk, there are some loose playing cards, some shovels, some molds, the magnifying glass that I had searched high and low for in September, and a handful of rank-and-file crayons (the dominant colors among them being brown and the color of goose poop, which are never used). The girls discover one of the great joys of existence: finding those things that you know by heart. Watching them absorbed in this ritual ceremony, I think I can steal away quietly to finish the new flower bed that I am in the process of making. The word "making" is a bit ambitious because the bed in question is only thirty square feet of yard to fill in and surround with stones. But in a little garden, each square foot is worth a park, and each transformation is an event.

"Where are you going, Bounoute?"

"I'm just going to finish something up in the backyard."

"Wait for us—we'll help you."

Alas, I know from experience that what would be useful for me bores them and what amuses them is destructive. They only like watering, which means drowning the bulbs that I just planted, splashing everything with mud, or manhandling the garden shears with their murderous blades. Fortunately, after about five minutes, they tire of this activity and move on to chopping up the iris and camellia petals, which requires them to requisition my kitchen shears, my plastic containers, and the coveted treasure, my old Roberval scale with its copper trays, and the wooden block base where you insert the weights into the little holes upon measurement. The two smallest weights had been lost last year and I swore to never let them play with it again. Paul glanced at me sorrowfully. He knew I was incapable of saying no, partly out of weakness and partly because, if I did lend it to them, it would guarantee a moment's peace for me so that I could trim my rosebushes, plant my lily bulbs, sow my sweet peas, all the while whispering to my garden to reassure it that I was finally back after a long winter away.

But the sky wasn't listening and a sudden shower chases us out of the garden. I only have a moment to yell out, "Not the irises in the living room—their sap leaves horrible stains!" They reluctantly brought bowls full of a leafy stew swimming in an inky glue back to the table in the backyard.

It was now time to seek the aid of one of my secret weapons for rainy days. Ammunition #1: a game comprised of fluorescent discs that could be cut up and "applied to any flat surface," which I bought at a toy store on the rue de Sèvres. The extremely competent saleswomen had assured me that this game exerted an irresistible and lasting attraction (the duration was very important!) for any human being between eight and fourteen years old. I set up my two little human beings at the big table in the living room and then made the most of the momentary calm to head back to the desk in my bedroom where Paul was still taking a nap. Because the little desk in the children's room where he normally worked was monopolized by Clémentine's stuffed animals and Violette's magazines, there was now only one desk for the two of us and we both waged unending maneuvers against the other in order to take back this precious terrain from the adversary. This time I had conquered the bunker and hurried to set up all of my cherished materials: multicolored pieces of paper, pens and markers in various colors, Scotch tape, and scissors. I even managed to write the first sentence: "I find myself quite moved to speak before an audience of scientists and specialists even though I am not any sort of specialist myself. My only titles consist of being a woman, which is in itself common enough (here I'm hoping to draw a smile);

a novelist, which doesn't really allow me to better know human nature (here, hopefully a modest grin); and, finally, a feminist, which is perhaps the most interesting qualification for it has allowed me to differentiate myself from the traditional vision of feminine sexuality (Aha! the room will think, she's a lesbian!)."

Feminine sexuality, my ass! I would have much preferred to talk to them about the smell of the earth in the spring or the red-throated robin that stations himself about a foot away from me while I dig with my spade, cheerfully under the assumption that I'm working just for him.

Come on, come on, Benoîte Groult! This is a serious presentation, fifteen to twenty pages, which will be published afterward in the conference proceedings. If only I had three full days to myself, I know that I would write intelligent things in the ensuing calm and concentration. The challenging audience of the medical school would be impressed, I would have rehearsed my lines, and I would deliver them with gusto.

But Zazate watches over me: Come on, come on, Bounoute! Your speech, that's all well and good, but you know that your first duty is not to be happy but to make everyone else happy! Your grandchildren wait for you, with their little beaks open, and your husband's lonely all by himself.

Virginia Woolf was right: "Killing the Angel in the House was part of the occupation of a woman writer." If I dared! But angels of domesticity are hard to kill, and in my case, I'd have to kill at once both the mother and the grandmother. Woolf underestimated the problem; she didn't have any children, and Beauvoir didn't either. I should have been warned a long time ago before this little bitch of a angel took possession of every fiber in my body, my reflexes, and especially the expectations of all my family.

An hour goes by. Silence falls upon the house. I work. Paul is sleeping in the bed and the girls play without fighting. I should know that silence is always suspicious when it comes to children. When I go downstairs, a surprise awaits: even though the sun has not yet set, it is completely dark in the living room. I look around me: three of the four windows are darkened by discs of every shape and color.

"They say that they stick best onto glass. It's like staint glass," Clémentine explains. "It's wonderful, isn't it?"

"*Stained* glass," I correct her automatically.

Violette has wisely escaped to the bathroom. Sidestepping their demand to give an artistic appraisal of their handiwork, I seek recourse with the Boogeyman Effect.

"If all of this isn't gone when Paul comes down . . ."

245

I don't even need to say anything else. The memory of the "terror" that Paul instilled in our daughters is part of the family saga and the anecdotes have only become more fleshed out as the years have gone by. "Tell us again about the time when Paul took off his belt in front of the whole terror-stricken family." He had chastised Constance after we had left her with her paternal grandparents for the weekend and she had disappeared for the night, almost causing them to die from worry. (That was what Paul couldn't forgive.) After hours of searching the empty roads of Kercanic with a flashlight, Grandpa finally found her in the middle of the night, sleeping in the hay at the neighboring stable. She had wanted to spend the night with the horse at the Tréguier's farm! "We heard her scream, poor Constance," the two older ones say, with a gleam of admiring fear in their eyes.

There was also the time that Paul, seeing me at the end of my rope, went upstairs with dread (for he hated taking on the role of the gendarme). He went into Blandine and Lison's room (Constance slept in the room next door), where, for hours, they both had been scoffing at my efforts to get them into bed. He said in a monotone, without batting an eye, "Well, young ladies, which one of you will receive the first spanking?" Lison had presented her bottom to him, playing the role of martyr while Blandine precipitously got back into her bunk bed, hoping that, if administered from below, the spanking would lose some of its intensity.

Now that our children have children, the exemplary value and miraculous effects of corporal punishment still work, as long as it remains rare and memorable. It must be suited to the seriousness of the deed, and meted out regretfully, reserved for when more talking just won't cut it. The most miserable applications are the single slap or the poor spanking in the middle of the street by a parent who has been publicly humiliated by his child (who, though amply covered up by his coat, still breaks out into accusatory sobs anyway).

We only needed two or three episodes of this sort for Paul's authority to become established and to show me that all of my love for them only merited permanent disobedience and their uncontrollable restlessness. As soon as Paul's key was in the lock, their faces changed: the harpies became little angels receiving their first Communion with lowered eyes, and mellifluous tones in their voices. Their rooms were miraculously cleaned up and they got into bed at my first warning. "They were just awful today," I tell Paul, who doubts my appraisal upon seeing these three goody-goody little saints. Were these really the same creatures who, just a few minutes earlier, had turned the bathroom into a swimming pool, beating up on their little sister, tearing each other's eyes out, and laughing in my face? Paul just had to appear at their door, cold and distant, without showing the slightest sign of any affection, and they turned into a doting little fan club, fawning over him.

"Yes, Pau-aul. . . . Would you like your whiskey, Paul? I'll get it for you. . . . No, it's my turn tonight! Yes, we're certainly going to run right up to bed afterward. . . . Will you come tuck us in?"

Ah, those bitches. This was when I lost my respect for all children. In the end, they only respond to brute force.

Today the heroes are tired. Paul doesn't want to be scary anymore. He prefers to keep himself at a distance. But swirling behind him, like the tail of a comet, are the memories of his exploits. Yet, alas, the new generation is tougher. There won't be any miracles today.

There are about two more hours until dinnertime and it would be good for them to get some exercise if I want to be able to put them to bed at ten o'clock. I resign myself to pushing the furniture against the walls and I take a seat on the couch to attend an exhibition of rhythmic dance and acrobatic gymnastics.

"Violette's quite gifted when it comes to gymnastics. You should stay a minute and watch her." Paul shoots me a blasé look and goes back upstairs into the bedroom. He wouldn't have troubled himself willingly to go see Nureyev!

I suggest some of my music tapes. They are "super-stupid" but Violette brought some of her own, some "good" ones. The spectacle begins. The girls display the miraculous grace that suddenly appears, for a few brief moments, in every child, leading you to believe in her ge-nius. But this grace never survives past innocence. The living room, which seemed spacious enough for Paul and me, has rapidly become a narrow cage that continues to shrink as the excitement of the dancers mounts. Alas, one of them ends up falling, hitting her temple against the corner of the heavy oak coffee table. Screaming ensues for five minutes, then whimpering for another ten, followed by a hot compress and arnica ointment. Violette lies on the couch, her face drawn, the compress covering half of her face. She has always taken life very seriously. During this episode, Clémentine, who is helping me set the table, an-nounces, "Next time, I'm going to be the one to hurt my-self so I won't have to put out the silverware."

Paul, who had heard this retort, was suddenly revisited by his glorious past: he came down for dinner with a sign that he had made, announcing the election of "Queen of the Flibbertigibbets." Underneath this inscription, there were two columns where each act of flibbertigibbetry would be

noted with a check mark. I could have never invented something so flibbertigibbety myself, but the word pleased them.
Already, the spirit of competition was painted on their faces,
and they fought each other for who would clear the table,
laugh the hardest at our jokes, or offer to go get the milk at
the farm. They worried about what sort of punishment the
queen might incur. "I will give her a very flibbertigibbety
present," Paul said. "And don't worry! I'll find one. As for the
other, if she doesn't have too many points against her, I will
give her a Swiss knife with her initials engraved on it."

Night came. I had counted on the famous sea air to en-
tice my little madams to sleep. My usual visitors, who are
in the prime of their lives, are always wiped out the first
night they come to our house. However with my granddaughters, I have to revise my expectations to the contrary: the iodized wind has wound them up and, since
there wasn't any school, it would be completely inhuman
to send them to bed so early.

"What are we going to play, Bounoute?" I'm an under-
achiever when it comes to recreational activities. I don't
have the strength to teach chess to beginners, Monopoly
doesn't amuse me, and I cheat in order to lose the games
more quickly, which annoys them. I would rather punch
tickets in the subway than play camp counselor! Meanwhile, upstairs, I know that my public grows impatient:

"Ladies, gentlemen, dear friends, I am more and more impressed to find myself here in front of you . . ."

"What if we played a hand of Happy Families?" Violette cried.

"You'll play with us, Bounoute? With just two, it's no fun."

It's their first night so I can't say no. Adieu Aristotle, Hippocrates, mythology, and feminine sexuality. Hello Soots-the-Sweeper. It was completely useless to make little imploring eyes at Paul, who was luxuriously ensconced at the fire's edge and plunged deep into reading the newspaper and his sailing magazines. He wouldn't be coming to bail me out; he was on vacation.

Always hoping to perfect my methods, I had planned on reading them, once they got into bed, a list of rules that I had concocted for these ten days. Article 1: Put your clothes away each night on a chair. Article 2: No cavalcade downstairs at 6:00 a.m. You must wait until 8:00 a.m. before coming down to the kitchen. Article 3: Don't go out into the wet yard without boots and don't walk down the rocks in slippers. I had ten of this nature. I suspected that all of them would go unheeded, but I continued to hope that someday I would wield the iron fist of my grandmother Groult and then everything would unwind calmly around me. What a dream it would be to frighten them! I know women who are sweeter than I, but their every order is followed without a peep. And what's more, it's executed happily, for deep down children much prefer to obey than to disobey, as long as they don't have the chance to hesitate. If they detect the slightest indulgence in your voice, then you're finished. I never knew how to be firm enough and then they know exactly what they're dealing with. From birth, children figure these sorts of things out.

It seems that elsewhere Violette and Clémentine are less wild. The other two grannies love to take care of their grandchildren. These saintly women ask for three or four of them at a time! Is it because I refuse to be called granny that I'm an unworthy grandmother? My granddaughters are proud to say in class that I'm a writer but they deplore the fact that I refuse to wear my label of grandmother. Children want the world to follow ritual. They may even prefer a rigid world, where each of their ancestors are placed in a neat directory. "Daddy is an engineer (or doctor or mechanic) and Mommy stays at home," they continue to respond when asked at school, hoping to deny the evolution of mommies everywhere, and reconstituting through force the family of their dreams.

A few of my friends, whether women with a sense of duty (a rare species in the process of disappearing although a few specimens from my generation still remain today) or women who are sincerely enthusiastic, ask me why I balk at taking care of my granddaughters, who will eventually be accompanied by their friends, for school vacations that reoccur . . . oh, I don't know, say five times per week, as the Ferré song goes. Why did I prefer instead to invite friends of my own to Brittany? To them it seemed as if I abandoned my post and refused to accept an external sign of aging. And why then did I reject the name "Granny" even though I had always gone by "Mommy"? I argue that my name, "Behnwatte," is unpronounceable for a child. When she was two, Clémentine could only muster "Bounoute," which was then adopted for lack of anything better.

"I don't think I have ever heard a more undignified word," Paul had remarked. But I was used to my bizarre first name, which no one found graceful. I also suspected that Paul found me graceless in many ways in my role as a grandmother, which left me no time for him, or for myself.

At 10:00 p.m., finally, lights out. I was off duty. But I went back before going to bed myself to watch them sleep. I like them when they're in bed, their mouths open but silent. Clem was drowning underneath a sea of hair and Violette was buried under her comforter with her feet sticking out. Their sneakers were in all corners of the room, underwear, jeans, and socks strewn all over the floor wherever they had fallen. In this miniscule room, which doesn't accommodate any disorder, I couldn't set down one foot. A true granny would have known that it was necessary to invoke Article 1 right away and tell them in a tone that forbade any retort, "Young ladies, wake up and put away your things." Everything could turn around. "Bounoute has changed," they would think admiringly. But they were sleeping so peacefully! And they were so tired! It was vacation, not prison camp. I was also tired. Terrible reasons, I know. Without making a sound, I gathered up their clothes and left them on the ladder of each bunk bed. I had lost.

The next morning, the weather was on my side and everyone was out in the yard. My three acres were soon transformed into a riding school and I benefited from the presence of the bellowing instructor and a stubborn stallion. Tiresias walked up and down the little alley with a bang, leaping over my flower beds, and flying between my bushes. Their small silhouettes played over the sea. The tail of Clem's horse fluttered. The lighthouse at the entrance of the port seemed to be posed there to illustrate an ad for Finistère; the morning closely resembled happiness. But it took its toll on my garden: two squashed heather plants and my only peony was decapitated. It takes three years before a peony deigns to bloom after it has been planted. And this was supposed to be the year! I put a rod along the upper half of the stalk where you can make out the bulge of the bud. But what if Tiresias falls onto the rod? I abandon my peony; I'll try to make a splint for it after my two vandals have left.

At noon, in the sun, we sample some crabs, crayfish, and langoustines that I had picked up. One of the girls decides to make a collection of their pincers and puts them on the wall to dry out. The other one refuses to eat because she had just seen these creatures alive only moments ago when I came back from the market in Quimperlé.

"You're so cruel," she tells me.

Endive, they hate. And rabbit? Clémentine's teacher is vegetarian and her views have wrought havoc on our menus at home. Paul can no longer serve a roast chicken without getting a homily. We hide little pieces of minced ham under her noodles so that she'll eat meat without knowing any better. If we serve roast beef, we might as well be assassins. "There's blood there . . . just like our own!"

"And do potatoes also have a soul, Clémentine? Have you thought of that?"

A scornful glare. I tell her that I love to eat frogs and it's as if I have killed her father and mother. I know that I'm only aggravating my case, but I keep at it.

"And where do you stop in the hierarchy of creatures to save? Do you allow snails to be eaten for instance?"

"I refuse to eat any creature that feels pain. My teacher says . . ."

"I won't ask you to eat flies, but would you allow me to kill them with a swatter?"

"In India, people make a special detour in order to avoid squashing an insect. My teacher says that in India . . ."

"Fine, in India people won't kill a mosquito but children die there from malaria transmitted by mosquitoes. And if you saw dogs in India, they're skeletal, beaten up, covered with vermin. . . . You know, if we didn't eat chickens, they would all be devoured by foxes; and sheep by wolves; and shrimp by crabs . . ."

"Well it's no use being more intelligent if we continue to act like animals."

I suppose she's right. No use putting a check mark on the flibbertigibbet chart. Clem is already a formidable polemicist.

Paul keeps giving me despairing looks. I won't achieve anything through quibbling, and I'm a dreadful reformer. Clémentine is at the age when the teacher is always right because she has delivered you from the omnipotence of your parents. As for your grandparents, don't even mention them, the poor old dears. Our own parents didn't know how good they had it. "Finish up your plate, please . . . We'll serve you the same spinach again tonight if you don't finish it for lunch. . . . A child must never contradict his parents and in any case, we didn't ask for your opinion. . . . At nine o'clock, I'm coming upstairs to turn out the lights." Me: I suggest, legislate, pussyfoot around, retreat. "Wash your hands." "They aren't dirty." "Put on your slippers." "I don't know where they are." "Put on your sweater." "I'm not cold." "Put it on anyway." "Aaargh!"

It's best not to even discuss it. The orders should be simple and short, just like in the military. But it's no use being intelligent if it means acting like a drill sergeant, Clémentine would say.

Finally, that night, Blandine would arrive and there would now be two people to square up against them. I could go back to my Hippocrates, Aristotle, and that whole gang of misogynists from antiquity to today.

The afternoon got off to a bad start: the sky grew dark and the air was full of a perpetual rain (they call it drizzle in Ireland). What did it matter: the riding school would be moved into the living room. They just needed to roll up the rug and tuck it under the armoire, put a few jump ropes between the chairs in the kitchen and the door of the bathroom (which will be off-limits), and then pile up on the ground the couch cushions to simulate the hurdles. The room soon resounded with the stallion's whinnying and the cracking of the whip.

"Is it not possible to find games that aren't so noisy?" groaned Paul, who in the meantime had regained possession of our desk and pretended to be working there.

But how could I say to the children: No more horse races. No more silly laughter. No more living room Olympics. No more music (while Clémentine, who played some delightful old songs on her clarinet yesterday, was now hooked on playing our electric organ and intoxicating us with rumbas and jazz accompaniment).

At five o'clock, we finally left to go pick up Blandine at the Lorient train station. "Lucky you, your mother's coming!" Clémentine says, suddenly realizing that she misses her own. "Being happy isn't everything unless other people aren't," a remark that is particularly apt when it comes to children.[113] For them, the grass is always greener on the other side. Violette believed that she was going to have her mother to herself, forgetting that Blandine was first and foremost my daughter, in order of appearance on the scene. Barely arrived, Blandine announced that she was going to go to bed because she was exhausted and could hardly stand one minute longer. I knew well that it was to sleep and to have some quiet that she had come. That's exactly how I conceived of my role as mother: at my house, they became little forty-year-old girls and I gave them a round of maternal therapy. But first of all, my daughter wasn't forty. She was thirty, plus ten years. That was a more satisfying formulation. As for me, I didn't have an age because I was the mommy. No one ever asks if I'm exhausted.

Blandine closes the curtains to her room, takes out her old cashmere blanket and disappears under her comforter until evening. After dinner, she goes back to bed at nine o'clock, which at least encourages the children to retire early as well. But tonight, Violette refuses to sleep in her bunk bed because she has seen a spider. She lets out some inarticulate cries and shudders in horror. I put a check in her flibbertigibbet column. Clémentine insists that we can't kill the little creature, following as usual the dictates of her teacher. Violette ends up sleeping in her mother's bed, leaving her cousin to confront her contradictions: she's also terrified of spiders.

They brushed their teeth without protest but when I went to kiss them good night, I noticed that their clothes were all over the floor as usual. Blandine didn't seem to care.

"We can't wage a war on every front," she said. "It's too tiring. Their teeth are important, but a mess isn't serious. I don't want to wear myself out with the little things."

I can well remember a time when Flora and I brushed our teeth *and* put our clothes on a chair, without wearing anyone out! But Dr. Spock put an end to these ways. It seems that they were inhuman and destructive to young characters. It's not nice to talk about discipline while on vacation. And so I buckle.

The next day the damp yard sparkled under the rising sun and Brittany gave us one of those days that allow you to believe in the world's innocence again. The wet earth smiled at the first mild day of the year. A fisherman returns to his anchorage, and moors his dinghy with a few quick moves. These sounds make that particular noise of calm mornings when no one asks what their purpose is on earth. It's enough to just be, and each thing is in its proper place. It's low tide and the girls climb down to go fish in the river. This afternoon, we'll go to the beach.

Around 10:00 a.m., Blandine emerges, her face covered in a greenish plaster.

"I have three days to get back a human body," she declares.

"Big undertaking," Paul remarks, but Blandine can't laugh because it might crack her mask.

"Three days? You're not spending the whole week here with us in Doélan?"

"Mommy dearest, I need to take a vacation from being a mother. That's what will truly allow me to unwind. I speak so much in my work that I have only one desire: no telephone, no talking. So I'll spend three days at your house to get back into shape and then a friend is coming by to pick me up. We're hoping to spend three days touring in Morbihan, stopping in a few nice restaurants. Because I have to go back to work on Monday, I'll just return on Sunday to get my Violette, if that's all right with you."

"Ladies, gentlemen, dear grannies . . . oh, excuse me, dear friends. What could I possibly have to say to you on April 15?"

In any case, dropping everything, we go to the town of Dourveil that afternoon. While we were eating lunch, the sea slowly retook the river bed, the boats flapped and sat up, the mullets came back chasing each other among the shells, starring the water's surface with the silvery reflection of their wings. By the time we will have returned home in the evening, the water will have reached the last step of the stairs and our house will feel like it's on an island.

At the beach, I relax in the sensation of being nowhere, somewhere between the earth and sea. I feel suspended between a dream and reality, as the memory of my origins wells up from deep with the years. The calls and the childish disputes dissolve in the blue of the sky among the birds' cries. Time stills, nothing happens except for one wave breaking onto the back of another. We play silly games, amuse ourselves by walking in the water and loudly splashing the surface as if we were five years old. In the evening, we return with a vague feeling of melancholy without knowing why.

Like most men, Paul doesn't like the beach. Women are better able to remember where they came from.

Clémentine and Violette dared each other to go swimming. They're at the age when you have to keep your bets, no matter the cost and so they plunged boldly into the freezing water. I envied their folly. Do you remember what that was like, Rosie?

On our way back we stop by the Bay of the Dead after the storm. The girls had wanted to put aside the fruits of that morning's fishing expedition to study them more closely later. But the hundreds of periwinkles had escaped from their enclosures and were glued everywhere between the tiles of the terrace. The tables in the backyard were weighed down by the kelp that had been prepared for the crustaceans' dinner. The crabs decided to hide in the grass and the shrimp were dead in their bucket, no doubt from having ingested a breadcrumb or two. While they were bringing these things back to the sea where they belonged, I inspected my garden as I did every night. Tonight the hollyhock that had grown along the wall for years was broken on the ground. Every spring it surged up from between the stones, turning at a right angle to become vertical once more, then climbing toward the sun like all the others. It was even more beautiful than the others that clung to the façade, as if its secret roots, which seeped into the granite and cement, were better protected from the insects and other diseases that strike all hollyhocks.

Beginning the next day Brittany went back to its capricious spring ways. It rained as if it had never been nice. Blandine opened her curtains and then shut them quickly. She only loved the south of France and her schedule for the day—a bath of essential oils, ginseng shampoo, manicure, pedicure, and waxing—left her only enough time to accompany us to the crêperie. As my rainy day reserves had been depleted, the only things left were the bottom of the barrel: we would go admire Gauguin's *Yellow Christ* at the Trémalo Chapel, see the Sérusier[114] exhibit at the Pont-Aven town hall, and buy some cookies at the famous Traou Mad shop. No doubt there would be pouting, but I would console myself with the Sérusiers.

The next day—divine surprise—the sun appeared and brought a weak breeze from the west that allowed me to flip to the sailing and nautical sports chapter of my playbook, since today there was no risk of seeing my two sirens driven to the mouth of the port by the fearsome east wind that rakes up and down the river. They would have been incapable of fighting against the current, losing an oar and getting farther and farther away in their little nutshell, without the presence of mind to use the remaining oar like a rudder to reach one of the two rivers before being thrust out onto the high seas. I had little hope for Violette. She was a Savoyarde at heart,[115] not really interested in boats, and Clémentine a pure intellectual who didn't display the slightest interest in sports, other than her horses.

And so—time for an obligatory rowing lesson. They were forced to wear life jackets despite their protestations. But the whole time I didn't dare take my eyes off their little boat when, after I went ashore, they were quick to take up some lousy little paddles, giving up on the noble oars, which they claimed were too difficult to handle. After some paddling around, a collision with the kayak of our little neighbor who controlled his boat with a masterly skill, and one or two trips around the river, claiming to buy a pastry at the café across, they came ashore at the house, pretending that they had correctly moored the dinghy and announcing that they would rather play shopkeeper.

And so my second generation wasn't going to give me the Florence[116] or the Isabelle[117] that I dreamed of. Maybe, just maybe, Pauline, who was still so young, would show endurance, dexterity, and a spirit of adventure. But in ten years, I'm afraid that all I'll have left is the spirit of adventure and no longer any means of putting it into practice.

For the moment Violette's goal is to own a perfume and souvenir shop in Chamonix and, for Clémentine, a grooming house for dogs in Paris. Some of the check marks for the flibbertigibbets disappear. And I get a cross of honor for myself, lamenting that these girls don't have the noble ambitions that had come my way at the age of forty!

Later, damage assessment: the girls still don't know how to row; nevertheless they managed to fall into the water as they disembarked among the algae. They beached the pram onto a rock following their slapdash mooring and let go into the current an oar that, fortunately, a sailor brought back to us. Still, these qualify as adventures at sea, which they can recount to their friends when they go home. After all it always takes a few mistakes before you get your sea legs.

On the third day Blandine's sleep treatments finally worked their magic and we watched a dreamy creature appear before us, her hips encased in a swathe of stretchy fabric that I would call a girdle but that she insisted on calling a skirt by Alaïa, and wearing a silvery jacket upon which curling-ironed wisps of her hair fell. Venus Anadyomene had come to our humble cottage and deigned to break bread with us. We had grown accustomed to a mummy spiked with rollers, with a chalky face and toes fanned out, separated by cotton balls to let her dark purple nail polish dry. And we knew that this creature, just arising before us, would be nothing but a brief apparition. She was destined for other eyes. Those of the two girls caressed her with ecstasy, for these silly goslings already dreamed of lace girdles, pushup bras, miniskirts, and maxiflirts. I felt like I was from another planet. I wore Petit Bateau underwear until I was fourteen years old, maybe even longer, without ever dreaming of my mother's garter belts. The silly young things of today jump from *Bambi* to *Nous Deux*,[118] from fairy tales to soap operas, tossing aside those long, timid adolescences where future dreams are quietly forged. The silly young things nowadays demand to wear bikinis when they're eight years old, envisioning without any fear their destiny as a sexual object. They lust after various prepubescent boys, knowing how to make use of their sexuality in theory, and are all too impatient to put it into practice.

I contemplate them with melancholy, thinking about that indecisive childhood that long kept us on the margins of reality, thinking about those long years during which boredom serves a purpose, far away from real boys, giving time to the imaginary heroes of French history and literature, the boys from the great red and gold series of books

by Jules Verne, Hector Malot, Jules Sandeau, all the way to
The Lost Estate,[119] during the years when the devil hasn't
yet taken over your flesh.

It makes me sad that Barbie is held up as the ideal as
soon as you leave the nursery. I try to explain that I want to
retch if, for Christmas, I have to buy Barbie's boudoir and
Barbie's hair salon and Barbie's horse, which resembles
some sort of manatee in venomous colors with a platinum
mane, but I'll lose even more ground compared to those
other grannies if I show myself to be too intransigent. It's
better just to keep a low profile.

In a waft of perfumed air, Blandine left us. I'm able to
take back her room and set up my virtual audience there
in preparation for my conference presentation, which remains even more virtual. On Sunday she'll be back to col-
lect her daughter.

After Violette left, a strange peace fell over the house. I
discover that one child isn't half of two; it's an entirely different quantity. With her fecund imagination and her gifts
fit for a Club Med activity coordinator, the elder had wiped
out the younger one, four years her junior. Clémentine slept
all afternoon on the big couch, the sun lighting up the gold
highlights in her hair. I had also changed in my status:
now I was listened to; she asked for my opinion; we talked.
Delivered from the tyranny of The Doors, Telephone, and

Nirvana, we listened to Anne Sylvestre, Barbara, Gilles Servat. In the evening, I told her stories. That's one of my strong points. I still have some success imitating the ogre and Tom Thumb with his seven-league boots.

When the girls were together, they hid out in their fortress, united in childhood, secreting selfishness and the unconscious cruelty that belongs to that age. Their duo formed a watertight wall against which I couldn't gain any foothold.

Did I really have three children at home for so long? How was I able to keep enough energy to live, to love a man, to love them back, to write? The answer is limited to a few words: I was thirty years old.

The day of Clémentine's departure, Paul, suddenly moved by tenderness (although I don't know if it was because Clémentine was leaving or he was getting me back all to himself) accompanied us to the airport. As she went to leave, I hugged Clem in my arms and all the emotions of her arrival came back: I thought she was magnificent, I had a tear in the corner of my eye, and I felt stupidly proud to be a grandmother. As I watched her disappear, so little yet so big for her eight years, I let out a sigh, which I swear wasn't strictly out of relief.

Tomorrow I'll expel all the stuffed animals and the collection of pincers, dead crabs, and stinking shells.

Paul will go back to the desk in the children's room. I will get back my big desk and I'll begin my presentation from scratch: "Ladies, gentlemen, dear friends," was actually superstupid. I will simply say "Hello everyone" and that will come off as much more young.

I didn't end up wasting my time this week after all!

CHAPTER 10

Salt on Our Skin

Benoîte—Going back today, when I'm eighty-eight years old, to *Salt on Our Skin*, which came out in 1988 when I was sixty-eight years old (not exactly the age to write a novel about a passionate love affair), I ask myself how I dared write it and how Paul had the grace to accept it. And also, now that he's dead, I ask myself how he lived with it.

Josyane—All the same, you dared to do it because you were confident that you lived with a man who didn't have any of the stereotypical baggage that generally governs male/female relationships. The real question that people can't help asking and which I will ask you now is: How, and at what price, were you able to take such a liberty? Your attitude takes for granted a certain relationship based on transparency with one's husband—and you were married when the book came out. How does a woman authorize herself to do what you did with this book?

—I realized that I had never dared to talk about pleasure. I wanted to approach it in a completely feminist fashion, shaking up the traditional image of it as a gift of one's self in order to show the selfishness of making love. And then I wanted to talk about it without any poetic metaphors, but by using the real words that designate the organs involved. I wanted to try to give these words a sort of innocence, perhaps a poetry, occasionally a vulgarity. Love needs that too. Above all, frankness.

—Very few women novelists have done that.

—It's not a genre that women were allowed to use! George Sand did it, of course, but she was used to breaking boundaries and she has been poorly judged by posterity. Critics emphasize her lovers more than her talent! It's the same with Colette, for as Pierre de Boisdeffre said, she "let her most basic instincts speak." And then there's Anaïs Nin, whose *Diary* I had just read and it showed me that it was possible to speak about sex with jubilation and without guilt, a rare thing in the erotic tradition, for this subject is most often treated with a frightening seriousness. But it was also about finding new words or treating things in a new way. Here, I ran into the utterly impoverished vocabulary that exists to describe the experience of female sexual pleasure. In the same way that I began *Ainsi soit-elle*, starting at the National Library by searching under the word "woman," for *Salt on Our Skin*, I looked under "anatomy" in the big Quillet encyclopedia from 1936 that my father had passed on to me. I thought that nothing had changed in feminine anatomy since 1936. But then, it had! On the full-page anatomical plates titled "Man/Woman," the female sex organs were reduced to a triangle. The clitoris wasn't marked or drawn. The word vagina didn't appear. Meanwhile, on the "Man" plate, the penis, the glans, the testicles—all of it was recognizable. There was a troubling exclusion here. I wanted to reclaim the words to talk about our own organs. The word vagina, among others, was practically obscene. Yet all of humanity has passed through this glorious vagina!

—Did you feel, years after Ainsi soit-elle, *that you needed a different way of speaking freely, perhaps more individually? Could you have written* Salt on Our Skin *earlier, without having taken your whole feminist journey that preceded this book?*

—I wouldn't have known how to write this way and I wouldn't have dared before. I benefited from the autonomy that age gave me, a cheekiness that I didn't have when I was twenty years old or even forty. A long life experience, with mad love, everyday love, lasting love also helped. I could finally approach the mystery of passion, which, even though it was the age of computers, remained something life-altering, devastating, and magical. Maybe it was because I had read too many Breton epics, but I made my hero a wanderer, that is a sailor, and I named him Gawain, the name of one of King Arthur's knights, who also roamed the sea. I wanted in part to merge the archetypes of love and passion, represented by Tristan and Isolde, Romeo and Juliet, and the others from the ages. After their first night on the island, Gawain and George are bewitched by one another, as if they had drunk a love potion, like Tristan. Their love would be absolute in that they didn't have anything to exchange, no contract, no reciprocal services, no social life. Their relationship remained intense as long as it didn't interact with reality.

—*But is there any feminism in this novel?*

—I'm happy that it's not too marked by it because it's a novel, but the book is steeped in feminism. Without love, and freedom within that love, a part of the meaning of life and a dimension of how women come into their own is missing. It's a feminist story because, for once, passion doesn't lead to being cursed and the heroine doesn't sink into madness, unhappiness, or suicide and it doesn't lead to punishment from above. At the end of the story, it's a woman who succeeds in life and perhaps even a bit more than that.

—I see by the abundant mail that this book brought your way— and often from men this time—that people repeatedly asked you the same question: "Why did you make Gawain die at the end of the novel?"

—Ah yes, a good question, because no one would have been surprised if it was the woman who died! No one asks why Emma Bovary commits suicide. It's normal. Anna Karenina throws herself under a train, Madame de Merteuil is disfigured by smallpox;[120] Sade's Justine is struck down by Heaven.[121] Madame de Renal dies from unhappiness, and Marguerite Gautier is left to die of tuberculosis.[122] In literature women are expected to be moral and are systematically punished for having loved too much. I am sure that if George had to undergo a long and difficult illness, or if she had been killed in a car going to meet Gawain, people would have found her much more moving. It would have been a beautiful story of tragic love, like all the other mythic love stories. The idea that she survives her lover, that she still finds her life worth living, even without him, that's what shocked people, even more than the vocabulary. But I stood by this ending because I was nauseated, just oversaturated with all of these women: they were all unhappy, seduced, and then abandoned, cheated on, frigid, condemned to disgrace, misery, solitude, and madness. Traditional erotic novels, ones like *Story of O*,[123] with whips, chains, humiliation, and chic torture also made me sick—I could read them and enjoy them, that wasn't the question—but they made me sick because women were regularly reduced to slavery, falsely covered in shame, and victims of their lovers' violence, always shown in a state of inferiority and in utter submission. I felt an urgent need to describe the joy of carnal love, the shared fervor, and for once a triumphant woman without remorse, regrets, or punishment.

—Some people criticized you for this approach, claiming that it wasn't feminist.

—Yes, a few: people who hadn't really gotten the book, it seems to me. I believe rightly that the book owes its success to the fact that the heroine lives more fully because of this love. But women don't always tell their men that this transgression thrills them!

—A critic wrote that it was "an ode to the phallus" and he de-lighted in believing that you had "finally put down your weap-ons." People also reproached you for George's selfishness.

—But selfishness is healthy! It's condemned in women be-cause it's so necessary for them. It's considered a veritable act of treason and moreover it is. All of a sudden women cast off the image that had been pinned on them and they reject the role written for them. Selfishness is a virtue of deliver-ance. It's true that George isn't the most sympathetic char-acter in this novel. It's Gawain who moves people, because he's tormented and guilty of this love, which consumes him.

—Apparently because George isn't miserable, people find her unappealing! As for yourself did you reap the benefits of this blessed selfishness?

—Yes, I was lucky in that respect, due to a dose of indif-ference and the self-reconciliation that came to me in midlife. It's not that nice to say it, but I escaped from that strain of complacent tolerance for unhappiness that is de-veloped in so many women. "But you're selfish!" people say to me as if this was something unforgivable. Yes, I'm selfish. So what? To me it seems the reverse: in loving my-self, I at last became more generous with others. People who are perpetually depressed, those are the real selfish ones. There's nothing more demanding, more narcissistic and egocentric than a chronically depressed person! With men selfishness is better tolerated. "Oh, Alain's really selfish," people say, almost fondly.

—As you were writing this book, did you think that it would create a scandal?

—In some ways I wanted that to happen, but I didn't expect so much hypocrisy. To pretend to be scandalized by a passionate adventure without any perversions, vices, or torture, but simply a relationship as easy as pie, well that shows how far people deny a female novelist the same freedoms and even the same vocabulary as a male novelist. Who would dream of saying that Patrick Grainville, Philippe Sollers, Yann Queffélec, Michel Braudeau, Pierre Guyotat, and so many other male novelists "are going to make you blush"?

One detail in particular shocked people, I think: that I dared describe with irony the masculine sexual panoply. In erotic texts the cock is described as a divine organ in all its majesty. The idea that a woman could speak just as disrespectfully about the attributes of masculine power—that was practically a transgression! I remember when *Ainsi soit-elle* came out, the female readers said to me softly, "It's true that testicles feel like toads when you hold them in your hand—they're wet, cold, and flabby—I never would have dared to say it myself!" And they giggled, putting one hand over their mouths like children who mock the teacher behind his back.

—One question remains: perhaps the real question that people can't help asking and which I will ask you once more: How, and at what price, were you able to take such a liberty? What sort of relationship between a woman and a man can lead a woman to say what you said?

—That's exactly what Bernard Pivot asked me when he invited me on his television program. "Benoîte Groult, everyone agrees that women's lib has happened, but just a few years ago people would have found your novel a little pornographic, no?"

—And how did you respond?

—I responded rather poorly. I didn't expect this word— pornographic. Afterward, I was highly suspicious. From the beginning I should have defined the word pornography— the exploitation of the other's body. There's no love in porn. But I let myself be cornered into the role of the guilty party. And then the writer Michel Tournier was there, and he was quite amused watching me try to extricate myself from this word. The other guests, *Charlie Hebdo* editor François Cavanna and director and novelist Jean Vautrin, didn't come to defend me either. It was a bit ridiculous to explain a love story to these four derisive gentlemen. We can't forget that language is also colonized by men. As soon as a woman says "vagina," everyone cries pornography. With this book it's as if I went looking for success by talking about ass! I suspect my dear Bernard Pivot of having deliberately selected a panel of guests to give a "well-brought-up" woman a hard time. When I came back to the house that night, my daughters said to me, "You didn't do a good job defending yourself, Mom. There are people who are going to think that at your age, you went into pornography."

Pivot had also recalled, acting scandalized, that I was the wife of Paul Guimard. "And what does your husband think of a book like this?" Did anyone ever ask Sollers what Julia Kristeva was going to think of his novel which was titled in all simplicity *Women*? Focusing on pornography and scandal was a way to deflect attention from what I had wanted to say about sexual freedom. When critics underlined the gender of the author, the feminist aspect was tossed aside. Yet, as far as I know, feminism doesn't get in the way of having an orgasm, to the contrary.

—*That was the same reasoning for Annie Ernaux when she wrote* Simple Passion. *Right from the beginning of this text the words "sperm" and "dick" appear! People wanted to slam her. A man said on the radio: "She has the style of a stenographer given to pornographic fits."*

In any case, as soon as the body, or sex, is involved, or even actual pornography, relations between men and women turn ugly. With Ainsi soit-elle, *while it wasn't yet a question of "political correctness," you approached the problem with complete liberty. Certainly you express your disgust for a certain number of pornographic writings, but you conclude, which isn't often the case with other feminists today, "Fine, those texts, like all others, have the right to appear, to be read, eventually savored, put into practice between two people, three people, ten people, whatever your heart desires." I particularly appreciated the fact that, right from the start, you anticipated the deviations that could come out of your analysis. I must admit that I was profoundly hostile to everything related to that American movement of "political correctness," this fanaticism that ends up becoming a denial of art and artists. However I believe, once more, that through puritanism, through being locked into stereotypes, women are mistaken for the enemy. It's clear that artists, writers, even those who have written extremely violent things, are not the radical enemies of women. In fact, certain "men claiming to be feminists," the "understanding ones," are paternalists of every stripe who want, crucially, to oppress women, to avoid confrontation, and to put them, gently and definitively, under their thumb. After all confrontation doesn't necessarily have to be something negative. Just as with relationships between parents and children, we can be so much more open with one another when we can have an honest disagreement.*

—As long as you're not crushed beforehand. You need to have a healthy dose of self-respect and an awfully good constitution to escape from the despair of being a woman when you read a few of those texts!

—*Was it for that reason that, in* Ainsi soit-elle, *you deemed that certain writers, Henry Miller being a prime example, wrote pornographic texts that you judge to be too degrading to women?*

—I was deeply influenced by Kate Millett's book *Sexual Politics*. She shows how D. H. Lawrence, Norman Mailer, and Henry Miller transformed women into a "genital field," upon which whatever men wanted could be imposed, without any notion of reciprocity. In the long run, that's destructive.

—Perhaps. But then it's a slippery slope to go from observa-
tion and analysis to blame and censorship. Doesn't it seem
better, as you did when you wrote Salt on Our Skin, *to for-*
mulate your own response? Why choose to remain on the de-
fensive, lodging a complaint, as if that were the favorite mode
of women? I remember a debate where I shocked women who
had just attacked one of the writers present, Philippe Sollers,
for his book Women. *They couldn't get over that I said to him:*
"I don't reproach you for having written Women, *but I find*
it unsettling to belong to a society where no woman has yet
written Men."

—An American novelist like Erica Jong has written such
a novel. But it takes time before the former slaves dare to
write about their oppressors! For a thousand years, philosophers have deepened their reflections of a world where
they occupy *all* of the places in the hierarchies of thought
and power. There has been such a short time since women
have gained the right to think and the simple right to read
and to write!

—Yes, let's talk about philosophy. Like you, I don't really like this
concept called differentialism, the idea that women and men
could have such profoundly different, or even opposite, natures.
Some have argued that women, for instance, have less ability

for everything in the realm of abstraction. And actually, other than Hannah Arendt and perhaps Simone Weil, I find very few examples of women who have a true philosophical spirit.

—I believe that philosophy can only bloom from the humus of centuries. Maybe your grandmother should have thought philosophically in order for you to be able to approach these topics in stride and with creativity. We can't develop after a generation of sacrificed women or victims.

—*As always you have an optimistic outlook on things. Some could say that you have succeeded, for the most part, in es-caping "feminine neuroses." No doubt you have also had the opportunity to live a harmonious married life. With* Salt on Our Skin, *this relationship could have become problematic. You haven't yet said how this man, who was your husband, who lived with you, could calmly accept that you wrote this type of book.*

—Calmly, I wouldn't be so sure of that.

—*But hadn't you talked to him about it beforehand?*

—Of course but only vaguely. I never show my novels in the course of construction. They're too unformed. Paul only read it after it was finished and I would have preferred that he never read that one. But you mentioned something about "harmonious married life." That's easy to say. Fifty-four years of "married life" aren't lived without moments of dissonance, discouragement, sometimes even despair. Or sometimes one of the partners completely stifles everything inside himself or herself that could have displeased the other. Sometimes you have to be violent with one another in order to accept the other. We know that, since Jung, "a life not lived" is a poison that can destroy your whole being. Sometimes you have to risk not pleasing people.

—*Still, if you dared, it was because you had the certainty of living with a man who didn't have any of the stereotypical associations that normally govern male/female relationships.*

—Yes, without a doubt. Without that, I suppose that we wouldn't have stayed together for so many years. Paul knew my life as I knew his; you have to accept in a book something you would accept in life. We were committed to this idea from the beginning, without knowing that it could be so hard, so painful sometimes.

—*With Gawain and George's story, you affirmed a relationship that women writers have not dared to portray while with men, it's fairly common. In their novels, they voluntarily mix fiction and autobiography to tell about their love affairs. It's understood that it's their artistic liberty in operation and their wives are supposed to look the other way.*

—Yes.

—These masculine models dominate to such an extent that it's difficult to imagine a woman exerting the same "artistic liberty" without incurring repercussions. You didn't have the intention, I suppose, of breaking up with your husband. So you must have been sure that he would respect your choices?

—I didn't even ask myself that question. I just needed to write the book.

—What do you mean, "needed to"?

—The most important thing in the world to me, at that moment in my career (that word has a bit of an idiotic aspect to it, but in the end it's true that thirty years of writing begins to be called "a career"), was to describe passion, something unreasonable that you can't intellectually understand, that you reject pragmatically but it hits you in the darkest part of your being, where the most primitive and authentic forces reside. It was exciting to pin down the power of desire with words.

—*Were you aware that many men, even those who were extremely free themselves, could have done everything in their power to prevent you from publishing this book; and that the man with whom you shared your life had been pretty exceptional?*

—I never admitted that to myself, but you're right. You are certainly right. At the same time, our agreement from the beginning wasn't just concerned with sexual freedom but with freedom plain and simple.

—*Certainly, but I'm sure that many novelists, who had also affirmed their freedoms, would have pressured their wives if the wives were to write their versions of their own posturing.*

—We know that Scott Fitzgerald acted this way with his wife Zelda. So did Sylvia Plath's husband. And so many others. I didn't think about this as a possibility. In some ways it was in homage to Paul. But I could have said to him, "If you can't take this, let's separate for six months. If the book isn't successful, then everyone will forget." I couldn't have given up this book; it was like a child to me. I had truly become a novelist—at last.

—Because you were married to this man for so long, did it prevent you from seeing that he had had an exceptional attitude, not just compared to other men of his generation but also compared to men who could have been his sons, even his grandsons?

—First of all he respected other people, including his wife, which is rare. He found it repugnant to weigh down the destiny of anyone else, to the point that he would let someone else drown if that was their wish. I'm not exaggerating. There's something frightening but beautiful about this at the same time. Then he also respected writing. And my book was a novel, after all, not a confession. I never knew any fisherman-sailor! I rarely took men to be my heroes. Gawain was my first true novelistic creation, even if I was inspired by details from real life. My "real life" was an American pilot, someone who's also rarely at home.

Finally it must be said that Paul, less in his novels but more so in his life, had always kept a large amount of freedom for himself. We had started off by taking the contract that Sartre and Beauvoir had, regarding contingent loves and necessary loves. I often needed to make myself go back to the contract, to reread it, to make myself apply it to every circumstance. I was also very unhappy for certain stretches myself.

—Did you two commit to tell each other everything, like Sartre and Beauvoir did, even though in the end, they ended up telling each other too much?

—No. I think that's dangerous and, even more, a great cause of suffering. It was Sartre who spilled about his contingent loves. His letters to Beauvoir[124] are terrible. When it comes to other people's love lives, you understand so much, while you're blind to your own! I think that it's almost always men who are the beneficiaries of this sort of contract.

—I have great admiration for Sartre and Beauvoir, which I'll always have, but I'm not entirely sure that their contract was such a good idea.

—It's very important to me that you love the couple of Sartre and Beauvoir. It's a line drawn in the sand. I don't feel trust or kinship with someone who underestimates their work or condemns their lifestyle. As for their contract, they maintained it while keeping up the mythic image of a couple that lasts "till death do us part." I remain grateful to Beauvoir for that. So many of their enemies would have been happy if they had betrayed one another!

—With you two it was more like you had a tacit contract of freedom.

—That's right. Without any little secrets but also without detailed accounts either. I definitely wasn't aware of many things.

—Did you know the people involved?

—They're almost always known, alas. And this knowledge is unbearable to live with at certain moments. But I had agreed upon the principle. I find it inhuman to demand that someone, today and in our Parisian milieu, in our careers where the temptations are never-ending, give up everything if it doesn't relate to their partner. I marry you and that means, from now on, you won't touch another woman, you won't have any more adventures, and you won't have any more freedom? That's horrible! What's more, I didn't feel up to imposing that.

—Ultimately do you think that you were right to bet on this reciprocal freedom?

—It seems to me to be the most honorable attitude. But it's hard to live by, especially for the person in the relationship who loves the most, or the longest. I will always remember the evening when we celebrated our first two years of marriage and Paul said to me, with so much innocence and joy: "I drink to my two years of faithfulness. I never thought that I could keep this up for so long!"

—*When you can say that with humor, is it all right?*

—All right for whom? I took that news like a cold shower. First of all, it implied that the period of faithfulness was now over. But fine, that was in my contract, there weren't any dates voided in white. He began to be once more the man I knew from before. My mother had sufficiently warned me. There was nothing left to do but take it in stride, which I did because we got along so well on the whole.

I learned only later that you can love two people at the same time. "For each thing has a different worth," as Gide says. Paul always knew that. Two, three, ten . . . he took pleasure in being a generalist and not a specialist.

—*But he stayed with you? We come back to Sartre and Beauvoir, to contingent loves and necessary love.*

—That's what he told me every time.

—*Today, in hindsight, does this arrangement seem satisfactory to you?*

—We could say that it worked. But, at a certain point, I needed to write *Feminine Plural* to blow off some steam, and to cry with different eyes. With this sort of arrangement, there will be a shipwreck from time to time and you have to open up the hull against unknown reefs. You need to know how to swim, caulk up the holes, smile at other people, at your children.

—*Perhaps it's a mistaken impression that you would like to fix, but listening to you, people are convinced that you two escaped the thing that, above all else, undermines couples and can ruin their relationship: resentment.*

—Yes . . . yes. Because we just about managed to live up to our promises.

—*While a majority of people who live together end up with some bad feelings, you didn't seem to harbor any, either one of you.*

—No, I don't see why people get upset at someone for being who he is. It would have been better not to choose that person in the first place. You shouldn't marry someone in order to remake them in your image. Nor should you remake yourself. I already tried that once.

—*It's probably thanks to this freedom that you were able to escape these feelings.*

—Yes, and what a poison resentment is, in a life shared with someone else! But there's another poison that's harder to escape, and that's jealousy. It's unpredictable and it can destroy you. But life is like that. It's infantile to believe that you can cut down on suffering. Today a life together can last fifty years! It's unacceptable to tell yourself that during fifty years—half a lifetime or longer—you won't begin a love affair, you won't live out the first minutes of desire, or deny yourself an exciting sexual encounter in a train or on a plane. Are you going to deprive yourself of these uniquely enjoyable moments just because of a vow of faithfulness that often no longer has any intense physical reality? What's more, for writers, these moments provide raw material for the creative process!

—*That said, was* Salt on Our Skin *some sort of revenge?*

—Not in any way. Not for one second. It seems to me that I would have written it no matter what. Maybe even earlier if I had a husband who had been totally faithful.

—So, did you know, when you began this text, that you were going to push the boundaries of your freedom as a writer as far as you could?

—I didn't say that explicitly at the time. Afterward I thought about it. In the moment the most important thing was finishing the book.

—At the heart of the matter, you were motivated by the thing that drives all writers: a sort of necessity. Nothing could have stopped you. But you told me that Ainsi soit-elle *gave you the greatest satisfaction to write. Did* Salt on Our Skin *bring you even more satisfaction?*

—Not really, because I had reached a point where I needed less reassurance. This time around, there was the perverse pleasure of disconcerting the critics, at least the misogynist ones: "What, this feminist? This sexagenarian lady, has written a story like this and with such indecent vocabulary?" Yes, it's hard not to feel a bit like the little girl who isn't allowed, unlike little boys, to say bad words. It thrilled me to tarnish my image!

—The book is much more provocative than Ainsi soit-elle. *For one thing, it denounces social conventions more strongly. Were there negative reactions from feminists to* Salt on Our Skin? *Feminists, unfortunately, can be prudish and pretty moralistic.*

—Strangely, yes. The "real" feminists didn't appreciate it. But it's the same sort of thing when you say a "real woman." It's doesn't really mean anything. To accept such restrictive definitions is a bit like getting into bed with the enemy.

—How do you explain this sort of moralizing—I always find it a bit surprising—from so many women who claim to work for women's liberation?

—It can't really be explained; it's just one facet of feminism. You don't explain the "morality" of a given religion, or of a given fundamentalist group; you just notice it and then look away. People always want feminists to be in step with one another and the smallest difference between them is held against them. It's not fair and, frankly, a bit ridiculous. With the Socialist Party, there are different currents, as with the Communist or the Green Party. Now, we're much more numerous and diverse than a particular political party. When you include sexuality in theory, as it's inevitable to do, well then you have a huge mess. Look at the tiffs between sex therapists and other psychiatrists already. I refuse to castigate anyone, no matter who they are. It's all just part of the richness of feminism.

The moralizing feminists that you were talking about are the radicals who claim that every woman should become a lesbian. Their slogan is: "A heterosexual woman is, at best, a reformist, and at worst, a collaborator." I agree with them, in theory. But at the same time, I want to be able to "collaborate," if that's what appeals to me. Renaud said essentially the same thing on his television program and I agree: "A woman who votes for a man is like a crocodile going into a luggage store." Pretty clever, as my granddaughters would say.

—*So you agree to live in contradiction with your theories?*

—Yes, it's that or suicide! In fact, it's Stalinism, this sole way of thinking, and its offshoot "political correctness," that are unacceptable, not contradictions. Contradictions are the salt of life. Sometimes they make you crazy, but they also make artists, poets, the utopists. You love life and constantly risk death. Or you fall in love with a man but despise all males, especially in a group. You like to make love but you hate the dependency that can come with it. Life is nothing but gratifying contradictions.

—*Before you came out as a feminist, did you have difficulties getting along with other women? For example, with those women who seem to be comfortable with their conventional role?*

—These women were the ones who rejected me the most often. I always hoped to pull them out of their situation, to sow a seed of revolt. Sometimes it just takes the smallest thing. I'm going to sound a bit like those priests (whom I can't stand) who try to win over unbelievers on their death bed: I'm convinced that all women are feminists unconsciously. Even Margaret Thatcher—when I see her on television, I still want to salute her. Albeit briefly! If you watch all the international meetings, the European summits, all you see are guys—old guys, young guys, black guys, yellow guys, but just guys—who decide our fates. When I see one woman, the only one, impeccably styled, with her fearless blue eyes among them, I'm inspired. Even if she hasn't lifted a finger in favor of women, she has done them some good just through her image and her courage. As for those women who betray themselves, I say to myself, What must they have experienced in life never to have understood?

—You said earlier that your book was all the more shocking because it was written by a sixty-five-year-old woman. How have you dealt with aging? And with the illusions surrounding aging women as well as the constraints that are imposed upon women?

—People want to make you feel guilty, even of aging, because you're no longer offering men the image of a woman as a sexual object, which is the only image they will accept! I'm irritated with our magazines, which belong to this conspiracy, and reject all women older than fifty years old. Even a woman in her forties is suspect. Supermodels are younger and younger these days. They aren't twenty-eight or thirty like the models that my mother used. They're between fifteen and twenty years old today. Or even younger! We're also shown that, at the same time, no woman is too young for any man, as long as he's not blatantly a derelict. Anthony Quinn, who's seventy-five, just got married for the fourth time—to his twenty-eight-year-old secretary and she's now carrying his child, even though he's got six others! And Sylvester Stallone's father, who was seventy-seven in 1996, brought a baby into this world through an intermediary—a young woman forty-five years younger than he is! It's pathetic when men rush to have a child like this; it's like they're little boys comparing their weenies! Now when moralists start squawking because there are a few dozen women in the world who want to get pregnant and they're over fifty years old, I think we're targeting the wrong people. A fifty-five-year-old woman has a longer life expectancy than a seventy-seven-year-old daddy! Those ethical committees so concerned about women's morals would do better to concentrate on masculine morality which so often runs into pedophilia and prostitution. Silence can only be read as approval.

—*How have you responded to all of this? What about physical appearance? Have you sought the help of plastic surgery?*

—I have become, little by little, accustomed to my physical appearance, with the idea of being irremediably a woman. I discovered that if I don't have any appeal, it's because I don't like myself. Such a banal discovery! I was under the impression that my first readers were the ones who had given me back my self-confidence. It was all their letters telling me that I had offered them a taste for life, and the courage to be themselves. But just as I was becoming young in my head, my face betrayed me! I wanted to reconcile the inner, intimate me with my appearance. So I sought out the means of plastic surgery and had a face-lift.

—You couldn't stand the imbalance between your inner rejuvenation while you were physically getting older?

—Exactly. When I was twenty, I didn't know I was young, or at least, I didn't know how to use it. All of a sudden at fifty, I felt more confident, happy, working at a career that I loved, having the man that I loved by my side. There were all the usual difficulties, sure, but overall, I felt as if I had achieved my dreams. And right at that moment, my skin fails me! It wasn't really my body for I've always been athletic—skiing, rowing, fishing, gardening. It was really a problem with my face. And so since I could cheat, I decided to thumb my nose at life by saying "Tomorrow I'm going to take off fifteen years with one cut of the scalpel!"

—You didn't agonize over the idea of an operation, or of changing your face, your very person itself?

—Less so than at the idea of aging slowly. I had really made up my mind and nothing could have stopped me, for there comes a moment when you can no longer look at yourself in the mirror. In the morning, you wake up young, full of verve and you go out. You're walking in the street without a care in the world and then suddenly your reflection takes you by surprise in the mirror of a shop in the terrible pale morning winter light. You're shocked. "That can't possibly be me. There must be some mistake!" I was given the chance to fix this mistake (well, given isn't exactly the right word; it's not a gift at all). Let's just say that I found a way to take away fifteen years within a few hours, and in so doing, to play a trick on life, and on society!

—*Do you think that you gave in to societal pressure?*

—Everything played into it: the fact that age is completely discredited today; there's no longer any advantage to having gray hair. People run up to help the young blondes on the train with their suitcases, not the "grannies," as people say condescendingly.

—*You let yourself be affected by that?*

—Yes, I let myself be affected. And men don't escape it either. It's no longer possible to be an old executive. They all have to have some work done, especially men whose faces are their calling card: actors, television hosts, politicians. They have to get hair implants, suck in their jowls, get rid of their varicose veins so they can run across the beaches of the Antilles next to their newest girlfriend. What's terrible is that, for those who resist, who refuse, they soon seem to belong to a different generation than their peers! I'm thinking about a certain actress a little bit younger than me, at the Césars, and she could have been the mother of Micheline Presles or Danielle Darrieux or Michèle Morgan—any of those women who have held on to faces with a surprising youth. Someone like Elizabeth Taylor—she lasted two times longer than she was supposed to. The Creator, thanks to the advances in plastic surgery, has seen an increase in believers.

—*One of my friends, who has had plastic surgery several times because she has one of these careers that depend on her image, said with a sort of refreshing lucidity: "In any case, the alternative is to seem like an old woman or to seem like an old patched up thing, but you're not getting any younger."*

—I don't agree. If you find yourself without bags under your eyes, or crow's feet, or laugh lines, or a double chin, you rejoice. And rejoicing is good for your health, for it produces endorphins and that makes you younger. Between forty-five and sixty-five, you can have a sort of indeterminate age, which is useful professionally, romantically, and personally.

Besides I was a year older than Paul and almost all of our friends, including my ex, Georges de Caunes. When these men remarried for the second or third time, it was to women who were twenty, sometimes thirty, years younger than they were. Whenever we found ourselves out among the trendy types, I sometimes felt like I was my husband's mother!

—Would you say that Paul Guimard didn't leave you for a younger woman because he was more discerning than the others?

—It wasn't a question of intelligence for these other men. It was more their desire to return to Venice for the first time. With someone young and new.

—But this ends up costing them much more than they thought. All you have to do is look at their pathetic attempts to appear young, forcing themselves to take up windsurfing or dancing all night long. These efforts even end up killing some of them prematurely.

—I imagine that they prefer to have five or ten years of love and then a heart attack as opposed to fifteen or twenty years of retired life and then a heart attack all the same.

—*Since we're on the subject of aging, I'd like to talk about the subject that, for so long, has given women nightmares—menopause. People say that this angst has become a thing of the past. However men still haven't stopped making fun of it. All it takes is one woman around fifty years old to be in a bad mood or whiny and immediately you can hear them whisper that she's in the throes of menopause. You seem to believe that menopause is nothing but an occurrence and that feminism, in some ways, helped you to get through this period with serenity.*

—In the spirit of the expression *panem et circenses*,[125] I'll respond to you by saying: to age gracefully, I recommend feminism then estrogen. People want to make you believe that menopause is the doorway to decrepitude, but women today are magnificent at sixty and at seventy! And I'm not even talking about fifty. Everything can still happen to you at fifty: falling in love, out of love, a new career, a new artistic talent. . . . The list goes on and on. Unfortunately too many women don't dare to take care of themselves and in France, they aren't encouraged to do so. Our doctors are men before being doctors. As doctors, they're supposed to take care of us, but as men, they hate it if we're not oppressed by our biological cycles! For this reason, I myself have always preferred a female gynecologist. But for so long, women have either withstood menopause silently at best or were disgusted by themselves at worst, so they're often reticent to ask for treatment. Nevertheless it's the last screw, the last infernal process that keeps us in denial about our own physiology. How do you accept being sidelined for a quarter of your life? A quarter?

—*Just because of shame, a shame that had been sadistically cultivated over centuries.*

—And, as usual, through the help of language. Vocabulary and images regarding the woman in menopause were made to sap her spirit, to humiliate her, and to destroy her. In the book that Professor Rozenbaum dedicated to the study of menopause in 1993, he noted that American doctors put all women between puberty and the disappearance of their period into a category called "premenopausal." That's like describing life as a "predeath" state. Why must it be about deferred agony?

—If an aging woman can feel badly, miserable even, because of this hormonal change, doesn't it also seem likely that her discomfort also comes from society's treatment of "the menopausal woman"?

—First of all this hormonal imbalance can be treated, as long as you don't accept the dictates of certain doctors. Second, as for society's treatment, here again you shouldn't let yourself be affected by this. I still remember, when I came to live in Hyères twenty years ago, some guy, not even young himself, had yelled to me from his car as I was trying to park in a tight spot, "Get out of the way, you menopausal old bag!" I was in the car, in the narrow streets of the old city. I hadn't come close to denting the body of his car but this man, quite simply, wasn't comfortable with the idea that a woman had the right to drive. He belonged to that group of men who previously had been against the right of women to vote and he was convinced today that she was incapable of sitting behind the steering wheel. I admit that this scorn stunned me! Can a woman ever dream of replying, "Get along now, you old prostate!" Maybe that would put an end to this sort of aggression.

—In the end we haven't gotten away from tota mulier in utero,[126] *from this reducing women to their sexual organs?*

—Because it's just too much fun to keep humiliating us! Another example of deadly vocabulary is an expression that you hear all too often, "They gave me a 'total'" or "They took it all out."[127] For so long, women have been reduced to their role as sexual or reproductive objects that they have forgotten that they are first and foremost human beings and not cows. And without a uterus or breasts, they are all the more human. Once again, I'll say that a feminist awareness can free you from these slighting judgments. It's sometimes hard. Diderot was on my reading list for my exams in literature. He was one of my favorite authors and seemed to be a friend of women. I was all the more despondent when I discovered what he thought about the other sex once they were past youth, "In menopause, what is a woman? Neglected by her husband, abandoned by her children, nothing in society, devotion is her only and last resource." What an image!

—*You were able to find some effective remedies in order to live each stage of your life in a positive manner in spite of everything.*

—It's your morale that counts. Turning to replacement hormones isn't enough because no medical prescription can make life pleasant, or worth living, if you feel empty and ugly and if you think you're useless. It's imperative to escape from this image of the perfect wife, of the devoted mother, of the perfect housekeeper, to take a little bit better care of yourself. That lasts your whole life; it's an escape. There's always time to redo things.

—*We come back to your cherished selfishness.*

—Yes, but also to friendship, to camaraderie between women, which could be called "sorority" if this word were used in the same way as "fraternity," which represents such an honorable and useful concept for the masculine ego! This evolution is on its way. Look at films like *Thelma and Louise* and *Fried Green Tomatoes*, or the marvelous *Strangers in Good Company* by the Canadian Cynthia Scott, or more recently, *The Hours*. We need to call for more films like these and we need to boycott those films that fall squarely into traditional misogyny, like *Les Mamies* (The grannies), which from the title alone locks you into the character of a menopausal woman.

—*In regard to* Salt on Our Skin, *I would like you to explain more fully the very phenomenon of its success. For close to a year you remained at number one, then two, on the best-seller list in Germany. Only Jean-Paul Sartre, with his memoir* Words, *had achieved this distinction. You sold a million copies in hardback and 900,000 in paperback. How do you analyze these figures, when in France you sold 150,000 copies, which is close to sales figures for your other novels? For example, your book* Les trois quarts du temps *(Three-quarters of the time) sold close to 200,000.*

—I can't explain it at all, but I think that sometimes a sort of love affair develops around a book and it snowballs. I didn't expect this, especially since I don't speak German and had never even crossed the German border until I had this success. My publisher, Droemer Knaur, who has had all of my books translated there, with decent success, beginning with *Diary in Duo*, didn't expect this either. *Salz auf unsere Haut*[128] sold ten times more over there than in France and I ended up thinking that my success was dependent on latitude. In Germany, in Holland, and in other Scandinavian countries, including Finland, there were record printings! However, in the Mediterranean countries, the book never managed to get off the ground.

—*So it was in northern Europe that this story was recognized and appreciated while it didn't strike a chord with people from the south. No doubt a question of cultural differences between "the Latins" and the others.*

—In any case, as I traveled through Germany for conferences and readings in many different cities, I had the opportunity to talk about this phenomenon with academics and female readers. Even with male readers, for in Germany I didn't run up against any of that particularly French irony when it comes to feminism. I was a normal author (*Autorin*, a feminine noun in German, which is not afflicted by the same grammatical complexes as we have in French!), and not a feminist who was writing a thesis novel. I was also quite touched by the consideration that the public there has for writers, which you don't find anymore in France. Over there, writing remains a prestigious activity, and it's still imbued with magic. People came from Cologne, Hamburg, Wiesbaden to listen to me read pages from my novel in French even though they hardly spoke the language themselves. But they listened . . . with devotion, as if they were at mass. This respect for literature, for an author, for her face—I find it moving. In France, people don't go out of their way to listen to an author unless it's something read by Fabrice Lucchini![129] You need fifty writers in a festival if you want the public to come out!

—*Thanks to these encounters, were you able to better understand the reasons for this geographic success?*

—I came to two hypotheses. The first one is that the image of the woman in the novel resonates with the place of women in Nordic, Celtic, Viking, or Germanic civilization. Among these northern peoples, you can find strong female characters in a great variety of roles. While in Rome, the cradle of the terrible "Roman right" that we sadly inherited, women don't have any name (they can use the name of the "gens"), or any rights. Some of these things remain the same in Italy, where women are so often painted in the role of tragic Messaline[130] or as a saint. It's either the mama or the whore. It's possible that in Mediterranean countries, my heroine provoked a certain rejection because she projected a reversed image of women's own submission.

I also benefited from one other advantage: it was because I was French that the German readers could allow themselves to enjoy my novel. I believe that they would have been less willing to pardon my marital sin if I had been German. *That*, they said indulgently and longingly, ever so slightly scandalized, "That's typically French. Only in France can you end up experiencing and writing such things!"

It's also true that in German novels, masculine/feminine rivalry often plays out in a violent way. I'm thinking of *Lust*[131] by Elfriede Jelinek, which was on the best-seller list at the same time as my novel. In this book, the male characters are brutes and sexual deviants and the women are abject victims.

The second hypothesis: deep down, women—for that's who bought the books, surveys prove it—had had enough of projecting themselves into the traditional despairing characters. In *Salt on Our Skin*, there was an image of freedom that made them dream, especially in a puritan country. And contrary to what had often happened with *Ainsi soit-elle*, husbands didn't forbid their spouses to read it because it was just a novel.

—Was Ainsi soit-elle *really a book that was forbidden by certain husbands?*

—To my great astonishment, it still happens. I have personally known two or three of these couples. The husband fears that these seeds of independence would eat away at his "household." "Don't read that; it's not good for you." In fact, it's not good for *him*, for his status as head of the family! Men still don't understand that only with emancipation can you construct a true relationship—with sustainable development, as they say today.

—*I had noticed the same thing with* F Magazine. *For example, a country doctor that I knew who, at the time, must have been around forty years old, dynamic, athletic, a trendsetter* avant la lettre . . .

—Dynamic? Athletic? Those are the worst!

—*He made his wife terminate her subscription to* F Magazine, *saying, "It's for lesbians. I don't want to see it around the house anymore." If we know you all too well, this sort of reaction probably only encouraged you to continue. But with* Salt, *you don't seem to have had any doubts in writing it.*

—That's not true. Toward the middle, I asked myself if a story based solely on desire and pleasure could hold its own for three hundred pages. If I could keep floundering around with this love story. At some points, I was nauseated. I wanted to write about the Gobi Desert instead! So I gave the manuscript to my daughters and they were the ones who encouraged me to continue. And then there was the preface, which no one liked. Myself included. I can't even read it out loud! In Germany, during the readings, I was asked every time to begin with the preface and I realized that I was incapable of doing that. I couldn't look people in the eyes and read those words!

—Why?

—There are some texts that just can't be read out loud. I could write it, even though I still find it too raw. Today I would redo it differently. But I needed to have some sort of preliminary explanation. Jean-Claude Fasquelle, my editor and friend, had told me, "You don't need to write an excuse to announce that you're going to approach a risqué topic." But I hung on to it. I had written it before beginning the novel, as a sort of shield. I hoped to show that I wasn't writing a love story in the American sense, nor a French melodrama.

—With good reason, because your book is the opposite of a melodrama. It's rather a book that can touch and excite people who haven't necessarily liked the rest of your literature. The most gripping thing, which surpasses the strict question of feminism, is your ability to go right to the heart of the problem of male/female relationships. You sensed that, on a deep level, all of society tries to make people enter into a social framework. But love, and especially here, the passion between George and Gawain, is destroyed if it becomes bogged down in society. In Salt on Our Skin, *many things along this line are said or suggested. Without theorizing it too much, you allow us to understand that, for a majority of the time, what truly*

happens between a man and a woman is the most asocial thing in the world.

—Exactly. And because of this, passion is fundamentally different than love. Passion can't be reduced to the social hierarchy and its criteria. It's unbearable, yet . . .

CHAPTER 11

Dick and Jane, septuagenarians, go fishing

"Did you know that, while I'm very young, at another time I was even younger?"

—Henri Michaux

A violent beating thrashes the windowpane that faces east toward the rising sun. Well let's just say east; the word "sun" is a bit much.

"The wind is from the east this morning," Jane murmurs in her sleep as she burrows a little deeper under her comforter. She hasn't even lifted an eyelid to glance at the time while Dick still sleeps—or pretends to. What good is it, anyway, to note the direction of the wind? In Ireland, whether it comes from the east, the south, or anywhere else, all of these winds bring rain. From deep within the bed, the thought of getting out—damp clothes awaiting them, the boat that must be bailed out before getting on its way, and two yellow silhouettes fighting against the fog and the downpours, determined to take up any old lobster trap, like the shepherd who won't return home without his lost sheep—seems laughable, unreal, absurd. But menacing.

"It might be time to head out," a muffled voice insinuates from under the pillow.

"We still have time," Jane responds. "The marine forecast doesn't come on until four or five in the morning . . ." The voice trails off.

"The sea's rising. In my opinion, it's only going to get stronger with the tide. But we don't have to go out if you're tired."

Tired? To respond, Jane jumps out of bed. Well . . . she gets up. In her head she jumped. She had always leapt in her head and until now, nothing had ever slipped in to gum up the process of an order from on high and its execution. But for the last little while, there had been a subtle lag in operation. No longer a faithful servant, the body has become an occasional burden. For so long, she had been one with her body, but today they were two. She refused to admit this and ran to open the curtains.

The windowpane is spangled with overlapping drops, superimposed onto each other in a metallic pitter-patter. Through a torn part of the sky, a violent sun drowns part of the Bay of Derrynane, giving a leaden look to the areas

that aren't lit up. It's sublime, as usual. Here, modest ad-
jectives fail. The sky always has two types of weather in it.
Out the southern window, offshore, they glimpsed a saw-
toothed horizon, a sign that the sea churned below. But by
the shelter of Lamb's Island, it seems possible to set up the
trammel net for an hour or two, just enough time to fish or
rig the last traps. They had only put two into the water. Dick
and Jane had been in Ireland already for several days, yet
had not actually been able to get out fishing due to a thick
fog that prevented them from taking the *Lil' Chicken* out
from its mooring. Turquoise blue, round, and potbellied, a
bit like a VW Bug, the *Lil' Chicken* looks like a chicken when
she bobs on the waves. She's a solid little boat nevertheless,
running about fifteen feet long and equipped with a reassuring double hull for this reef-fraught sea. She was made
by Beneteau, another reassuring fact in this country where
the fishing boats are patched together by planks left over
from old carts, and the modern little polystyrene dinghies
have the heft and thickness of an egg carton.

"Saint Beneteau, watch over us," they prayed each time
a swell brought them a bit too close to the hazardous rocks
that the lobsters liked and that, in bad weather, seemed to
pull in, then vomit up waves in an infernal movement of
suction and expulsion.

"At least it's not too cold," Jane reassuringly cries, opening up the shuttered door. "Fifty-three degrees Fahrenheit for August at 8:00 a.m., that's not too terrible."

When it was cold, she said: "At least it's not raining." When it was raining and cold, she said: "The rain has calmed the sea and we won't have too much trouble with the traps." And when it was raining and cold and the wind was strong, no one said anything. They just wanted to laugh in the face of this country's determination . . . and their own.

This morning, nothing to report, it's bad, as usual. Outfit number 2 would suffice: underwear, canvas pants, oilskins, peacoats, southwesters, wool caps.

Jane feels a throbbing pain in three out of ten fingers this morning, an indicator of humidity. (A laughable concept here, where the hygrometer is always above 80 percent.) Her two index fingers are already deformed so that when she points her hand to the south, the phalanx points west. You just needed to be warned. As for the right thumb, it's swollen and crooked. It doesn't bother her, at least not for the moment as she waits for the next flare-up. One day, the tips of her hands will be as gnarled as the trunk of an old vine.

"You should avoid putting your hands in the water," her rheumatologist said. "Try to wear rubber gloves." Ha, Jane had thought.

In any case, the Irish air penetrates to the depths of your joints, making itself at home. It refuses to dry the laundry or burn the vegetation, and it moistens the linens in the armoire, completely defeating any sort of effort to the contrary. It would transform Jane's colored and permed hair into oakum if the application was recent, into sticky tagliatelles if the perm was at the end of its course. There was no use fighting it: the wind and the rain were king and queen. And something in Ireland frowned upon effort.

Since they only spend one month per year here, they occasionally benefit from the burst of energy that comes when they disembark from the ferry in Roscoff. The first week in Kerry, Jane is determined to put four rollers on her head, despite the lumpy look it gives her woolen cap. She would never dare to go out bedecked in such a manner in Brittany, but here anything goes. And nothing sticks either. As soon as the curlers are out, all she has to do is open the door to the Irish air and her undulations collapse. By the end of the first week, she gives up. The second week, she renounces lipstick, then her nails. She no longer needs to file them because she tears them, urgently, each time she traps a finger in the mesh of a net or in the gills of the fish that need collecting every day. She then has a good excuse to finish them off tranquilly in the evenings while rereading, as she does every year, Synge's *Aran Islands* in order to reassure herself that on "The Island of Sorcerers and Saints," as it was dubbed, you truly are very far from Europe. Here Poetry is more real than History.

The third week, Jane watches her true face emerge without any of civilization's affectations. It's nothing to be thrilled about. By the fourth week, she doesn't even look at herself in the mirror. She's stripped of any artifice like a newborn baby. Seventy-five years later.

During breakfast each morning, Dick takes his five pills. He has been under orders to do so for the last two years already and has come to recognize that the efficacy of the diuretic produces impressive results in just a few hours. No amount of preliminary precautions before disembarking can prevent a perilous operation from unfolding once on board. Jane prepares herself for capsizing each time the captain is forced to let go of the helm and straighten up his tall frame, making the frail skiff wobble. He grabs the hull with one hand while the other attempts to undo his three outer flies: the Velcro one of his oilskin, the zipper on his jeans and the slit in his underwear (none of them happen to be lined up with each other) in order to free the poor bird tucked away down there. It was written on the label: "frequent urge to urinate." Can't Dick go sitting down? Jane wondered to herself. It seemed that was not possible. Men are strange.

Finally he sits back down, his center of gravity sinks and the vessel ceases its disorderly movement so that Jane can breathe again. She had never been afraid on the sea before. Not in Concarneau on her grandfather's boat, nor on any of the many other boats that she and Dick had known in their lives as sea-fishermen. But as Dick lost his stability, as his deliberate slowness, so essentially calibrated, became tentative and as his always precise motions became awkward, while their boats became smaller and less safe, Jane discovered anxiety. She knew that she couldn't leap about to hand him the gaff, and hoist it on board. She imagined him toppling into the sea, his red K-Way jacket puffing up briefly like a piece of bubblegum, until his boots dragged him down to the deep. He disappears. The sea closes around him. He doesn't even try to swim; she's sure of it. His heart stops quickly, this heart that already struggles on land.

Everyone tells them: they are stark raving mad to come to this corner of the world, to insist on sailing in this inhospitable sea where so many boats have already been swallowed up, from the remains of the Invincible Armada to the boats of General Hoche's expedition which went down in Bantry Bay, right around the corner, in 1796.

Yet, beginning at dawn, Dick and Jane "bust their humps." Dressing to go fishing is itself a challenge, when you have to slip on stiff and damp oilskins, reefer jackets that stink of fish, and heavy boots. Dick still looks dashing with his Celtic hair curling under his captain's hat. Jane, under an unbecoming woolen cap and squeezed into layered jackets, resembles an old cabin boy. She also works like a cabin boy while Dick, like all captains, waits for the work to be done. She bustles about, gathering the baskets, the shelling tool, the lines, the new Swedish paravane, and the Japanese plank, and extricating from her jute bag the old trammel brought from Brittany, which had a good seven or eight years of loyal service under its belt. Loyal isn't the right word. Nothing's loyal at sea; everything tries to betray you, to fail you, to leave you hanging. That's the ultimate goal of every wave.

The old transparent nylon trammel had been poorly put away last September. The day they were stripping the boat, Dick mocked Jane's perfectionism, as usual. She had wanted to gather up the knots of the top half of the net as well as the weighted bottom half before putting it away in its bag for the winter.

"It's not going to tangle itself up all alone in there. You tied up the holes. That should be good enough."

But nothing's good enough for the sea's instruments. They hurry to make the most of the smallest weakness—especially those things that haven't been done according to the rules of their art—in their own good time. These are the things that transform themselves, when the moment arrives, into a major catastrophe.

"Let's unwind it once, just to make sure, before stowing it away." Jane had suggested.

But Dick won't make any extra effort unless there's a knife to his throat. "Listen, the top part looks impeccable. The bottom will follow."

Jane deferred. The temptation to put in the least amount of effort is contagious in the long run.

Their Guest, kitted out in oversize apparel that had been left behind last year by a friend who was 6'2" and wearing boots that were too small, which had been left behind by someone else, climbs down and waits for them on the dock. He's an old friend whom they like a lot. On land. For the last ten years, he has been coming along with his new wife and they preferred the old one. And then it has to be said that friends have the bad taste to age at the same time as you. Consequently they help you less and less. You reach an age when everyone around you is either sick or dead. It's difficult not to be mad at everyone! Furthermore, the Guest has always been incompetent, which somehow doesn't prevent him from being game to go fishing every morning while Dick and Jane would have preferred to get their sea legs alone, in peace, away from everyone's eyes.

In a few days, they'll have recovered their familiar movements and then they could go through the motions without any effort.

On the seawall, Jane drags along her plastic green Sportyak dinghy. Last year, it weighed less, strangely. She puts into place the wooden slats that she had made to keep from sitting on the bottom, along with the rowlocks, the light aluminum oars, and puts to sea to go and find the *Lil' Chicken* where it's moored, a few hundred yards off because there isn't even a port in Derrynane! She's the one who makes the rounds because the dinghy is too small and too fickle to contain a man of 5'11" and nearly two hundred pounds and who could no longer bend over backward. The Guest is slight, but she doesn't trust him. He had the misfortune of explaining that he had learned to row on Lake Geneva! He's also the type who thinks too much before acting. The ocean makes short work of people who hesitate. He was an intellectual, one of many from his generation, who boasted of never having known how to do anything with his own two hands.

"I won't help you clear the table. It's for your own good because I break everything I touch," he warns, beaming.

In saying that, he gives himself permission to stay in his chair while Jane clears the table. He fills up ashtrays without ever emptying them. He's simply lazy and irresponsible, yet he thinks he's endearing. There are times when his discourses on Franco or the origins of Nazism—their friend happens to be a historian—seem much less interesting to Jane than a good old unclogging of the sluggish sink pipes.

Docking at the back of the blue vessel, because there's a bit of surf, Jane has to control her heartbeat. For the past year or two, this has become the moment of truth for her—getting out of the dinghy and into the boat, a feat that requires a mastery of all sorts of divergent movements unfolding around her, along with the menacing vertigo. The day when she can no longer overcome this fear, they'll have no choice but to sell the boat, their last boat. The next mode of forward propulsion would be a walker—that was clear. Therefore she must get over it for one more year. And then the next year and the one after that. If only there were a real port here, with a harbor wall and rings instead of this outlying anchorage, they could keep sailing until they were a hundred! But the Irish don't care for functional arrangements or even useful tools. They have an art for letting these things go for so long that they become useless: the seawall had given in, the access ramp was broken. It would have been silly to take on this work indeed! That was another reason why they loved this country: they were certain that they would find it the same each year, just a little bit more dilapidated, like themselves. The roads had the same potholes in the same spots. There wasn't any construction "to better serve you," no concrete mixers or work teams. Everyone knew how to do everything, poorly, but it would last for a while. Tools were always strewn about a ship's dock—nails, all sorts of iron work, broken oars—in the effort to make everything work, through the genius of "close enough" and a spirit of mutual help that balanced out their negligence.

Nothing to latch onto on these plastic dinghies, for the love of God! No peg or handle. The plank that serves as a seat along the sides is removable and it comes off in your hand if you grab a hold of it. The central bench is made of molded plastic. Why should Monsieur Beneteau have foreseen the need for a handle? His boat isn't a handicapped bathtub; we're at sea, not in hospice! Just yesterday all you needed to do was raise your left leg high enough— when the dinghy was flush with the sea and the freeboard was elevated—and swing it over the top. It was the simplest movement in the world. But now the leg stops halfway up! On land, in order to climb over a wall, say, you might get a little help, and no one's the wiser. At sea, every crew member has his own work to do and can't fill in for others. It was a joke, Jane thought, the first time it happened, a stiffness, a passing cramp. But the next year, the leg went up a little less. You can't try to trick the sea; it doesn't forgive those who hesitate or fumble about. It's a killer. Standing up in the wobbly dinghy, Jane reprimands herself. A little wobbliness, which was passing through, brought by a wave, lodges in her throat. You should never wait, for these little beasts will squeeze your heart all the more tightly if you let them. "Come on, go on, Rosie. You can do it!" She still obeys under this name, but just barely. She overcomes the difficulty by quickly putting her knee onto the gunwale. It makes her seem a bit impotent, but only the algae will notice. Then the other knee and voilà, she's on board. Well, not really voilà, more like a harrumph. The important thing is to get on board quickly.

Aging, it must be acknowledged, means losing the beauty of your movements. You get farther and farther from the ideal motion, which seamlessly joins precision and economy. Little by little your movements lose their spontaneity. They require more gesticulation, and they run up against a painful limit, culminating in the useless and awkward. For a little while longer, as long as you don't let go of the reins, the head will pitch in to help out the body and disorient the reflexes.

Aboard the *Lil' Chicken*, Jane finds her routine: unhook the carabiner, tie up the Sportyak in its mooring with a round turn and two hitches (what would the guy from

Lake Geneva do? A "granny knot"?), grab the large oars, and pass back by the pier where the boat stops short with a swift oar stroke the length of the steps. Dick gets in without having to do a thing. Jane doesn't tell him about any of her problems. Describing them would only make them worse. He sits down at the helm of the outboard and begins to pull the cord of the Johnson. It takes time to tame a motor. They don't like to follow orders until you've figured out all their little quirks. This one liked to be titillated. It never responded to the first advances. The steering wheel locked.

"They told me at the garage that they'd just made it turn over."

The two of them knew not to count on "they." On the telephone, the motor worked impeccably, "everything A-OK," "they" had said. Waiting there, the familiar little scene played itself out on the outboard: it coughed and spat and then went quiet.

"The Mercury started better, don't you think?" the guest commented.

The previous motors always worked better because you forget about their defaults. And then the next remark, well . . .

"Did you see in *Boating*?" the Guest said. "They've unveiled a new Yamaha with an electric starter!"

"You don't have a boat," Jane says, "but you buy nautical magazines?"

"I don't make love anymore either since my bypass, but I still buy romance novels!"

"It's not that this Johnson is so bad," Dick says, wearing himself a bit thin. "I have a bad rheumatism today in my wrist. I must have sprained it doing something funny."

Do "good" rheumatisms exist at our age? Aren't all our movements a little "funny"?

"I can help you. Pull the string," the Guest politely proposes.

But on board, Dick, whose manners are so polite on land, becomes intractable: a nonsailor is a species that you must prevent from doing harm at any price.

"Fortunately there's not a breath of wind," the innocent adds.

Dick and Jane don't even need to look at one another. The Guest is even more useless than they had thought.

"You can't tell from here," Dick says, "but look offshore, you can see that clouds are gathering. However there's a good breeze."

"Good" means that it's beginning to get bad. At sea, euphemisms are standard. So many shipwrecks that dwell down below were carried off by a "swell"—you never say by a mountain of frothing water even though that's what they saw before they went out—or were drowned by a "good breeze." But the Guest, who doesn't believe in this sort of thing, laughs to high heaven.

"We'll put out the lines?" he asks.

The lines! If he thinks that they're going to let him keep a line in hand, he's kidding himself. First he needs to let the others fish and he can take the fish off their hooks, if he knows how to correctly handle the fish by the gills. Then they'll see. Maybe.

The *Lil' Chicken* leaves the bay and sets out on its route. The landscape widens, opening itself up a bit like an immense book, showing to the left, in greens, mauves, and browns like a tweed, the bare, powerful Beara Mountains that must just reach nearly two thousand feet. To the right, on the hillside, there are hundreds of tiny fields; some of them look almost vertical, bordered with walls made from brittle rocks and flecked, all the way up to the summit, with the white coats of sheep.

Were they looking at all this beauty, which they found again every summer with incredulity, too intensely? Or had Ireland's ocean played one of its tricks on them, that same old story, reminding them that you should never take your eyes off it? The boat crosses through a pillow of floating algae and the motor stops short. When silence falls over a motorboat, it doesn't bode well. All three of

them lean toward it: a long trail of the algae that Grandfather called *Chorda filum* is wound around the propeller. Jane knows what to do: rush to get the oars to keep
the boat on course and to keep it from heaving over. On
top of everything else, they find themselves in the vicinity of the "breathing rock," over which the sea pokes out
like a tongue, then pulls back inside with a hideous suck-
ing sound. They had thus renamed it, as they had done
for many of the rocks in the bay because they had trouble
memorizing all of the names these rocks had been given
in Gaelic on the marine maps. Dick releases the motor
and with the help of the gaff, the boat hook, and his Opi-
nel pocketknife, tries to shred the filaments of the aptly
named *Chorda filum* while Jane rows her heart out, with
her eyes fixed on that rock against which they could be
driven with the slightest wrong move. She knows that
she's not as indestructible as she used to be, but what
would happen if she eased up on the oars? They'd be
screwed if they had depended upon the rower from Lake
Geneva.

But what were they doing there instead of lolling about
at the Château de Rondon on the banks of the Cher River,
an old folks' home for aging writers? What the hell were
these two wet willies doing in their sailors' rags, one gripping her oars and the other bent over his sticky algae?

Who would come recite "Oceano Nox" on their watery grave "while they sleep under the green seaweed"?[132]

Only one sound can chase away these morbid thoughts: that of the motor starting up again. The pin of the propeller doesn't give and the Johnson turns over. For the moment, Dick is a wizard and, with Jane at his side, they form the best crew in the world. Only one formality remains: setting up the trammel.

Toss out the buoy, the rope, the rock, and the first yards. It's soon apparent that something is wrong. Sections from the central panel pass through the large mesh knots and prevent the net from opening up vertically in the water. They're tempted to move it around the buoy rope, or to reap the benefits of the hole made by a spider crab last year to foist the spiraled extremity into the gap. This is a move destined to fail. But Jane tries anyway. The Guest shakes the net uncontrollably. He shakes and shakes; that's all he knows how to do.

"Come on, we'll put this part into the water as it is. There'll still be forty yards to fish with. That should be plenty," Dick decides.

Thirty feet of trammel are weighted into the form of a plait, but it doesn't seem to go any better. There are more tangles; the weights end up over the floats and the net becomes a vast, balled-up mop, twisted in the hands of a crazed housewife. There's a growing desire to just take to it with a knife. "If we just cut this link here, I think it would untangle the whole thing," the Guest advises. This might seem obvious, but experience has shown that this solution is always worse than the problem itself. Discouragement and shame wash over them. Jane can no longer claim to be the Queen of Tangles, capable of unswaddling in record time a crab grabbing its half-devoured prey or a spider crab caught in the mesh as if in a straitjacket.

On the horizon the cowardly solution beckons: a new trammel. They actually have an immaculate one in the attic, without any holes, which wouldn't cause them any problems in the near future. Dick orders them to give up. The Boss is the Boss. At sea Jane never questions orders. They take up the thing and put it back into its bag. Spread out on the grass, perhaps the trammel would reveal its secret. Now the only thing left to do is rebait the two traps that were already out. The Irish sea would provide; she's never left them empty-handed. Ten minutes later two wriggling mackerel and a little black pollock are found, and they're instantly cut in two and ready to be strung up in the traps. As she winds back her line, Jane gathers up the beautiful lot: she brings in a four-pound pollock of perfect beauty, which will soon become dinner, along with shallots and some beurre blanc. The Guest widens his eyes. So their fishing stories weren't just boasts, coming at the tail end of their Parisian dinner parties?

Sometimes the sea provides for her dearly beloved a royal recompense after they have been maltreated. There are only two traps to take up, but beginning with the first one, which had been astutely placed the night before underneath a sandy hole at the foot of a slope, a "four-person" lobster, its pincers raised toward the enemy, is brought up to the surface. The poor creature doesn't know that a facetious Creator seems to have invented him to be easily eaten by Man. While at the bottom of the sea his sole predator is the conger eel, which lurks in the waters waiting for him to shed his skin, on the surface he seems to have been programmed for the pot. Easy to seize by the cuirass if you just avoid the pinchers, and easy to break into medallions or portions according to the number of partakers, his succulent flesh is properly gathered at one end, his entrails at the other, lacking bones of any sort. Lobster is almost like Japanese surimi—it's so well packaged. His tail falls down with convulsive jerks, banging around in order to frighten off the enemy, the poor thing! He struggles in vain as his pincers have become too heavy in the atmosphere. He doesn't know that he's worth 20 euros per kilo and this detail only heightens the taste of his flesh and the pleasure of those who have driven him out from his hole.

In the last trap, which is gathered lazily (for honor has already been preserved), two velvet swimming crabs and about ten and a half ounces of prawns complete the picture. It was a catchall trap with a fine mesh and everything that enters tends to remain.

The atmosphere on board relaxes and the sky brightens, revealing to the west the unlikely silhouette of the Skellig Islands. Little Skellig's high cliff, a peak above the water, is white with the droppings from thousands of birds who nest there in overlying rows: yellow-beaked northern gannets in the higher levels, then puffins, petrels, guillemots, white-headed gulls, and, down low, the black-headed gulls. It was a huge housing project for sea birds, protected from any intrusions: from saw-toothed reefs, from the jaws of sharks, devilish bottlenecks, where the furious waves, scattered by the wind, perpetually tear at and then vanish into trails of foam that line the entire perimeter of the island, rendering the very thought of approach unthinkable.

A few hundred yards away, the other Skellig, named for Saint Michael, stands tall, a rock of around seven hundred feet, with a few monks' cells, the ruins of a tiny chapel, and a bread oven perched on its summit. Four hundred and thirty-two vertiginous steps lead there, carved into the rock by a handful of fanatics, those Gaelic monks who first spread the Christian faith throughout the barbaric west from the sixth century onward. Whether or not Saint Columban or Saint Gall, the founders of the most famous abbeys in Europe, or the Breton nobles and Merovingian princes, had actually come there during its five centuries of existence seeking the source of mystic asceticism, the place remains the origin for one of those Celtic legends that form the weft of Irish history. It's a version of history that takes into account so many other legends throughout the ages, all of them hardly believable, yet proven to be true.

The sky itself was hardly believable, as it sought to prove that good weather was coming. But there's always something rotten in the state of Ireland: treachery is always hidden in innocence, bad weather within the good. You can sense it in a sudden gust of wind, in a chill that runs down your spine without any reason in the sun's full light, in a fog that comes out of nowhere and pervades the whole space within a few minutes, like a strange change of scenery.

Returning to land is a modest but triumphant act. Jane drops the two men off and then returns to anchor the *Lil' Chicken* to its mooring, wipe down the interior, and find her dinghy. Going back, the operation shouldn't present any difficulty. Jane always forgets that she has fished with this same childlike pleasure for over sixty-five years. With the same exuberance, she tends the oars and climbs up the docks, with the swaying step of a sailor, a basket in her hand and in her heart, the puerile satisfaction of having accomplished her task and having merited her pittance. It's an eternal moment that the sea sometimes bestows.

At the dock she often sees two of the five sons of their neighbor, who raises cows, about a hundred sheep, and traps lobster in the summer for the few hotels in the neighborhood. Somehow he manages to earn a living. Two of his sons have already left, for Australia or America, following the flood of immigrants that has bled the living flesh of this country for the last three centuries. Those who remain are rarely the business tycoons that the island could use.

The oldest of the sons, a colossal curly-haired redhead like the legendary king Brian Boru, had always found Jane to be a magnificent woman, sexy as all French women are. She appreciates this quid pro quo, which maybe wasn't even that. He stops to talk to her, rattling off sentences half of which she can't make out because of this awful Irish accent that makes their language closer to Breton than Oxford English. In his naive admiration, it's clear that he doesn't consider her out of his reach. Thirty-five? Fifty? Sixty? You can never tell with these over-dressed foreigners. He couldn't imagine seventy. That would mean comparing her to the old women of his country, who have been worn down by pregnancies and poverty, their faces ravaged by the four winds. But here everyone is the age they are and it's not an indictment that can lead you to be put to death. In France you've got to be eighty years old before you dare to pride yourself on your birth date. As you reach your forties, it's the first decade when you really begin to lie about your age and you enter into an indecent region where no one's quite sure how to behave.

The tall redheaded kid, with his child's eyes and man's look, makes her forget her age. He carries her basket and her oars all the way to the garden gate. Tomorrow she won't forget to put a bit of lipstick on.

The sweetness of the harbor, the treachery-free welcome of the yard, and the smell of grass are all the delightful compliments to the joy of sailing. Kerry's famous heath is still a bit harsh and Jane's "garden" is nothing but a little parcel of this heath, strewn with rocks, covered with heather and small gorse bushes, and bordered with, at the foot of the rocky walls that protect them a little bit, a few hydrangea bushes. It's a wild space where the will to survive can be read on each wind-tortured branch, on each leaf browned by the salt. It's a miracle that must be acknowledged if the petals of the hydrangea are able to preserve their velvety softness or if the sole rosebud, in the shelter of a rock as round as an egg, determinedly blooms all summer.

Jane likes these parsimonious gardens. The almost-indecent explosion of her garden in the Var in May nauseates her a little bit. All the rosebushes, all the perennials and the annuals, the climbing ones and the bushy ones, whipped up by the intensity of the light, rush together toward the sun and bloom in giddy blossoms, exhausting themselves on the spot. The myriad species elbow and overlap with one another, crushing you with admiration. She prefers her garden in the Midi in autumn as it recovers from the punishing summer when each plant, and each bush, finds its strength again and flowers as if the winter will never come.

Her garden in Brittany measures out its blossoms, guarding a portion of its treasures in order to bestow them at a moment's notice.

The word "treasure" doesn't work here in Ireland. On these coasts devastated by the salty wind, no plant, no tree reaches its intended size. Hunchbacked, bent by the domineering wind, sewn with scars, they subsist, unable to go, incapable of growing green some summers when their buds have been torn out in the spring. Yet they reappear courageously the following year, not knowing that elsewhere in the world, other vegetation grows unhampered.

Nature's eternal capacity for spring is perhaps the most moving thing about Ireland. Each rose is the first; each renewal is the beginning of the world.

I often ask myself how crazy we must have been to come here as Dick and Jane, each year, for the last twenty. And why we showed so much determination to see ourselves soaked, worn out, crippled, furious, cursing the weather, the sea and the years if not for each morning of fishing, each evening in front of the peat fire, blue like the flames of the bog, burning in silence with its fine, penetrating perfume, allowing us to forget the weather, as the future tense from then on conjugates into the conditional.

We discovered here that Dick and Jane were—at the same time—old parents who came to live inside of us without asking our opinion and incorrigible children that needed to be soothed. We didn't often know which of these characters was more annoying.

With the Guest, who became a friend again once he set foot onto land, and his companion who's not so bad after all (even though she's not my peer and she couldn't tell the west wind from the east), we talked over a salad bowl full of prawns, drinking a bit too much Paddy whiskey as evening fell. We talked about the great sailors and the lesser ones, of our trips around the world, and around ourselves. There was the inexhaustible subject—fishing and all of the boats we'd had at one point or another in our lives. All the fish that we caught and all the worthy vessels that we had, sold, wanted, bought again, who knows? There were the ones that Paul missed, that I hadn't liked, and the ones that only I knew how to drive (I'll always be particularly fond of those). There was the one upon which Paul and I exchanged our first kiss in 1949, under the gaze of the Glénan Islands as well as the gaze of our respective partners who contemplated the horizon without detecting the wave that served to send them on their way. There was the one upon which I almost drowned Yves, one of my potential sons-in-law who, alas, did not move beyond the level of fiancé. Or the one upon which we embarked with François Mitterand at Raguenès, one morning of bad weather, to take up an endangered trammel. If we had capsized, we would have only caused France to lose its first secretary of the Socialist Party, who didn't happen to be very good at sailing. And then there was the *Tam Coat*, our Breton boat and finally, the *Lil' Chicken*, which allowed us to keep coming back to play Dick and Jane in Ireland. In short, all of these boats had woven between us the links that became the moorings, constituting an outpost of our married life for the rest of our days.

As long as I know where to stay, as long as I'll be greeted upon arrival by the smile from my gardens, as long as I taste so strongly the desire to return and not to escape, as long as the earth won't have lost any of its colors, or the sea its cherished bitterness, or men their strangeness, or writing and reading its appeal, as long as my children bring me back to the roots of love, death can only keep silent.

As long as I'm living, death won't be able to touch me.

Epilogue

Just a few years later, in May 2004, death came to seize the more vulnerable of the two of us, the one who let it happen without any resistance. For a little while already, death had held him between her pincers like a crab, waiting to devour him. It had been four or five years since Dick had stopped writing, a sign that he was already elsewhere. The last activity that he made himself do on Earth was to go fishing in Ireland where, for twenty years, we returned each summer to cast our nets.

If it rained, if the wind gusted, each morning remained for me like the first morning of the world and I took it for granted that Dick, that Paul, experienced the same joy.

As I reread *L'Âge de pierre* (The stone age),[133] two years after his death, another truth revealed itself to me: I ask myself today if Dick, in those last years, did anything but keep me company.

From a certain point on, he showed a lassitude in all his activities that I attributed to his chronic fatigue, his legendary laziness, even if he made it a point of honor never to miss going out to sea. He went down to the beach every day at low tide, using the gaff like a cane. Because we no longer had the strength to get the boat out of the sand, we depended on the tide and sometimes needed to wait for a wave. We no longer had any friends to help us. That's one way to discover that you're definitively old. My brother-in-law, the Irishman, who had first brought us to Kerry, had died in London just a little while before my sister Flora drifted into unconsciousness, a consequence of Alzheimer's. My peers had all broken a femur or a shoulder and I suppose that younger couples were put off, after they tried it once or twice, by having to take the train, then the ferry to Cork, and then drive two hours only to spend ten days in the rain. As for our daughters, they had cleaned and untangled too many nets full of seaweed and dead crabs during their childhood to be able to still find pleasure in sharing our obsessions with listening to the weather bulletins that were so often alarming. Only Constance, Paul's daughter, comes with me to Derrynane for each high tide of the equinox, where we surrender ourselves to our reprehensible activities.

"Strong seas becoming large, then enormous." You need to have lived on the west coast of Ireland to understand the horror of those words.

After so many bright years when all of our Parisian friends had come, by turns, to discover the lush lands of the west and to be dumbfounded by our miraculous fishing, toward the end we found ourselves pretty much alone. But I got used to it, fighting relentlessly to make my corner of the heath flower, though it was scorched by the salt-carrying winds. I was always in the midst of a book, which let me write at the feet of mountains colored with the pinks of wild rhododendrons or the purples of heather, facing Derrynane Bay with its enchanting light cradling the illusion that I could be visited by the genius of Synge, Yeats, Joyce, or Beckett at any moment.

And then, perhaps as a remnant of childhood, I felt the same excitement upon seeing a blue lobster brought up in a trap or over a pound of prawns swarming in the bottom of a catchall.

I saw that Dick no longer savored the mollusks, sea urchins, and crustaceans that we brought back every day in our wicker baskets. Only the vodka that accompanied them still made him happy. He went back to bed after lunch, taking a nap that lasted until evening, when he woke up with the aid of two or three whiskeys. He then ate absentmindedly since he no longer enjoyed cooking and then he read even more absentmindedly until entering into his night.

"Hark, Love, my love, how softly steals the night,"[134] he liked to say ironically each time a gust of wind whistled in the chimney, making the blue flames of the peat shiver.

The strident call of my alarm ripped him in the early morning from unconsciousness, which had begun to seem like his preferred state. He slipped on still-damp fishing gear and dragged himself down to the boat which, unfortunately for him, bobbed quietly at anchor.

I say "unfortunately" for I came to understand only much later that Dick had perhaps been tempted, that last year, to escape from fishing duty. Though he possessed a mastery of all sailing knots and never bungled the mooring, he had apparently done a granny knot one morning to tie up the boat. An hour later, contemplating the horizon from the house, his new favorite pastime, he suddenly called out to me with a faltering voice:

"That's strange, there's an extra rock in the bay. Come look."

He seized the binoculars and glimpsed a vessel of a surprising blue color, drifting toward the Pigs, a strip of reef that deserved its name. I didn't even take the time to confirm it; Dick knew the bay like the back of his hand. It must have been our *Lil' Chicken* drifting toward the foaming sandbar. The western wind, the usual one, would have brought it back to us on land. But the eastern wind blew that day and it was carrying our boat offshore toward the Pigs which were already delighting in its eventual disembowelment. Without even slipping on my oilskin, I ran down the pier. Our neighbor Paddy, who was sitting on the steps, suddenly grasped the urgency of the situation and we jumped into his boat and he started his old outboard motor as fast as he could. Ten minutes later I managed to hook onto the gaff in the front of our *Chicken* and jump on board before she crashed. We brought her back in tow (and in triumph) to her mooring where I let Paddy do the necessary double-turn knot, promising myself to review that very evening the handful of important knots for our survival (which I regularly forgot each winter) in the *Breton Sailor's Almanac*.

Dick who was there waiting for us on the dock when we returned, said simply, "Nice maneuver."

At home he held me tightly in his arms for a long time, without saying anything for we thought the same things, the unsayable things. The boat had been fully equipped, with motor, nets, oars in place. It would have been a complete catastrophe and our fishing season would have been over. What more is there to say?

For a long time, I had wanted to believe that our sea excursions had comprised his last happiness, that I gave him the chance to be at the helm, just once more, for one more day, choosing his route and taking in the beauty begun in those early mornings.

Yet in the photos, which he didn't bother to take himself anymore, as if nothing stirred his interest, I detect today an absence. I contemplate his smile in one of them. It was the last day of the last summer in Ireland, the summer of our very last return to fish since we had decided to sell the house. Dick is sitting in the back of the boat, a trap on his knees, another in his arms, for we were taking them up. Lamb's Island was drowned in fog and he also had a gray look on his face underneath his sailor's hat. As he looked at the camera, he sported an oversize smile that he never had before, the fixed smile of someone having done his duty, revealing the semblance of contentment, the happiness of making someone else happy.

I wonder if he had been happy for any reason other than to make me happy those last few years. People don't just die from illness when they get older. They die because the taste for living leaves them.

Back when Dick was still called Paul Guimard, he wrote a wonderful and chilling novel, *L'Âge de pierre*, which takes place entirely in Ireland, the island of saints and scholars, the island of poets and madmen, the island of those who want to pass on.

"There comes a time when you no longer recognize the landscape," he had written. "Friends and lovers disappear at an accelerated rhythm and the interiors change before your eyes. When someone close to you dies, the easiest thing to handle is pain, a simple and unquestionable feeling. Then you notice that the dead person didn't go off alone, but that he took with him a part of you, more or less bleeding. I've seen friends die but also ideas, principles, habits, tastes, pleasures, pains, feelings. Nothing's the same anymore. I belong to a different race of the human species when I reach the end."

Paul wrote these lines in 1992, twelve years before he would reach his end completely. He had begun to feel himself die when he was still young, but I hadn't imagined for one second that *L'Âge de pierre* prefigured the retreat of the companion that I had "so closely held and loved so dearly"[135] for a half century. While no warning signs had yet appeared to me, his protagonist in this book described a sort of suicide at half speed. Paul had occasionally let it slip, lightly and in passing, that this book constituted in some ways his will. But we listen distractedly; we hardly ever hear someone. Novelists write so many things. And then what could we have done?

In the novel, Pierre is an aging man, a well-known architect who suddenly decides to abandon his Parisian life, to leave his wife and son (whom he loves nevertheless) in order to go die alone in Ireland, where he petrifies himself, little by little, becoming a mineral, beginning with a foot, then the leg, until he turns into a block of granite, a stone statue that, during one windy day, falls onto the rocks beneath his yard and disappears into the ocean.

"More inert than alert, he reached his end by uniting two principles: calcification and indifference. Death has no other remedy," the author concludes.

"Yes there is a remedy—a love of life," I answered him without letting myself be discouraged, although it was completely in vain.

What is married life, after all, other than the continual effort, the stubborn illusion of understanding and of being able to help one another, while words never have the same meaning, even between two human beings who had believed that with time they had learned to speak the same language, or even to understand each other without having to spell everything out?

They comprehend each other so feebly that, after death, misunderstandings persist. I hope that Baudelaire was wrong when he wrote "the dead, the poor dead, suffer so much pain," a sentence that my father repeated often during my childhood, always giving me the chills. It's the surviving ones, on the contrary, who torment themselves, who ask questions that will never receive any answers and think about problems that don't have any solutions.

I have never questioned myself as much as I have since the death of my Paul. Someone other than me, perhaps the woman he had loved for years (their affair had seemed like an eternity to me), had *she* figured out how to keep him from this slow and despairing slide into nothingness? Does such a means exist, perhaps a way of being that I didn't know how to find?

"Death's malady," as Marguerite Duras called it, can last a long time, though marked by lulls. Paul's career wasn't yet finished, for he went on to write another novel three years later. It was called *Les Premiers venus* (The first-comers) and he summed up its theme in two short lines, as was his manner: "Two young people steal an apple. They're condemned to death."

Between the verdict and the execution of the death sentence, eight hundred years go by because this book of course was about Adam and Eve, who invented a world that they didn't know at all, accompanied by the snake, their only true friend. The book was dedicated: "To my Eve" and I believed this to be a declaration of love, the first and the last in his entire body of work, in which, unlike me, he hadn't put very much of himself, or so it appeared. In the end, you always write with your own blood, or your guts, or your nerves. In any case, with your own unhappiness.

He had a way of putting an end to discussions with one definitive sentence that signaled that the subject was closed. We had agreed about several essential questions in our green years, one of them being the right to die, and we both signed the petition of the ADMD.[136] I had been a member since 1982, but I couldn't find Paul's membership card anywhere. His reluctance to belong to anything had no doubt prevented him from enrolling and he never wrote out a will. And as the years went by, it became more distasteful to bring up the subject. It was clear that Dick didn't want to fight. For him it was simply about living or dying.

It was true that, aside from the fact that we'd begun scanning the obituary notices grimly each morning, we weren't that concerned. The topic of the end of life hadn't yet taken on the scandalous tone that only recent sagas have brought to light, notably the heroic efforts of Marie Humbert to carry out the wish of her son Vincent, whose pathetic survival (completely assisted in every way), lasted for years.[137]

France, alas, is no longer a daring country in the ethical domain and I run the risk of having to wait several more years for the Leonetti law to be repealed.[138] But I'm

in no rush! I have made a refuge for myself against in-
clement weather, founded upon the knowledge of having
participated in the greatest of causes, on behalf of the exploited and humiliated half of the human race. We finally
are seeing women emerge from what Freud called "the
dark continent." The conviction of having given to this
struggle—even the smallest contribution—fills me with
peace and joy for the rest of my days . . . or my years?

I'm no longer ignorant of the fact that death crouches
not far off, watching its prey under crocodile eyelids that
never close in sleep. I comfort myself with the hope that
its jaws won't clamp down upon me so soon. But I know
that death has more than one trick up its sleeve.

Through what grace do we manage to forget death's
presence? What ruses still manage to make us delight in
the beauty of the world, revel in the joy of writing and the
thrill of waking each morning?

One must be wary of pursuing the question too deeply.
Accidents can happen all too quickly.

Notes

1   In the French, Groult makes an important distinction in terms, noting that she grew up without contraceptives and *IVG*, which is not to say without *avortements*. The term *IVG*, the acronym commonly used in France to refer to abortion, means *interruption volontaire de grossesse* or a "voluntary interruption to pregnancy," in contrast to the more general term *avortement*.

2   Mouvement de libération des femmes (Women's Freedom Movement).

3   These terms allude to Simone de Beauvoir's groundbreaking feminist text *Le Deuxième Sexe* (*The Second Sex*), first published in 1949.

4   Notably, Olympe de Gouges, who was guillotined in 1793, and Pauline Roland, who died while deported from prison in Algeria in 1852.—Author's note

5   Association contre les violences faites aux femmes dans le travail (Association Against Violence Against Women in the Workplace) cited in the wonderful pamphlet by Isabelle Alonso, *Même pas mâle* (Not even male) (Editions Robert Laffont, 2008).—Author's note

6   Groult quotes the blunt line "*Fumer tue*," which is emblazoned, due to government regulation, on most packs of cigarettes in France.

7   Fifty years early, my mother basically invented the ergonomic seat that is used today in hospitals.—Author's note

8   This sentence calls attention to the greater freedom that young men enjoyed, even in the vernacular language. Young men had, at this time, a slang term for friend (*copain*) and the feminine form of this word (*copine*) didn't come into use until many years later. Girls at this time could only use the more formal term *compagne*.

9   Colors typically associated with Mary.

10   By Clara Malraux.—Author's note

11   Morbihan is a small region in Brittany bordering the Atlantic Ocean in northwestern France.

12   A highly competitive civil service exam used in France to recruit teachers to secondary education.

13   The École normale supérieure came into being during the French Revolution and was meant to serve as a prestigious institution of higher education where young people were trained to become skilled teachers for the new republic. Today, the ENS remains an elite institution for France's best and brightest students.

14   Translation from the newest edition of Simone de Beauvoir's *The Second Sex*, translated by Constance Borde and Sheila Malovany-Chevallier (New York: Knopf, 2010), 737–8.

15   Salic law stipulated that women and descendants from the female line could not inherit any land or titles.

16   "Waterloo, sad plain" is a line from the poem "Expiation" by Victor Hugo.

17   This Molière satire from 1659 is translated in English as *The Ridiculous Précieuses.*

18   Translated in English as *The Learned Ladies*, this play by Molière (1672) satirizes women's education.

19   A reference to the 1922 novel *Ces Dames aux chapeaux verts* (The ladies in green hats) by Germaine Acremant.

20   See *Le Féminisme au masculine* (Masculine feminism) published in 1977 by Denoël.—Author's note

21   In this passage, Groult riffs on the prevalent use of the term *père* or "father" for masculine roles of power in society.

22   In *La Femme mystifiée (The Feminine Mystique)*, translated into French by Yvette Roudy.—Author's note

23   Jean Giraudoux (1882–1944) was a French novelist known for his refined prose. The young women of his novels were often rendered in idealist terms.

24   Latin term referring to laymen, or the greater common population.

25   "Oh! The sad life of a sailor / Our beds are hard, and our hunger's pierc-
     ing." The French lyrics paraphrase the well-known song "Vents et
     marées," with verses written by the popular poet Jacques Prévert and set
     to music by Joseph Kosma. It was most famously sung by Yves Montand.

26   Maison Deyrolle, which bills itself as a *cabinet de curiosités* and still sells
     various accoutrements for naturalists, has become an iconic Parisian
     landmark.

27   Ty Bugalé means "the house of children" in Breton, the native language of
     Brittany.—Author's note

28   The extreme western region of Brittany, bordering the Atlantic Ocean, its
     name derives from Latin *finis terræ*, meaning "the end of the earth."

29   To wit: monkfish, starfish, whiting, cod, John Dory, and mackerel.
     —Author's note

30   Service du travail obligatoire (Office of Mandated Labor).

31   A tradition in many French churches, the special privilege of crowning the
     statue of Saint Catherine was given to a young woman older than twenty-
     five who had not yet found a husband. The girl could say this prayer as she
     went about her task: "Help me, Saint Catherine. Please do not let me die
     single. Find me a husband, a good one, Saint Catherine, but rather one than
     none."

32   Georges Duhamel (1884–1966), a doctor, then writer who was eventually
     elected to the Académie Française.

33   The spahi was a famous unit of the French army. Its members were origi-
     nally recruited from the native people of northern Africa. During World
     War II, some spahis saw action in Syria, Egypt, and Tunisia.

34   Clovis (466–511), known as the medieval father of modern France, united
     all of the Franks into one kingdom, beginning the era of the Merovingian
     dynasty.

35   Saint-Cyr, or the École spéciale militaire de Saint-Cyr, is an elite military
     training academy in France located in Brittany.

36   The École polytechnique is a prestigious secondary school dedicated to
     math and the sciences.

37 *La République des instituteurs* (The republic of teachers), by Jacques and Mona Ozouf, (Le Seuil, 1992).—Author's note

38 Jean Marin (1909–1995) fought with the French Resistance and filed news reports from London to the French underground during the war. Close to General Charles de Gaulle, he also took part in the Liberation of Paris. After the war, he was an important figure in the French media, eventually serving as the head of Agence France-Presse from 1954 to 1975.

39 Léon Blum (1872–1950) was a French politician and served as prime minister on three separate occasions: 1936–1937, March 13–April 10, 1938, and 1946–1947.

40 "Dreyfusard" is a term referring to someone who stood on the side of Alfred Dreyfus during the notorious Dreyfus affair. The scandal was sparked by the accusation of treason and subsequent conviction of Dreyfus, a young Jewish officer in the French military, in 1894. He was sent to a penal colony in French Guiana. In 1896 new evidence came to light clearing Dreyfus, but this was suppressed by the French military authorities and new charges were created against him. These actions were brought to the public's attention by the novelist Émile Zola, who wrote an open letter titled *J'Accuse* (*I accuse*), which was published in a Parisian newspaper in 1898. For several years afterward, the French public was openly divided over the man's innocence and grouped themselves into Dreyfusards and anti-Dreyfusards. Eventually Dreyfus was retried and acquitted in 1906.

41 Colette is known for her numerous affairs with women, including Natalie Barney and possibly Josephine Baker. However she was also married three times to men.

42 The Académie de la Grande Chaumière, literally the Academy of the Large Thatched Roof, was a Parisian art institute founded in 1902.

43 Christofle is a French company known for their sterling silverware, porcelain dinner plates, crystal, and other home goods. Many noted artists designed for them, including Jean Cocteau and Man Ray.

44 The Incredibles is a reference to a group of fabulous dandies who called themselves *Les Incroyables* during the French Revolution.

45 In the original, Groult writes, *"Parce que ce n'était pas lui . . . parce que ce n'était pas moi,"* a winking reference to a famous quote from Michel de Montaigne on love: *"Si on me presse continue-t-il, de dire pourquoi je l'aimais, je sens*

que cela ne se peut exprimer qu'en répondant: parce que c'était lui; parce que c'était moi." In English, this quote has been translated as "If you press me to say why I loved him, I can say no more than it was because he was he, and I was I . . ."

46 The French town of Oradour-sur-Glane was the site of a Nazi massacre during the war. On June 10, 1944, without reason, a German unit of soldiers killed 642 men, women, and children in the town.

47 Most likely a reference to Colette's famous autobiography, *Mes Apprentissages: Ce que Claudine n'a pas dit* (1936), translated as *My Apprenticeships and Music-Hall Sidelights* (Vintage, 2004).

48 In the French, Groult uses the term *éducation sentimentale* (sentimental education), a reference to Flaubert's 1869 novel of the same title.

49 Mimi Pinson is the title character from a 1845 story by Alfred de Musset, "Mademoiselle Mimi Pinson: Profile of a Grisette." A grisette was a young woman who lived on her own, often working in the city, and associated with artists and other bohemian types. In Musset's story, Mimi charms two young medical students who admire her selflessness when she sells her only dress to feed a hungry friend and then manages to make a new dress out of curtains.

50 The Prix Femina is a prestigious French literary prize awarded annually to a novel; its jury is made up exclusively of female members.

51 Home to Le Moulin Rouge and other famous cabarets, Pigalle is a neighborhood in Paris famous for its numerous sex shops, and, at one time, the prevalence of prostitution.

52 From *George Sand in Her Own Words*, 1st ed., translated and edited by Joseph Barry (London: Quartet Books, 1979), 306.

53 Ibid., pp. 311–12.

54 Pétanque is a game like bocce, played with two sizes of balls, and popular in France, especially in the south.

55 Basque pelota is another popular regional sport in France, particularly popular in southwestern France. The game itself resembles tennis.

56 PMU, the French horse-racing betting office.

57 The promise "to obey one's husband" figured in the civil marriage ceremony until 1988.—Author's note

58   *George Sand in Her Own Words*, pp. 306–7. In this passage, Sand herself quotes from the Molière play *L'École des femmes* (*The School for Wives*) (1662):

> Marriage, my dear, is no laughing matter.
> The status of wife binds one to solemn duties,
> As you will ascend to that position
> In order to live a free and easy life.
> Agnes, your sex is made to be dependent;
> The beard is the symbol of authority.

From *The School for Wives*, act 3, in *Eight Plays by Molière*, translated by Morris Bishop (New York: Random House Modern Library, 1957).

59   See *La Voyeuse interdite* by Nina Bouraoui (Paris: Gallimard, 1991), translated as *Forbidden Vision* (Barrytown, NY: Station Hill, 1995).

60   *Le lait de l'oranger* (Gallimard, 1988), translated as *Milk for the Orange Tree* (Quartet Books, 1990).

61   *Leçons particulières* (Individual lessons) (Fayard, 1990).—Author's note

62   Jean-Jacques and Mireille Manrot-Le Goarnic decided to give each of their children a traditional Breton first name (which, during this period in the 1960s of Breton nationalist sentiment, was interpreted as a political choice). In turn the French state refused to lawfully recognize their children and to provide the standard allocations that were usually given to large families. (A witty poem on this subject by Charles Maitland Fair appeared in the June 1, 1963, issue of *The New Yorker.*)

63   Passed in 1975 and named for its main proponent, Simone Veil, the Veil Law legalized abortion in France up to fourteen weeks. It also legalized the "medical interruption of pregnancy" for cases of severe fetal malformation or if the mother's life is in danger at any point in the pregnancy.

64   Created in 1922, the Cognacq-Jay Prize is given out every year to three hundred French mothers of large families (at least five or more children). The award is named after its wealthy benefactors, the married couple Ernest Cognacq and Marie-Louise Jay, who could not have any children themselves.

65   A Latin author fifty years before Christ.—Author's note

66   The Danish city of Helsingør, also known as Elsinore, is home to Kronborg Castle, which famously serves as the setting, renamed as Elsinore Castle, in Shakespeare's *Hamlet*.

67   This line is a variation on the famous quotation from French philosopher Nicolas Malebranche (1638–1715) who said, "Imagination is the madwoman dwelling in the attic."

68   I tell the story in *Les Vaisseaux du cœur* (*Salt on Our Skin*).—Author's note

69   Office de la Radiodiffusion Télévision Française, the official government organization that provided public radio and television in France from 1964 to 1974.

70   The Tricoteuses, literally the Knitters, of the French Revolution were a group of women who participated in the events leading to the change of power in France. They attended governmental and revolutionary meetings, often bringing their knitting. During the Reign of Terror, the women continued to congregate and brought their knitting, this time to the scene of public executions.

71   The title of this book is a play on words. In French, the term for "amen" is *ainsi soit-il*. Here, Groult riffs on the masculine pronoun and substitutes the feminine one in its place, changing the phrase to *ainsi soit-elle*. Groult's witty takedown of the Catholic and masculine power structure might best be conveyed in English as something like "A(wo)men."

72   Moulinex, founded in 1937, was a French company that specialized in household appliances.

73   Jean de la Fontaine (1621–1695) was a French writer known for his *Fables*, a collection of tales often with classical sources, such as Aesop.

74   Groult quotes the line *"dans les goémons verts,"* from Victor Hugo's poem "Oceano Nox": *"Tandis que vous dormez dans les goémons verts"* (While you sleep in the green seaweed).

75   A process for creating soda ash.—Author's note

76   The masculine form was used by these women directors, in place of the feminine equivalent, *directrice*.

77   CNRS is the French National Center for Scientific Research, a government organization that collaborates with the French university system.

78   In French, this is known as the École des hautes études en sciences sociales, or more popularly by its acronym, EHESS. It is an elite research institution focusing on the social sciences.

79   Reissued in 1998.—Author's note

80   GAMS is the Groupe pour l'Abolition des Mutilations sexuelles (Group for the Abolition of Sexual Mutilation), created by Awa Thiam.—Author's note

81   Thomas Sankara was the first in Burkina-Faso.—Author's note

82   A French journalist for *Le Monde*, born in 1951.

83   *Académicien* is the masculine form of the noun. The feminine form should be *académicienne*.

84   These two members were Jacqueline de Romilly and Hélène Carrère d'Encausse.—Author's note

85   Published by Ramsay in 1979, and published in English by NLB in 1981.

86   This term is called "pharaonic" because it is described in a papyrus found in upper Egypt and dates to two thousand years before Jesus Christ. Eighty percent of women are infibulated in Sudan, in Ethiopia, and in Djibouti, etc.—Author's note

87   Professor Minkowski was one of the few who supported our actions. —Author's note

88   Even though excision is not prescribed anywhere in the Koran. See Claire Brisset's investigation in *Le Monde* from a refugee camp in Somalia, 1994. —Author's note

89   Savigneau is invoking different branches of feminist movements: feminist psychology asserts that psychological principles have been theorized based on masculine norms and perspectives; feminist political theory examines the state and public power structures as they regulate gender roles and their construction in society; and Choice Feminism maintains that women have the right to choose whatever societal path they desire.

90   In May 1968, French society and industry came to a standstill in the wake of widespread protests and strikes on multiple fronts. The movement began in Paris with student riots at several universities and soon spread across the country to different workers' unions. The massive riots and strikes brought de Gaulle's government to a halt and led to his eventual exit from politics the following year.

91 Claire Bretecher, born in 1940, is a French cartoonist whose creations deal largely with women and gender. Her most famous characters include the *Frustrés* (the Frustrated) and a teenager named Agrippine.

92 As opposed to the more common expression *femme abandonnée* (deserted woman), which is also the title of a novella by Balzac.

93 I'm thinking of Jeanne Deroin, Pauline Roland, Hubertine Auclert, and others.—Author's note

94 Lucie Aubrac (1912–2007) was an iconic hero of the French resistance during World War II. Her memoir, translated into English as *Outwitting the Gestapo* (University of Nebraska Press, 1993), recounts the numerous times that Aubrac risked her life to free her husband Raymond from prison during the war.

95 Germaine Tillon (1907–2008) was a French anthropologist who also played an important role in the French Resistance. She was eventually captured for this work and sent to the Ravensbruck concentration camp until the end of the war. In 1937 she published an account of her time there, combining firsthand experience with her anthropological training. In the 1950s she worked in Algeria and served as a liaison between the French government and the Algerian revolutionary force, the FLN, helping to broker several cease-fires.

96 Dalida was a world-famous recording artist, and was also known for her tragic and sensational lifestyle, marked by numerous scandalous love affairs and culminating in her own suicide in 1987.

97 As opposed to the standard default, which is the masculine form of the word, *écrivain*.

98 Savigneau makes the point that she chooses to use the feminine form of the word for editor, which is typically just *rédacteur*, even for women.

99 In French, the distinction is even more silly. The word for midwife in French is *sage-femme*, or literally "wise woman." There are no *sages-hommes*.

100 "Franglais" (a combination of the words *français* [French] and *anglais* [English]) here refers to the controversial adaptation of English words directly into the French language.

101 A reference to Molière's play *Les Précieuses ridicules*.

102 Élisabeth Guigou, a member of the Socialist Party, served notably as the minister of justice under Jospin (1997–2000) and as minister of employment (2000–2002).

103 Martine Aubry, a politician, became the first female secretary of the French Socialist Party.

104 Françoise de Panafieu is a member of the center-right UMP party. She unsuccessfully ran for mayor of Paris in 2008, losing to Betrand Delanoë.

105 Christine Ockrent, a Belgian-born journalist, became the first female anchor for a major French evening news program.

106 In their ordinance, published in March 1986, Groult and the other members of the commission suggested that female professional nouns should be used in official government documents. They also set out grammatical guidelines for how nouns relating to professions and titles should be made feminine.

107 Veil was referring to the official dictionary of the Académie Française, where the word *présidente* can only refer to the wife of the president, not a female president.

108 *Chef* has a variety of meanings in French. It can refer to someone in the culinary profession as well as more informally to "the boss," as well as any number of career terms related to being the leader or head of something such as a foreman (*chef d'équipe*), conductor (*chef d'orchestre*), or head of state (*chef d'état*).

109 Bedos is pejoratively riffing on two masculine terms here, the naval *enseigne de vaisseau* (the ensign) and majordomo.

110 Here Groult notes that when the word *doyenne* is used in its feminine form, it is mainly to connote the most senior member of a group. The masculine version of the word, *doyen*, is used for the dean of a university.

111 France's highest honor, the Legion of Honor, carries five levels of distinction. The highest level is *chevalier* (knight), and the form is generally masculine when bestowed on both men and women.

112 Camille Claudel (1864–1943) was a gifted sculptor who had a tumultuous relationship with her former teacher Auguste Rodin. Her final years were spent in a mental institution.

113 From Jules Renard's *Journal*, published in English as *The Journal of Jules Renard* (G. Braziller, 1964).

114 Paul Sérusier (1864–1927) was a French painter, an influential member of the Nabis movement. He worked alongside Gauguin during their shared time in Pont-Aven, a town in Brittany.

115 The Savoy is a mountainous region in France that shares its border with Switzerland.

116 Florence Arthaud is a famous French sailor born in 1957.

117 Isabelle Autissier, born in 1956, is another celebrated French sailor and navigator. She was the first woman to finish a solo yacht race around the world.

118 A trashy French magazine not unlike *Star*.

119 Popular authors of literature beloved by teenagers and young adults in France. Notably, Jules Sandeau was also linked romantically to George Sand and they cowrote a novel together, *Rose et Blanche* (Pink and white) in 1831.

120 Madame de Merteuil is the name of the female protagonist in *Dangerous Liaisons*, the 1782 novel by Choderlos de Laclos. The Marquise de Merteuil uses sex and other forms of manipulation to pit herself against her rival and former lover, the Vicomte de Valmont.

121 *Justine* is a novel by the Marquise de Sade. Published in 1791, it tells the story of a young woman who was continually subjected to mistreatment, sexual and otherwise, at the hands of various men until she was forced to commit crimes herself and was then sentenced to death.

122 Madame de Renal is an adulterous character from Stendhal's 1830 novel, *The Red and the Black*. Marguerite Gautier is the tuberculosis-stricken courtesan at the center of Alexandre Dumas's novel *The Lady of the Camellias* (1848).

123 *Story of O*, published in 1954, is an erotic novel marked by its extreme sadism and masochism, written by Anne Desclos under the pseudonym Pauline Réage.

124 *Lettres au castor*, literally "letters to beaver" (Sartre's pet name for Beauvoir) is the title of the collection of letters that Sartre wrote to Beauvoir. It has been published in English as *Witness to My Life: The Letters of Jean-Paul Sartre to Simone de Beauvoir, 1926–1939* (Scribner's, 1992).

125   The Latin expression means "bread and circuses," a shorthand term evoking a central tenet of Roman rule, appeasing the populace through food and entertainment.

126   This Latin expression means "woman is a womb." It is evoked in the beginning of Beauvoir's *Second Sex*.

127   In French, the word *totale* can refer to a total hysterectomy. Groult cites the expression *"On m'a tout enlevé"* which is like saying "I had it all taken out" to refer to a hysterectomy.

128   Like the English title, *Salt on Our Skin*, the German one departs from the original French title, which is *Les Vaisseaux du cœur* (The vessels of the heart).

129   Fabrice Lucchini, a Parisian-born actor, has starred in popular French films, such as Eric Rohmer's *Perceval*. In recent years he has staged theatrical readings of a number of French authors: La Fontaine, Louis-Ferdinand Céline, and Roland Barthes, among others.

130   The eponymous tragic heroine from the opera by Isidore de Lara.

131   Translated from the German [into French] by Yasmin Hoffmann and Maryvonne Litaize (Nîmes, France: Editions Jacqueline Chambon, 1991).—Author's note. Translated into English by Michael Hulse (New York: Serpent's Tail, 1992).

132   Hopefully Victor Hugo will pardon me this slight infringement upon his poetry.—Author's note

133   Published by Grasset in 1993.—Author's note

134   This line comes from Baudelaire's poem "Self-communion," translated here by Jacques LeClercq. *Flowers of Evil* (Mt. Vernon, NY: Peter Pauper Press, 1958).

135   The original line *Que sont mes amis devenus/que j'avais de si près tenus/et tant aimés* comes from a Leo Ferré song, "Pauvre Rutebeuf."

136   Association pour le Droit de Mourir dans la Dignité (Association for the Right to Die with Dignity).

137   Groult refers to the highly publicized case of Vincent Humbert, who was severely wounded in a car accident, and then left blind, mute, and paralyzed. With his mother, Marie, he openly wrote a letter to President

Jacques Chirac in November 2002, requesting permission for the right to die. After his request was denied, his mother administered a fatal dose of barbiturates to his drip, killing him on the third anniversary of his accident, September 26, 2003. In January 2004, she was brought to trial on charges of "administering a toxic substance," but these were eventually dismissed two years later.

138   The Léonetti Law, passed in April 2005, aims to ensure respectful conduct for the terminally ill by preventing medical professionals from exercising "unreasonable determination" to keep someone alive. It also requires doctors and others to pursue all palliative means at their disposal. However the law prohibits active euthanasia.